Art Life

Art Life

Catherine Ocelot

Translated by Aleshia Jensen

BDANG

Many thanks to Daphné B., Emmanuelle Caron, Natacha Clitandre, Julie Delporte, Micheline Lanctôt, Marcel Jean and Rafaël Ouellet, for their stories, confidences, and generosity.

Art Life
Catherine Ocelot

© 2019, Catherine Ocelot and Mécanique générale for the original French (Canada) version

Translation by Aleshia Jensen
First Editon
Printed by Imago in Turkey

Library and Archives Canada Cataloguing in Publication

Title: Art life / Catherine Ocelot ; translated by Aleshia Jensen.
Other titles: Vie d'artiste. English
Names: Ocelot, Catherine, author, artist. | Jensen, Aleshia, translator.
Description: Translation of: La vie d'artiste.
Identifiers: Canadiana 2019021807X | ISBN 9781772620467 (softcover)
Subjects: LCSH: Artists—Comic books, strips, etc. | LCGFT: Nonfiction comics.
Classification: LCC PN6733.O24 V5413 2020 | DDC 741.5/971—dc23

Part of the BDANG Imprint of Conundrum Press
BDANG logo by Billy Mavreas
Lettering by Catherine Ocelot

Conundrum Press
Wolfville, NS, Canada
www.conundrumpress.com

We acknowledge the financial support of the Government of Canada through the National Translation Program for Book Publishing, an initiative of the Action Plan for Official Languages 2018-2023: Investing in Our Future, for our translation activities.

We acknowledge the Canada Council for the Arts, the Government of Nova Scotia and the Government of Canada for financial support toward our publishing program.

Canada Council   Conseil des Arts
for the Arts   du Canada

NOVA SCOTIA

"There is as much mystery in getting close to a person as in moving apart."

— Dany Laferrière

"We have the right to exist, same as the trees and the birds."

— Julie Delporte

A president

SUNSCREEN
PROTECT YOURSELF

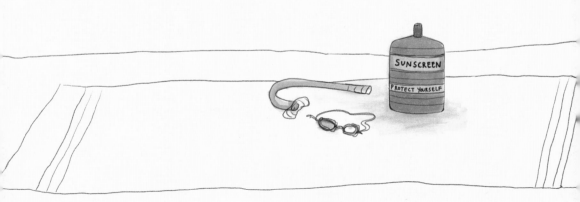

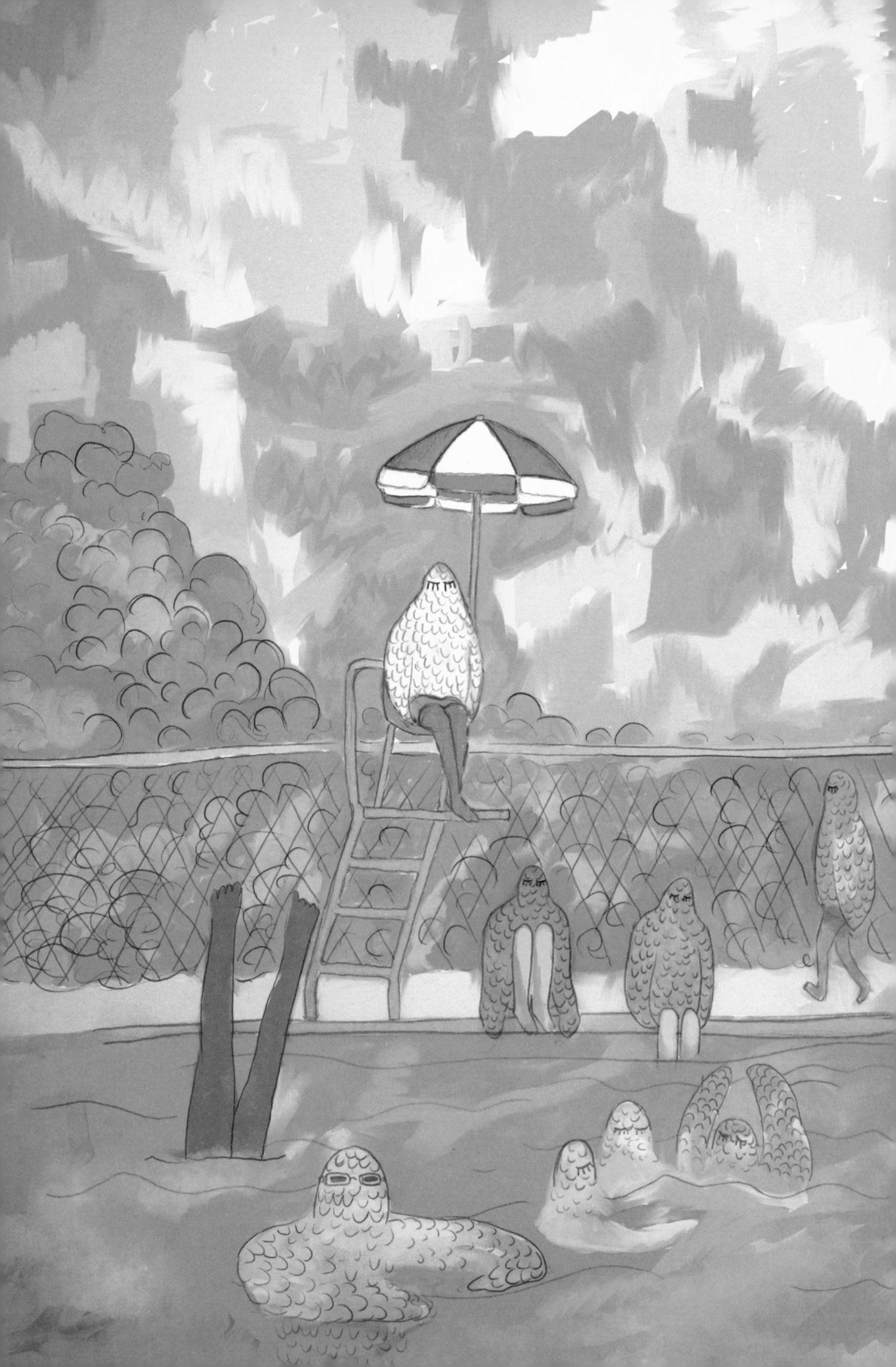

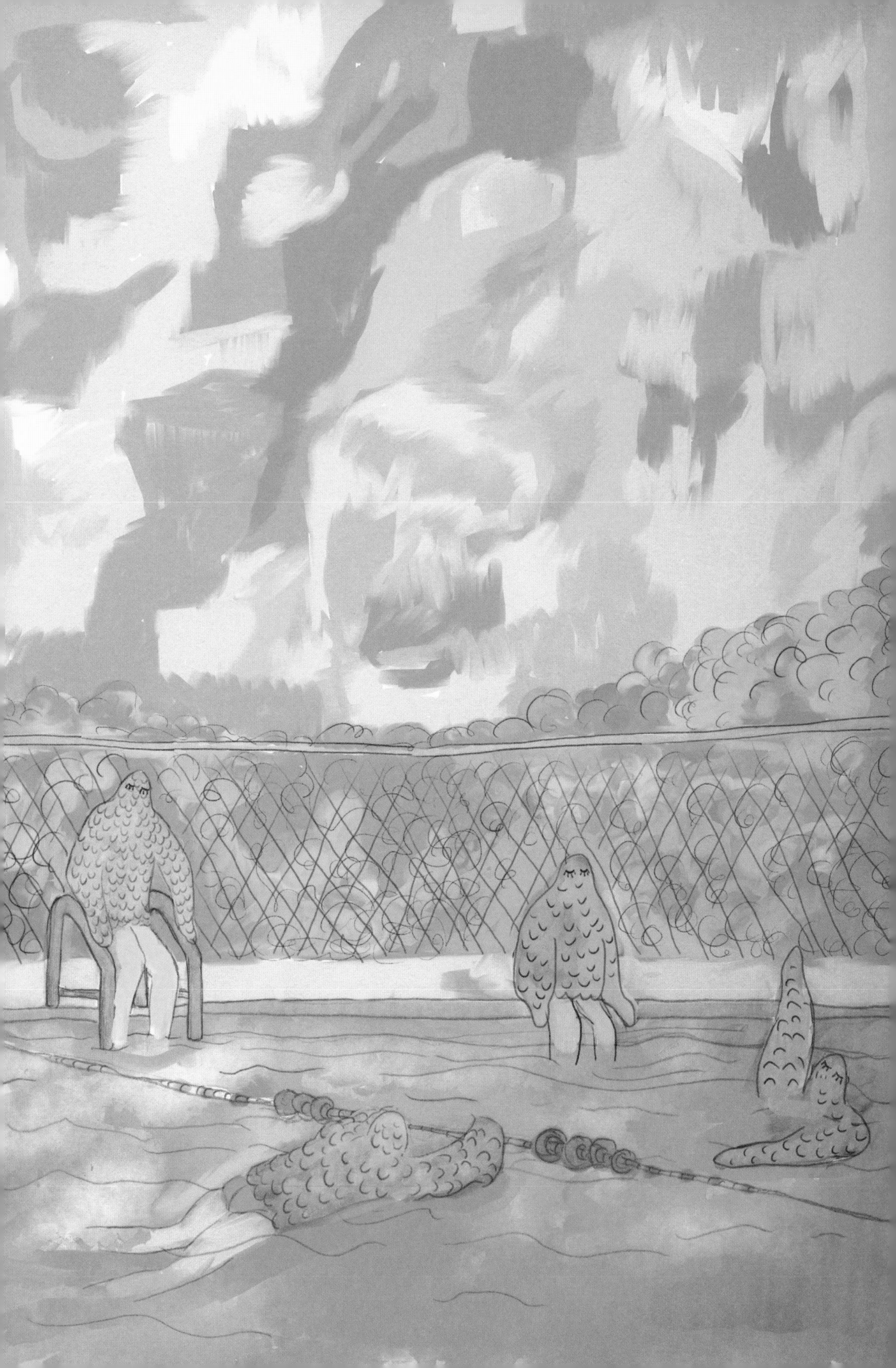

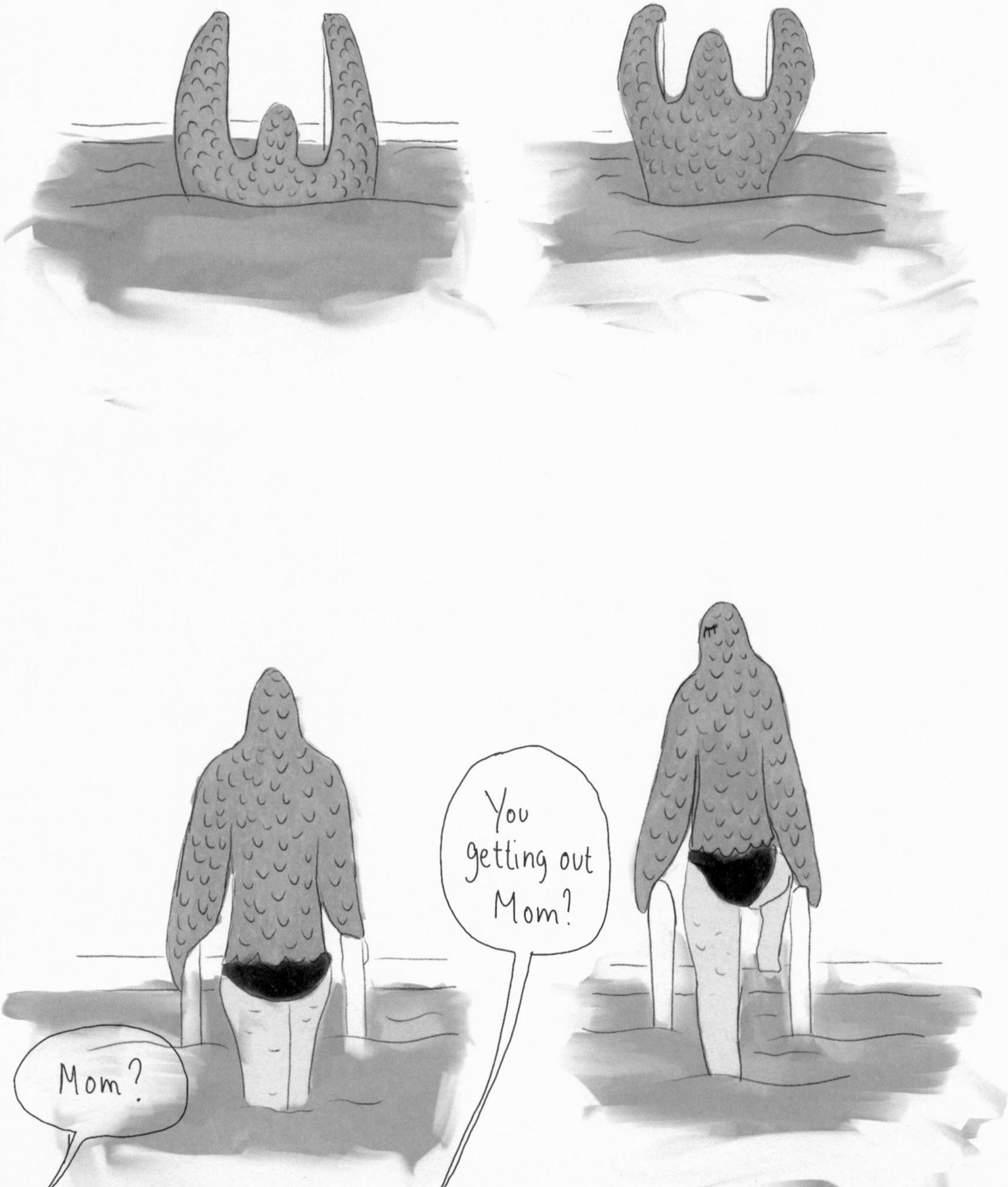
Mom?
You getting out Mom?

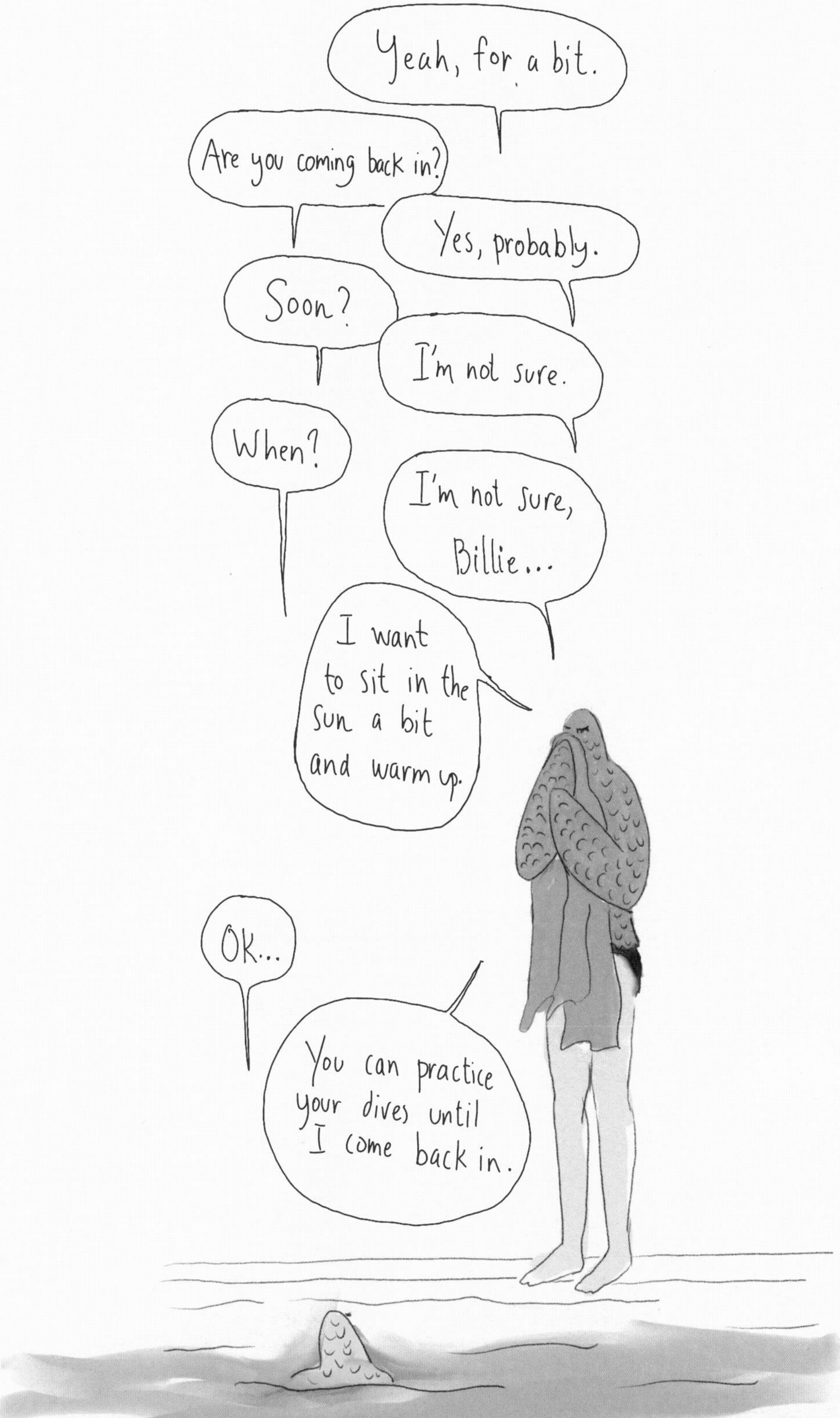
Yeah, for a bit.
Are you coming back in?
Yes, probably.
Soon?
I'm not sure.
When?
I'm not sure, Billie...
I want to sit in the sun a bit and warm up.
OK...
You can practice your dives until I come back in.

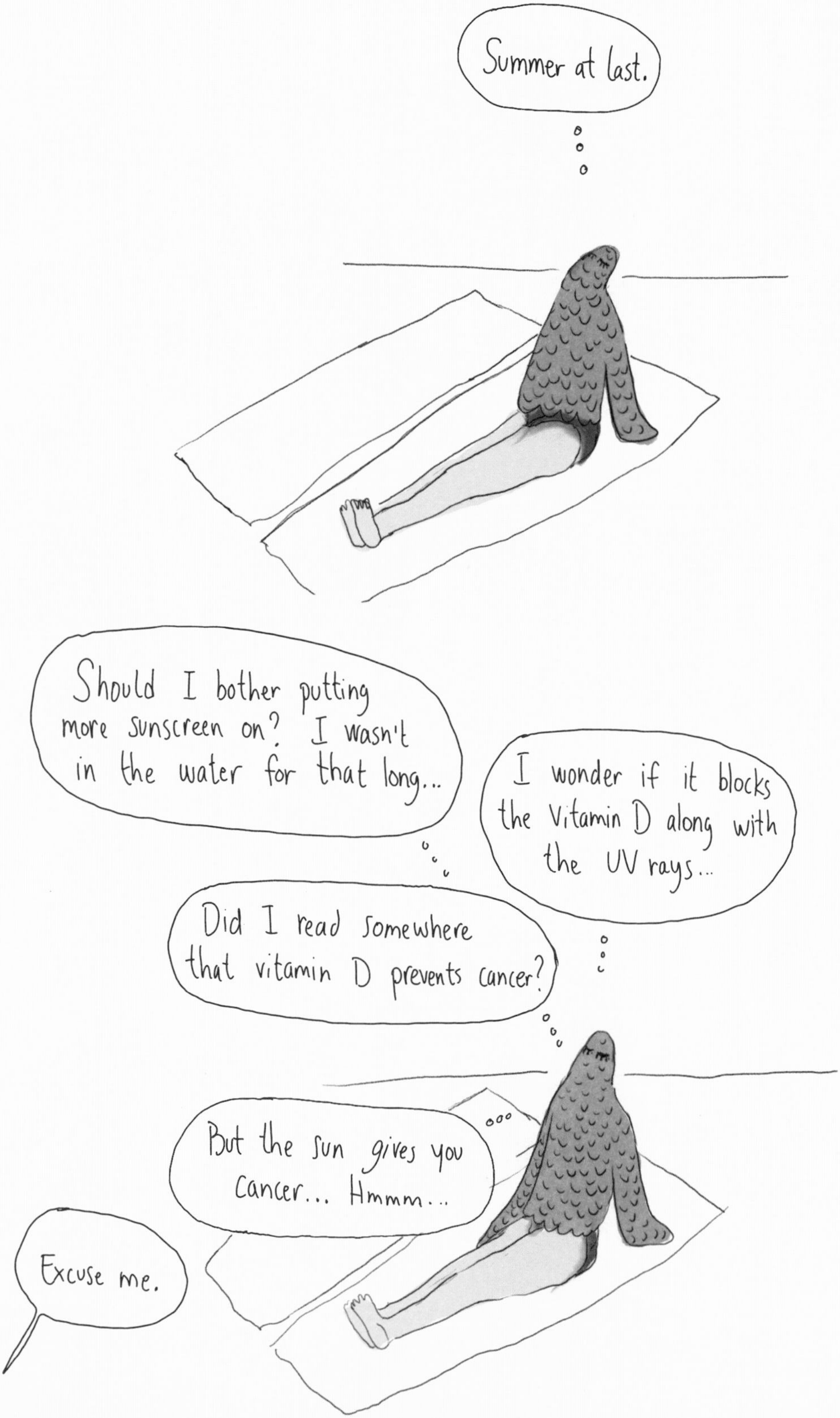
Summer at last.
Should I bother putting more sunscreen on? I wasn't in the water for that long...
I wonder if it blocks the Vitamin D along with the UV rays...
Did I read somewhere that vitamin D prevents cancer?
But the sun gives you cancer... Hmmm...
Excuse me.

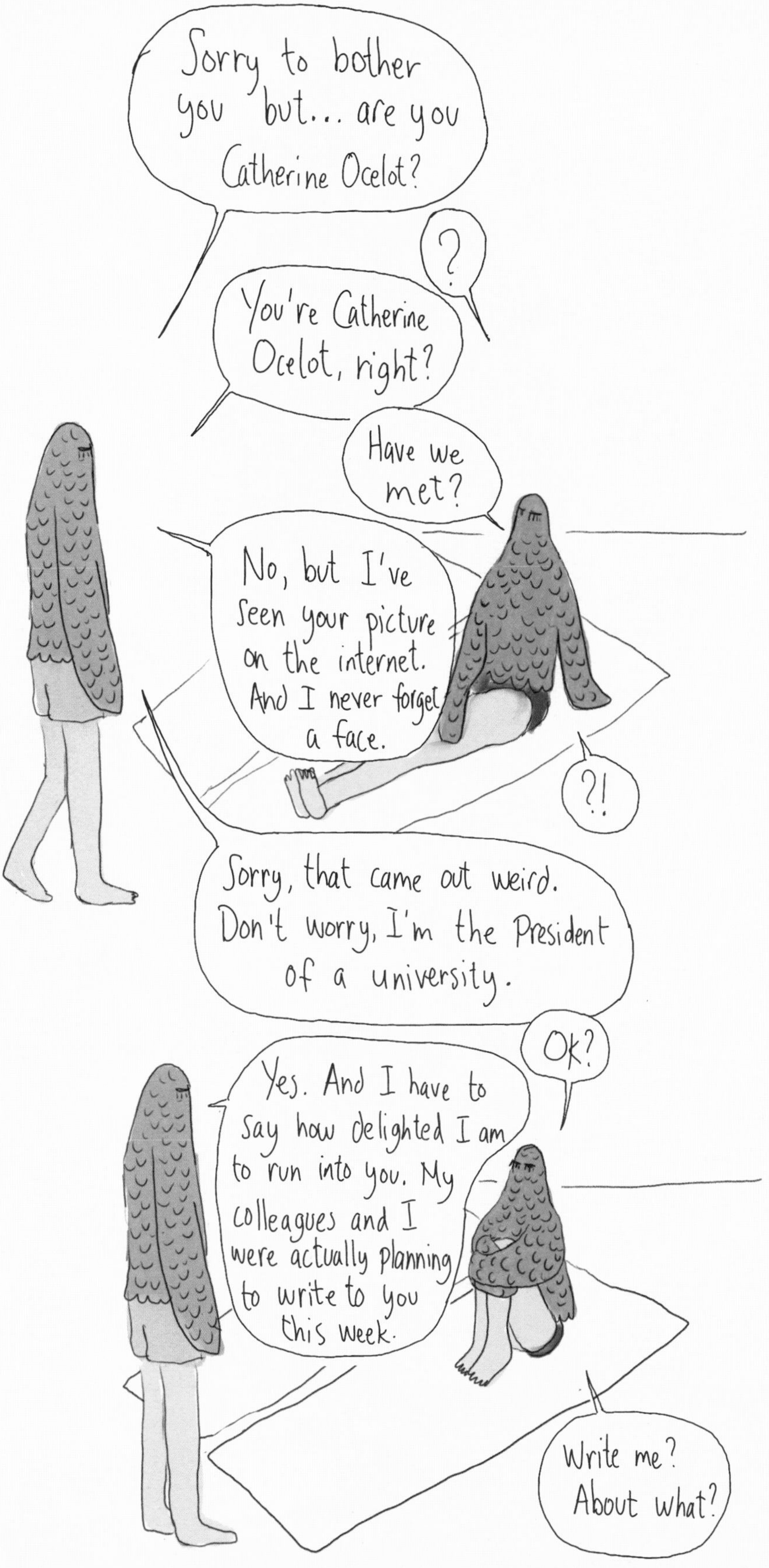
Sorry to bother you but... are you Catherine Ocelot?
?
You're Catherine Ocelot, right?
Have we met?
No, but I've seen your picture on the internet. And I never forget a face.
?!
Sorry, that came out weird. Don't worry, I'm the President of a university.
Ok?
Yes. And I have to say how delighted I am to run into you. My colleagues and I were actually planning to write to you this week.
Write me? About what?

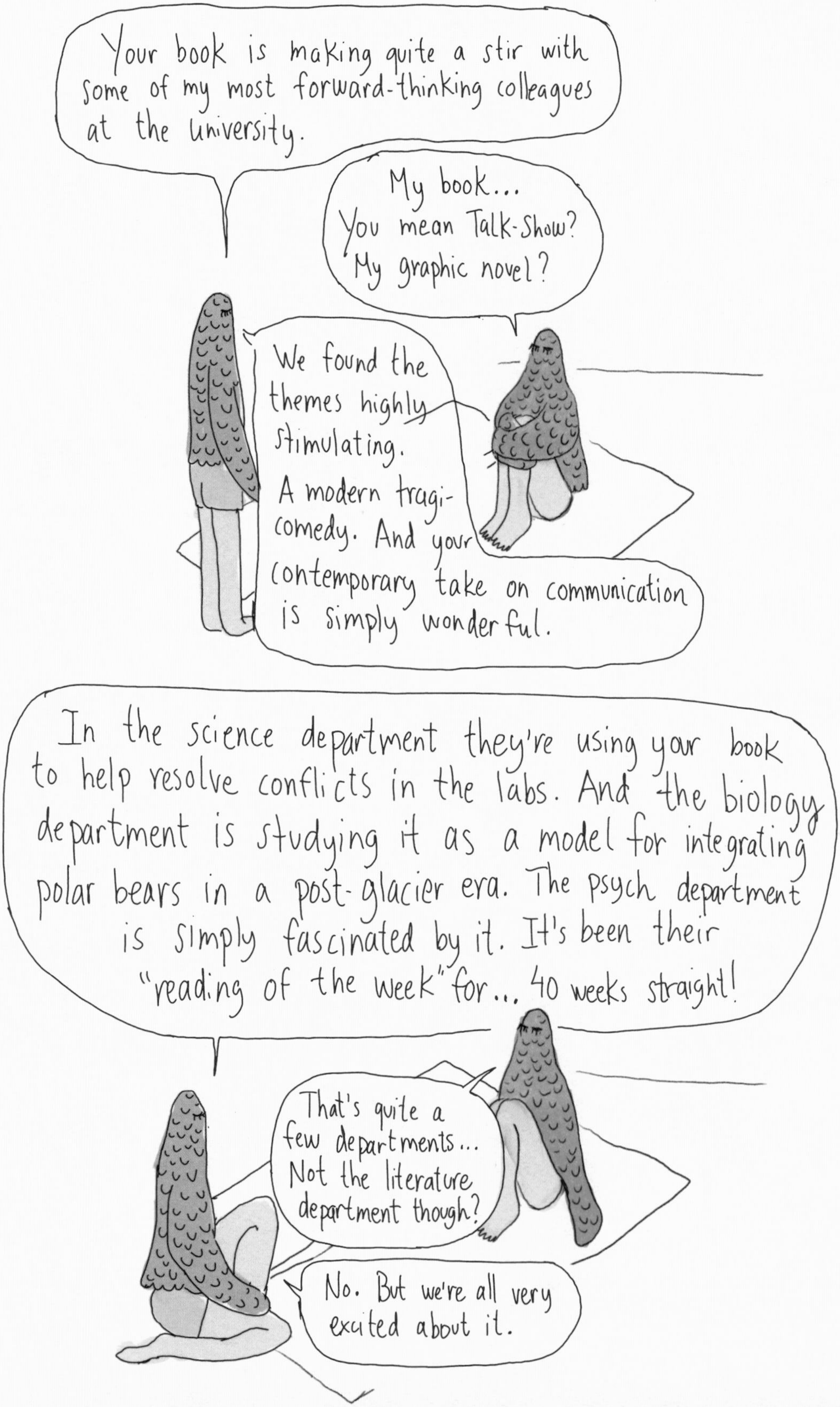
Your book is making quite a stir with some of my most forward-thinking colleagues at the university.
My book... You mean Talk-Show? My graphic novel?
We found the themes highly stimulating. A modern tragi-comedy. And your contemporary take on communication is simply wonderful.
In the science department they're using your book to help resolve conflicts in the labs. And the biology department is studying it as a model for integrating polar bears in a post-glacier era. The psych department is simply fascinated by it. It's been their "reading of the week" for... 40 weeks straight!
That's quite a few departments... Not the literature department though?
No. But we're all very excited about it.

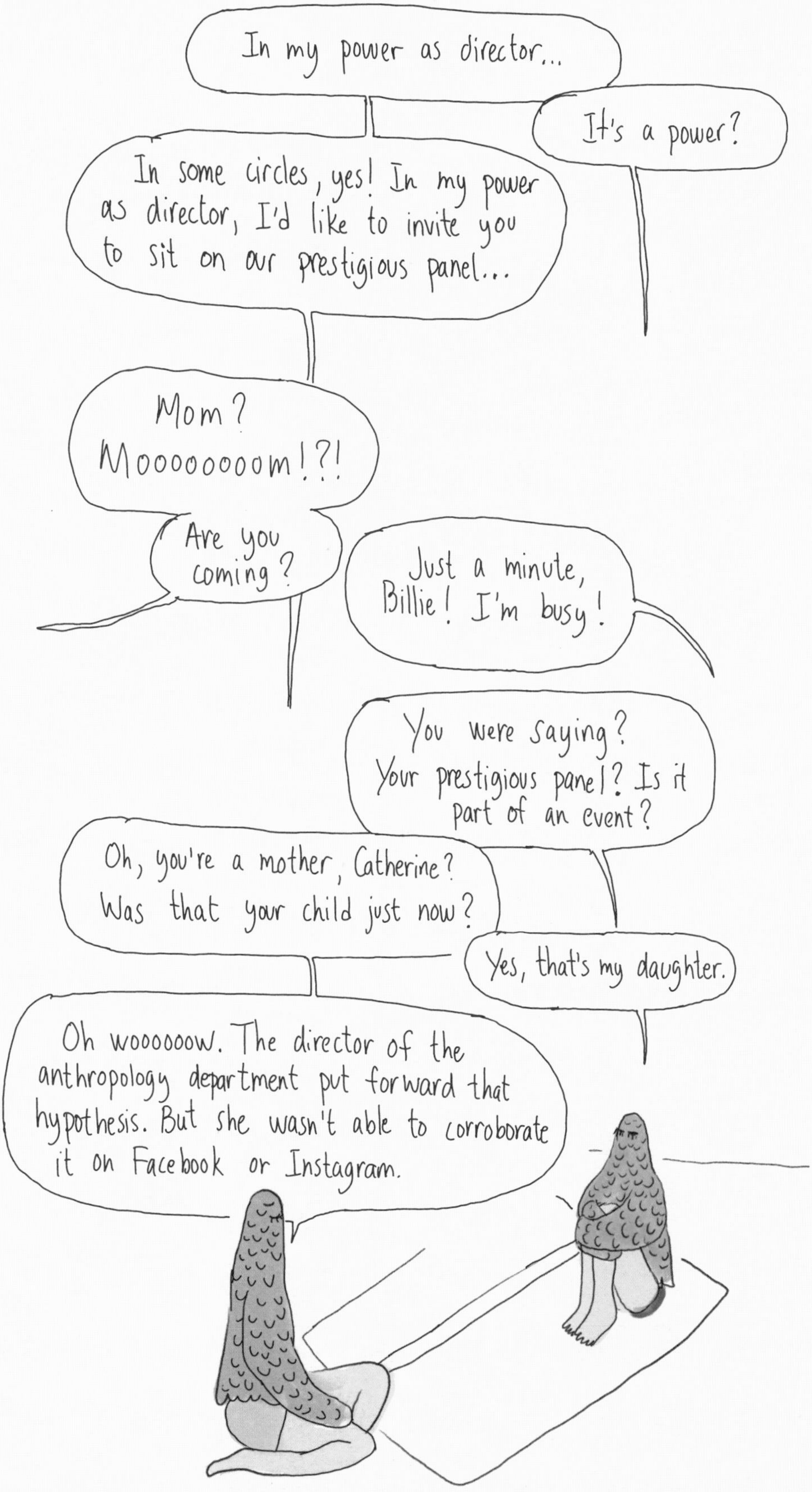
In my power as director...
It's a power?
In some circles, yes! In my power as director, I'd like to invite you to sit on our prestigious panel...
Mom? Mooooooooom!?!
Are you coming?
Just a minute, Billie! I'm busy!
You were saying? Your prestigious panel? Is it part of an event?
Oh, you're a mother, Catherine? Was that your child just now?
Yes, that's my daughter.
Oh wooooow. The director of the anthropology department put forward that hypothesis. But she wasn't able to corroborate it on Facebook or Instagram.

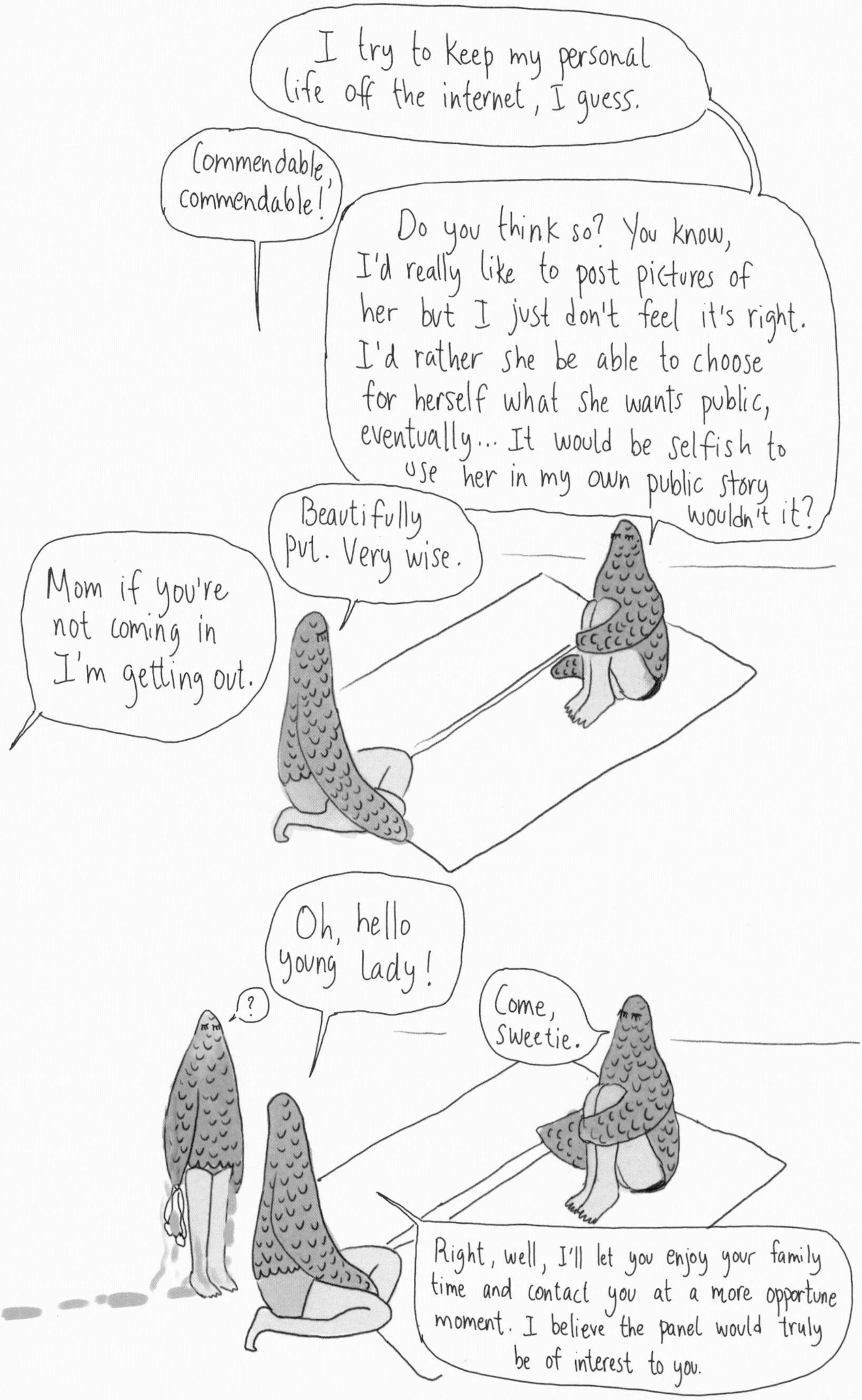
I try to keep my personal life off the internet, I guess.
Commendable, commendable!
Do you think so? You know, I'd really like to post pictures of her but I just don't feel it's right. I'd rather she be able to choose for herself what she wants public, eventually... It would be selfish to use her in my own public story wouldn't it?
Beautifully put. Very wise.
Mom if you're not coming in I'm getting out.
Oh, hello young lady!
?
Come, sweetie.
Right, well, I'll let you enjoy your family time and contact you at a more opportune moment. I believe the panel would truly be of interest to you.

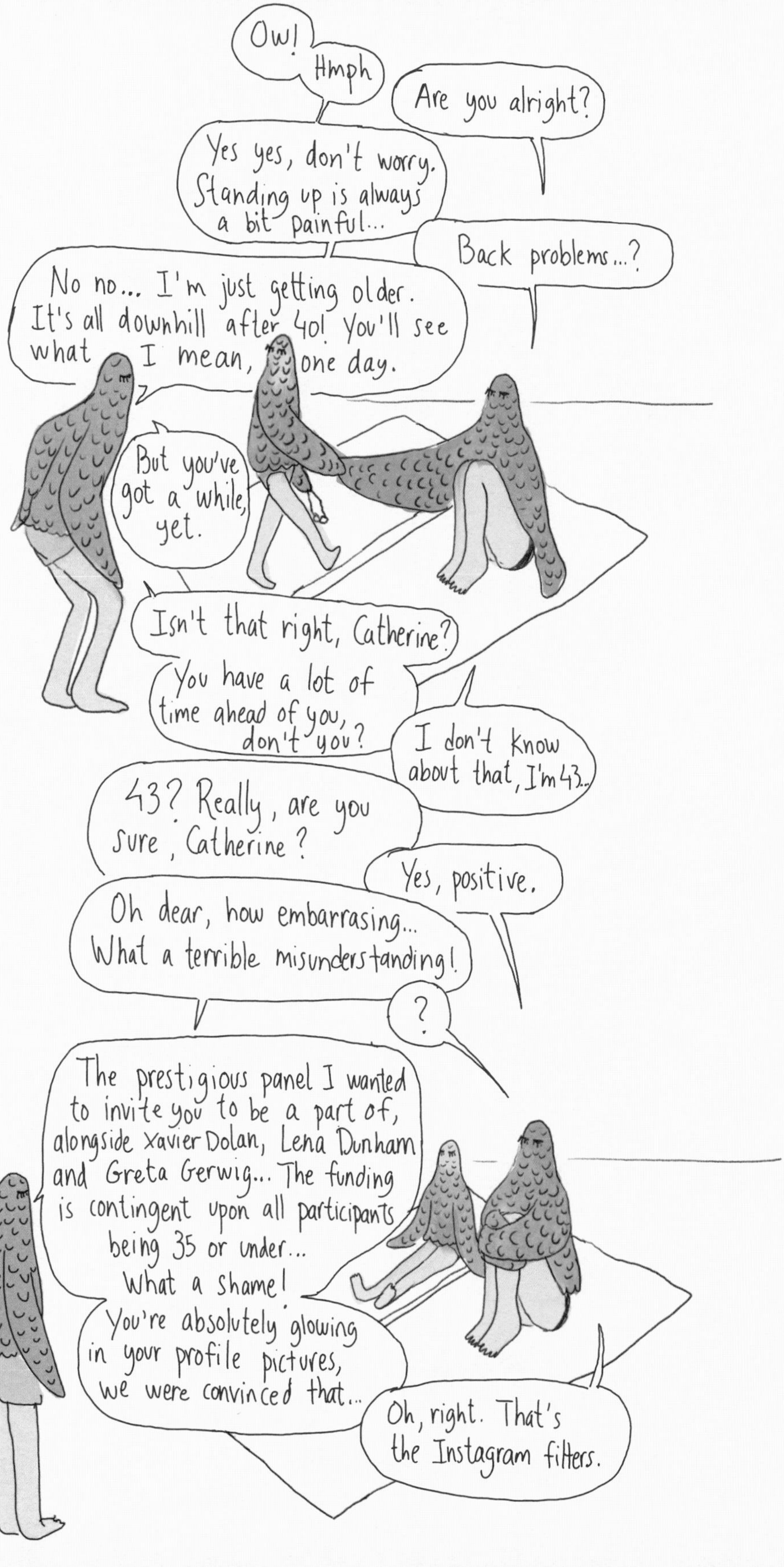
Ow!
Hmph
Are you alright?
Yes yes, don't worry. Standing up is always a bit painful...
Back problems...?
No no... I'm just getting older. It's all downhill after 40! You'll see what I mean, one day.
But you've got a while, yet.
Isn't that right, Catherine?
You have a lot of time ahead of you, don't you?
I don't know about that, I'm 43...
43? Really, are you sure, Catherine?
Yes, positive.
Oh dear, how embarrasing... What a terrible misunderstanding!
?
The prestigious panel I wanted to invite you to be a part of, alongside Xavier Dolan, Lena Dunham and Greta Gerwig... The funding is contingent upon all participants being 35 or under... What a shame!
You're absolutely glowing in your profile pictures, we were convinced that...
Oh, right. That's the Instagram filters.

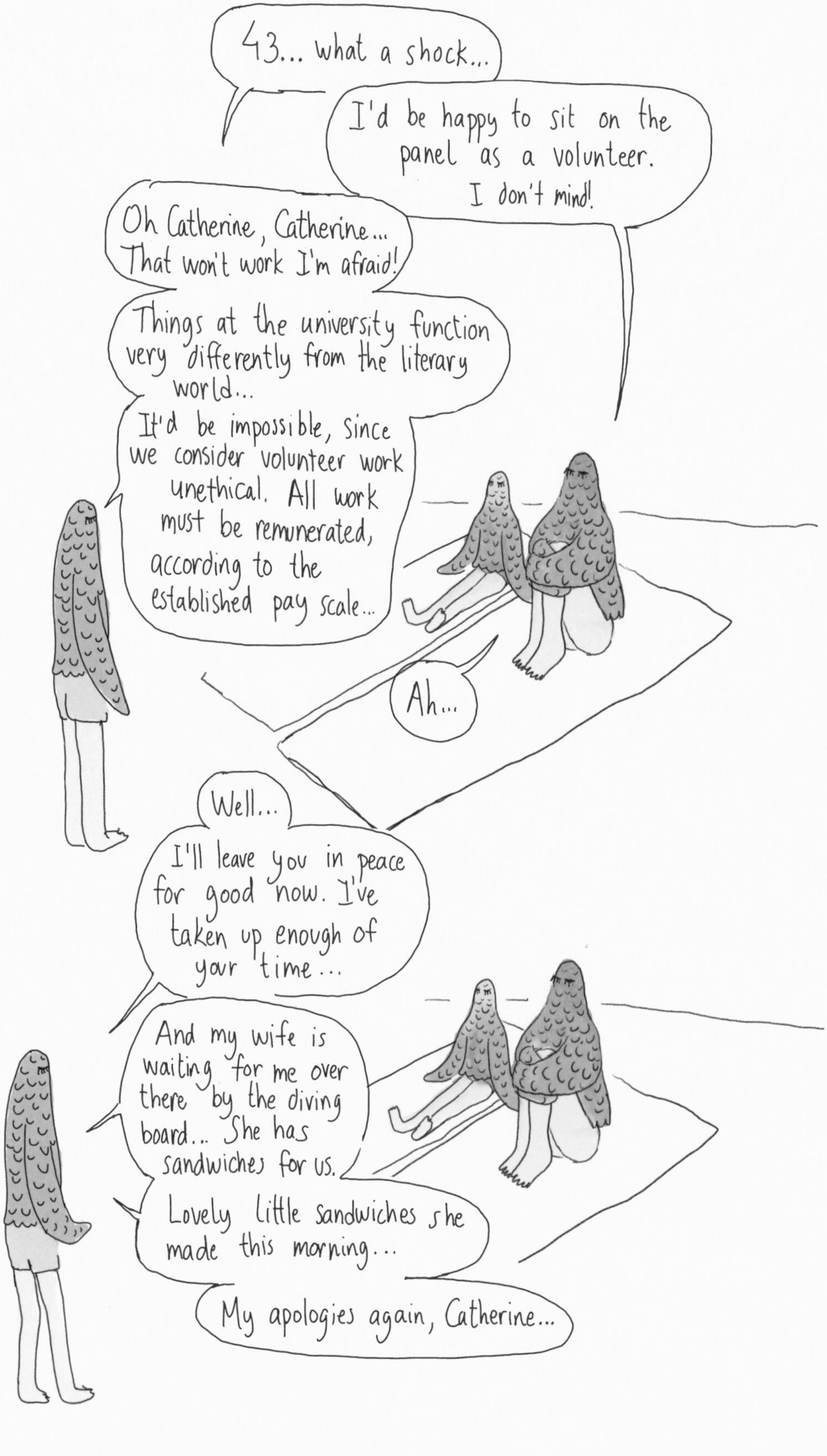
43... what a shock...
I'd be happy to sit on the panel as a volunteer. I don't mind!
Oh Catherine, Catherine... That won't work I'm afraid!
Things at the university function very differently from the literary world...
It'd be impossible, since we consider volunteer work unethical. All work must be remunerated, according to the established pay scale...
Ah...
Well...
I'll leave you in peace for good now. I've taken up enough of your time...
And my wife is waiting for me over there by the diving board... She has sandwiches for us.
Lovely little sandwiches she made this morning...
My apologies again, Catherine...

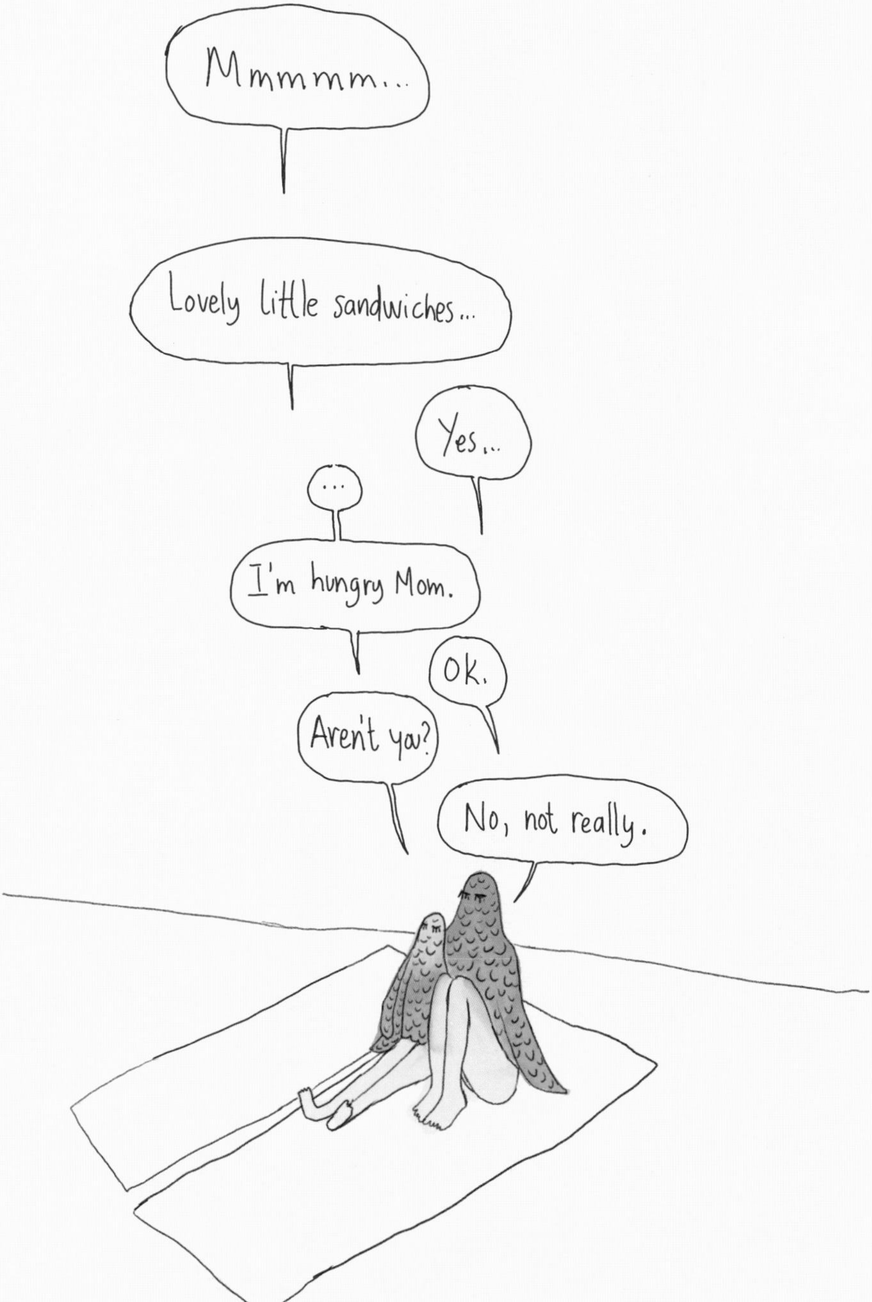

Mmmmm...
Lovely little sandwiches...
Yes...
...
I'm hungry Mom.
OK.
Aren't you?
No, not really.

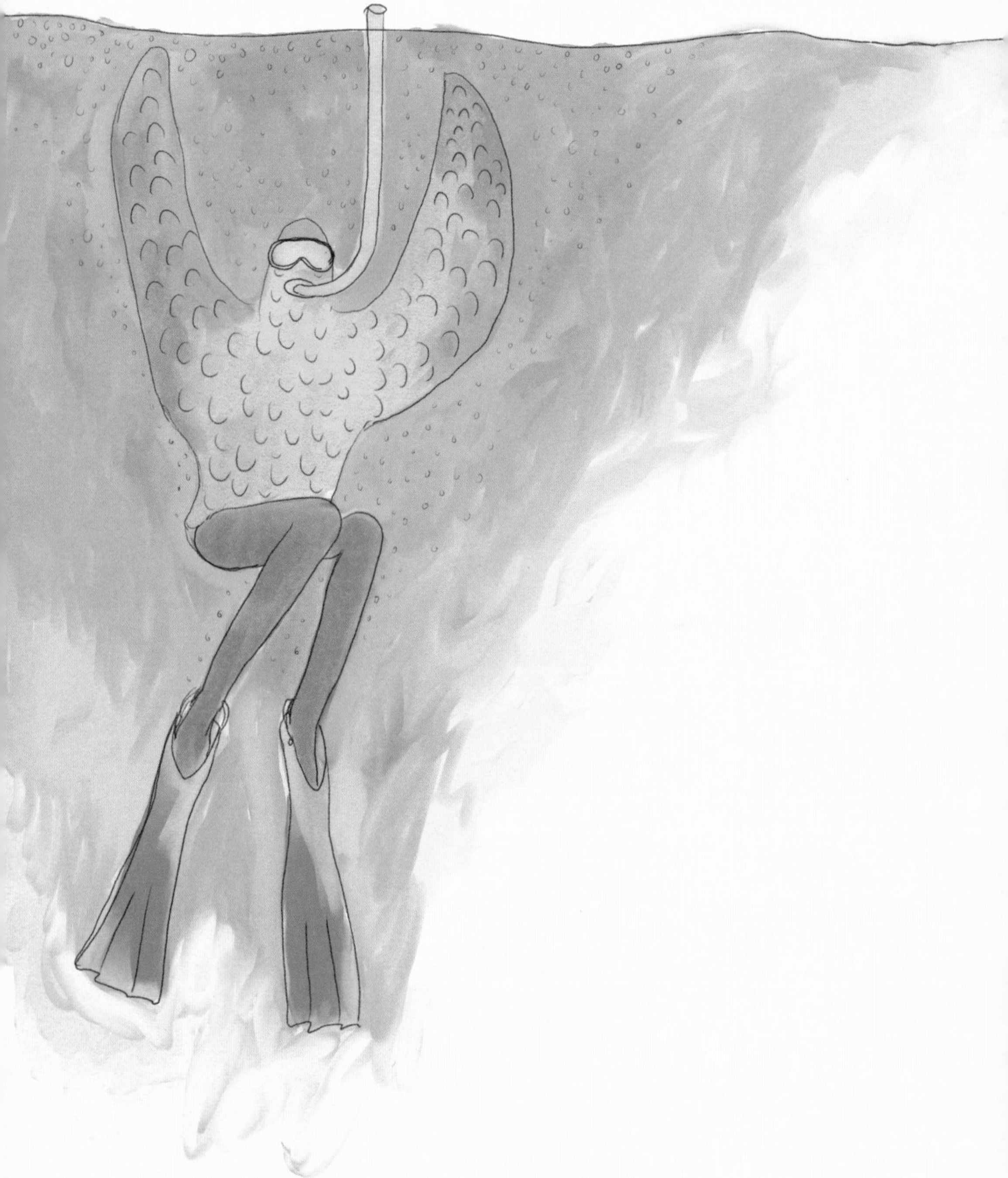

Natacha

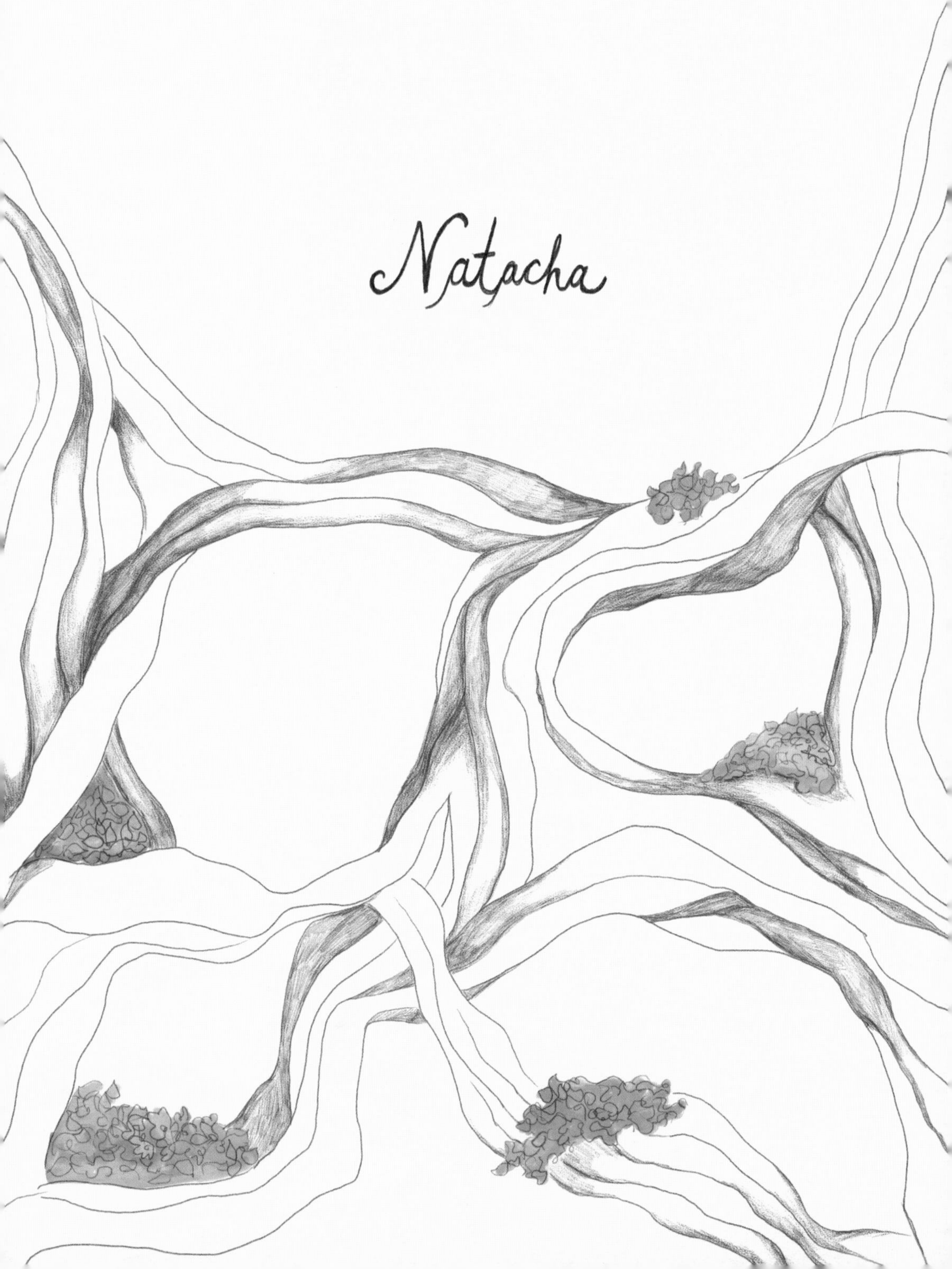

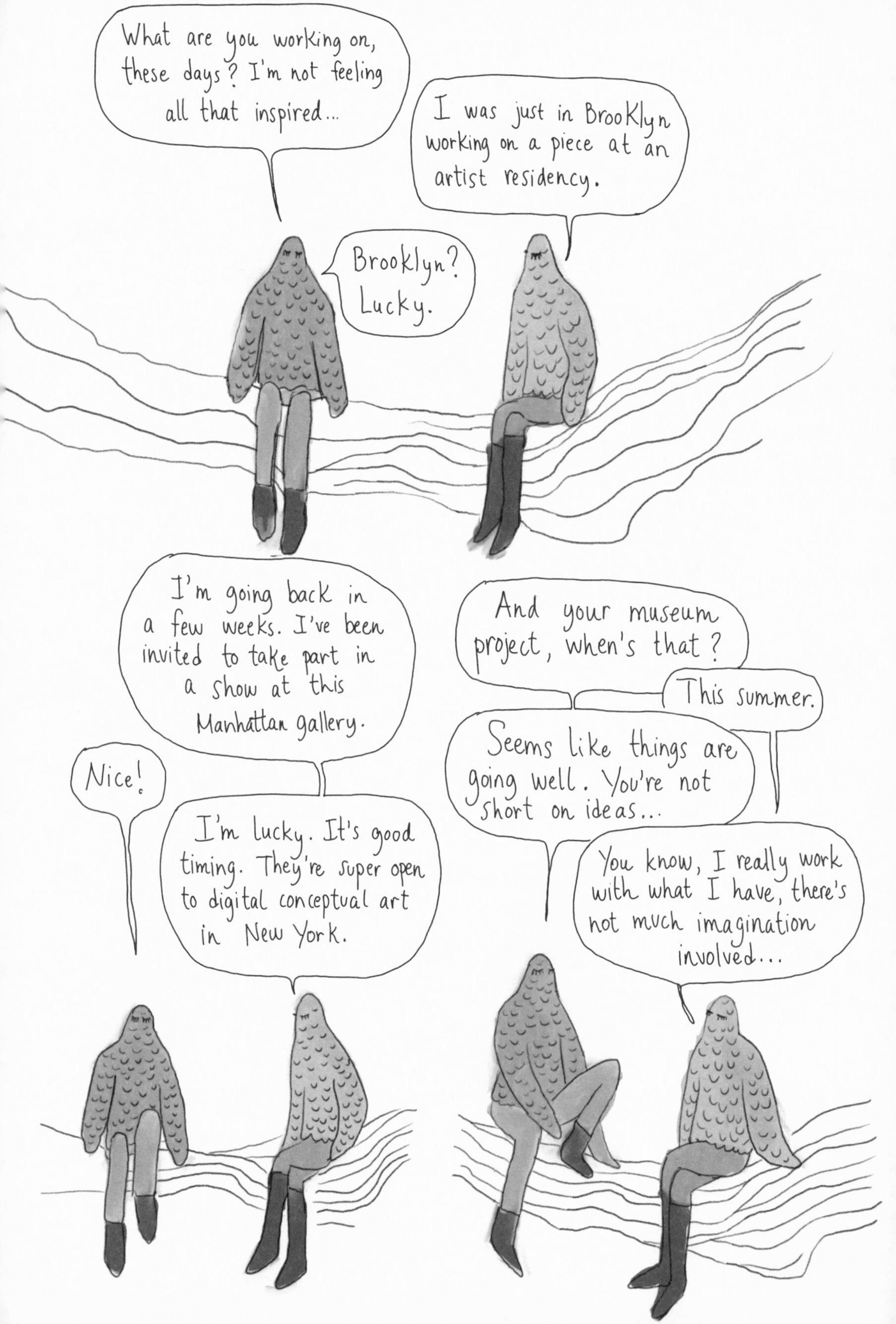
What are you working on, these days? I'm not feeling all that inspired...
I was just in Brooklyn working on a piece at an artist residency.
Brooklyn? Lucky.
I'm going back in a few weeks. I've been invited to take part in a show at this Manhattan gallery.
Nice!
I'm lucky. It's good timing. They're super open to digital conceptual art in New York.
And your museum project, when's that?
This summer.
Seems like things are going well. You're not short on ideas...
You know, I really work with what I have, there's not much imagination involved...

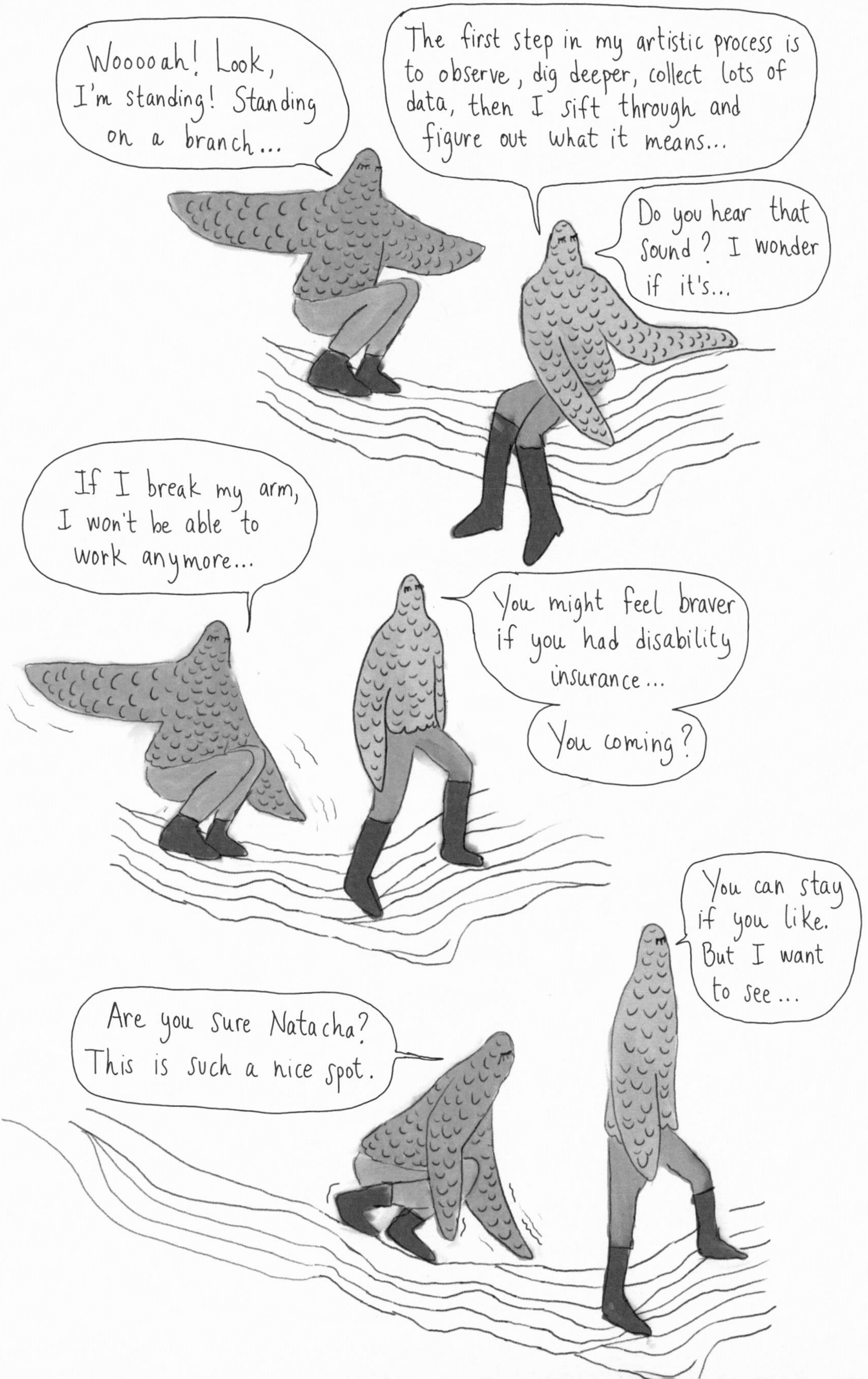
Woooah! Look, I'm standing! Standing on a branch...
The first step in my artistic process is to observe, dig deeper, collect lots of data, then I sift through and figure out what it means...
Do you hear that sound? I wonder if it's...
If I break my arm, I won't be able to work anymore...
You might feel braver if you had disability insurance...
You coming?
You can stay if you like. But I want to see...
Are you sure Natacha? This is such a nice spot.

I'm hyper-aware of my surroundings... The ugliness of the everyday is hard to handle...

For some of my projects, I task myself with finding different ways to watch and take in my surroundings.

For instance, every time I walk out of the metro station, I force myself to look at the colour of the sky, to note the smells and what kinds of memories they conjure. I'm so hyper focused on the experiment that I forget how ugly the street is outside the metro.

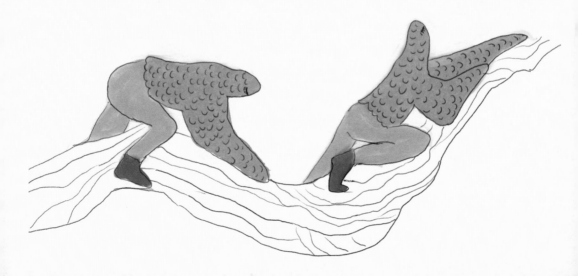

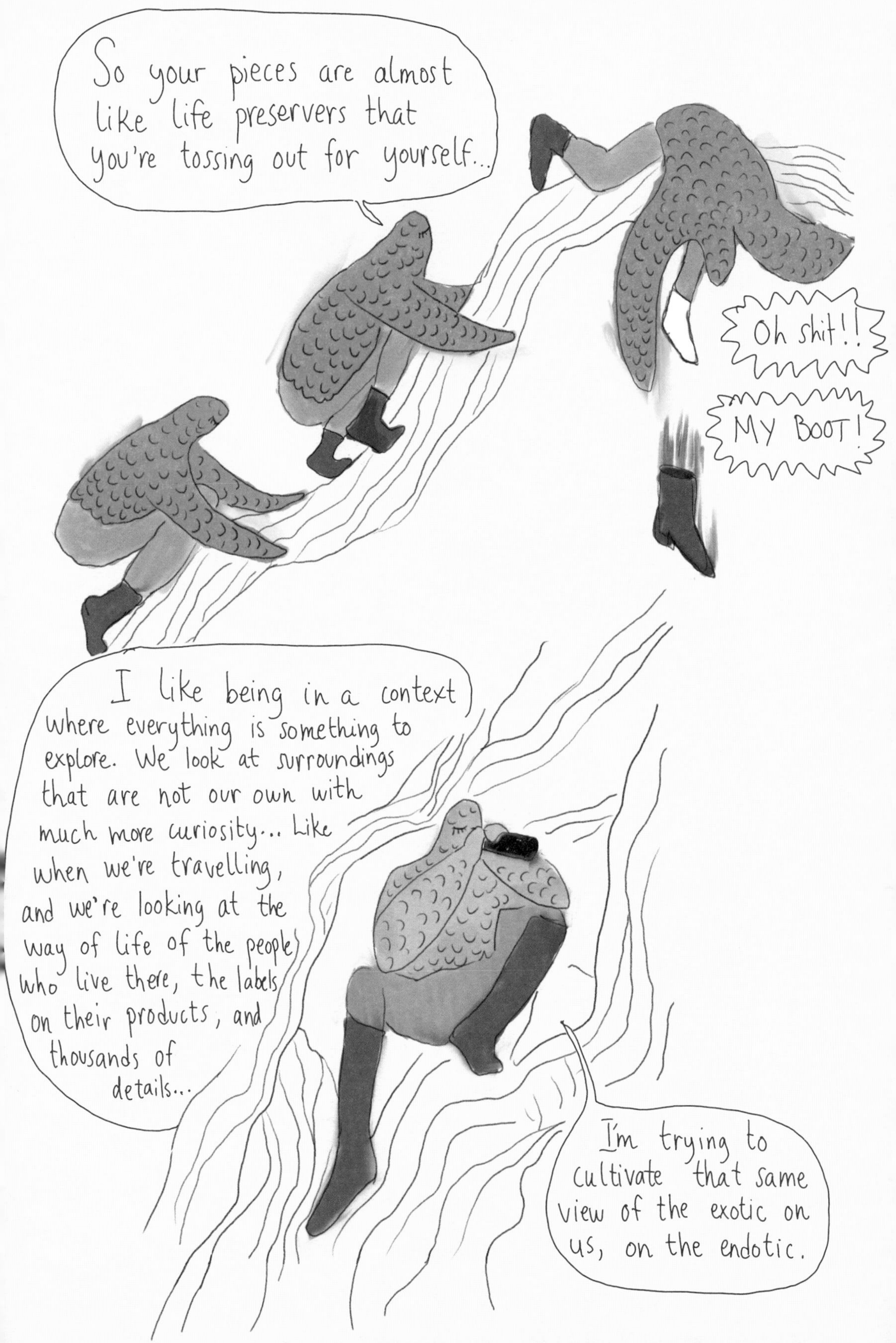

So your pieces are almost like life preservers that you're tossing out for yourself...
Oh shit!!
MY BOOT!
I like being in a context where everything is something to explore. We look at surroundings that are not our own with much more curiosity... Like when we're travelling, and we're looking at the way of life of the people who live there, the labels on their products, and thousands of details...
I'm trying to cultivate that same view of the exotic on us, on the endotic.

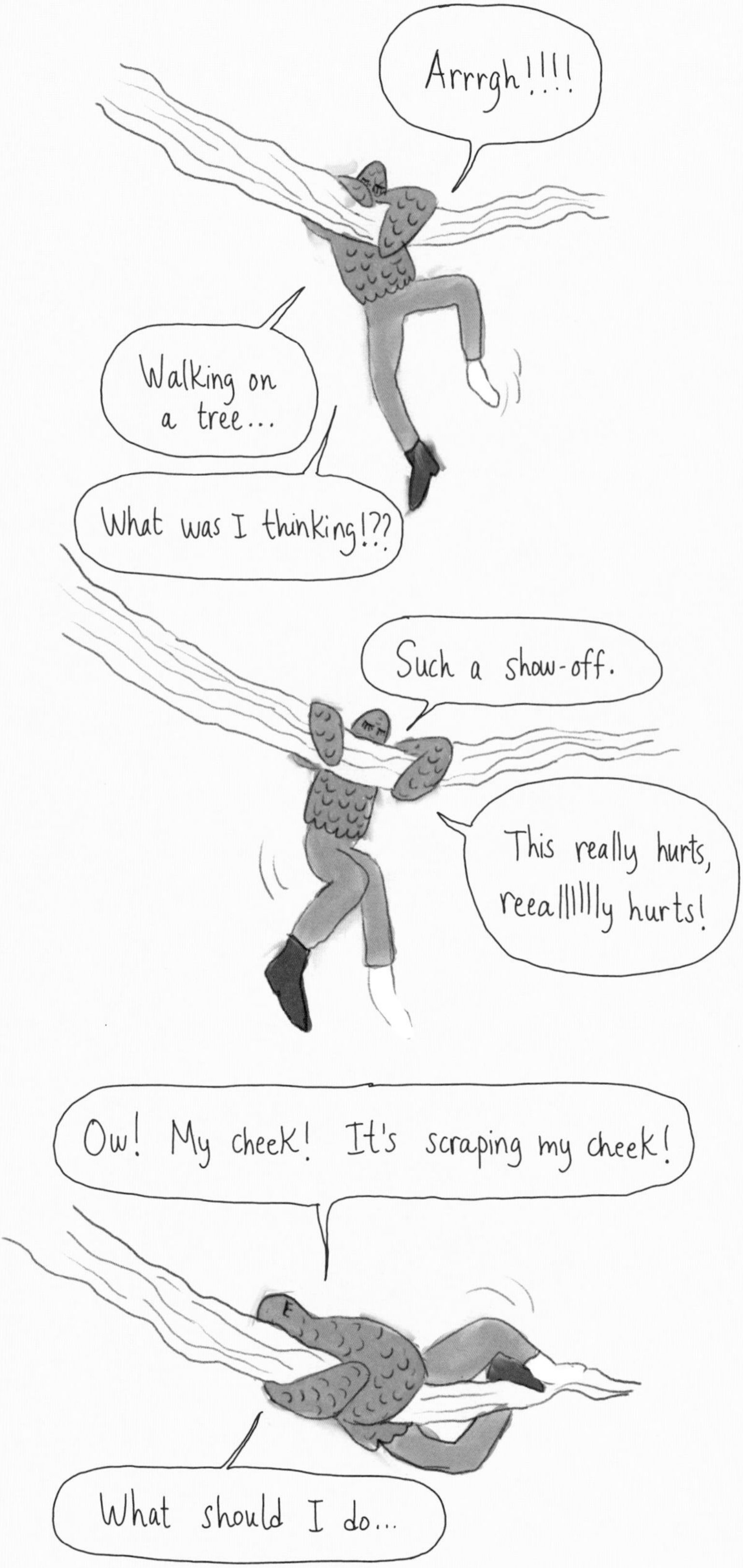
Arrrgh!!!!
Walking on a tree...
What was I thinking!??
Such a show-off.
This really hurts, reealllllly hurts!
Ow! My cheek! It's scraping my cheek!
What should I do...

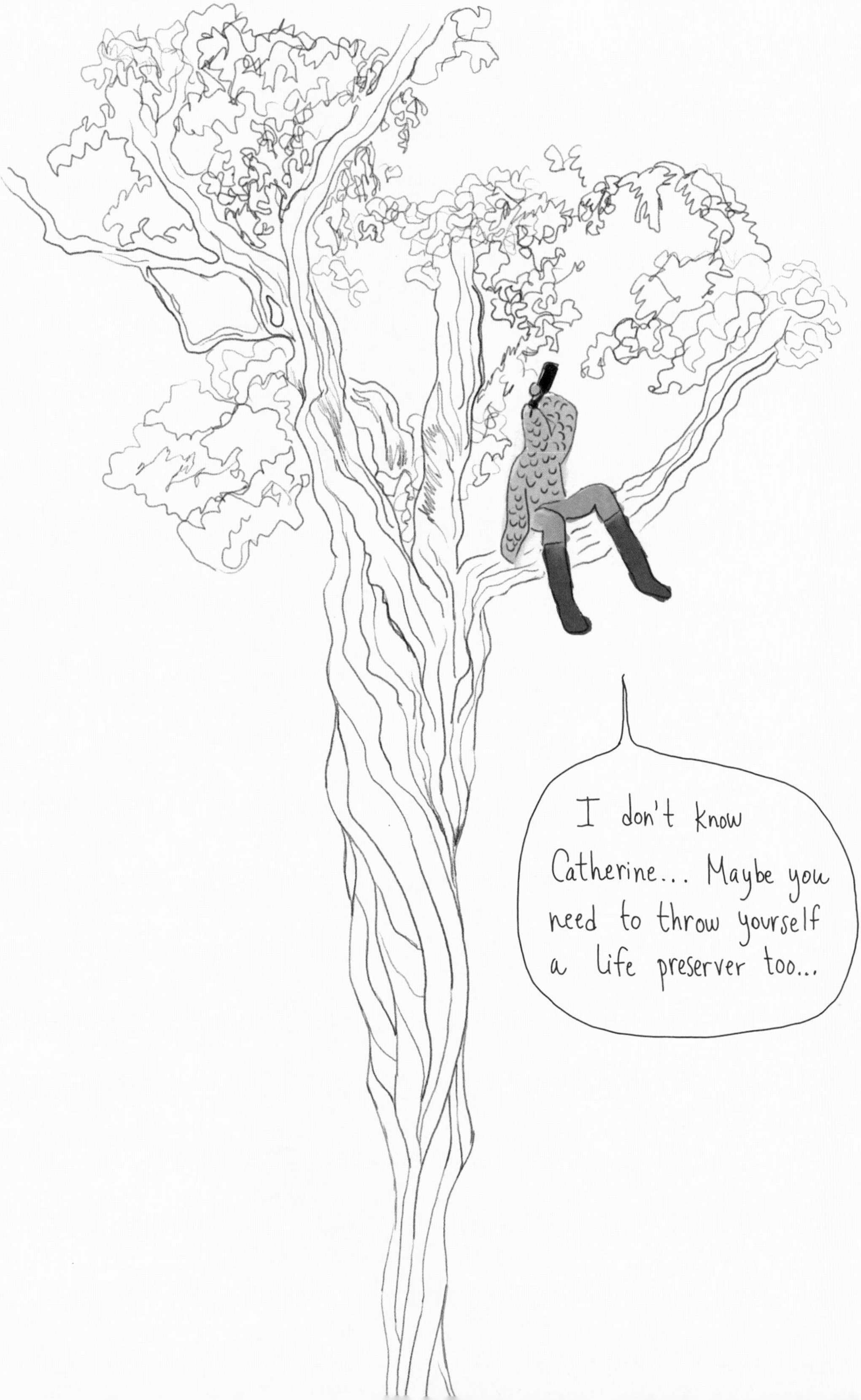
I don't know Catherine... Maybe you need to throw yourself a life preserver too...

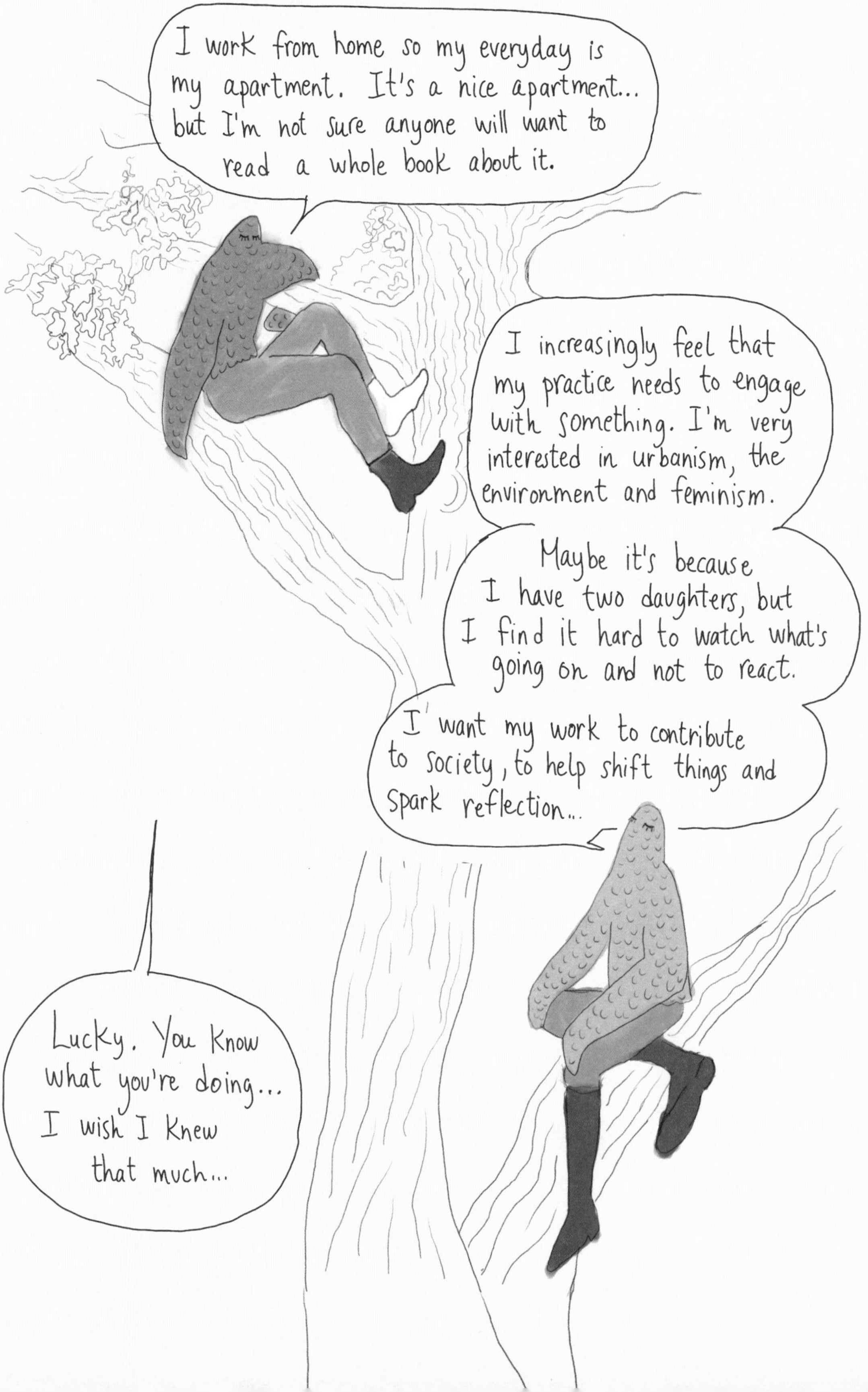
I work from home so my everyday is my apartment. It's a nice apartment... but I'm not sure anyone will want to read a whole book about it.
I increasingly feel that my practice needs to engage with something. I'm very interested in urbanism, the environment and feminism.
Maybe it's because I have two daughters, but I find it hard to watch what's going on and not to react.
I want my work to contribute to society, to help shift things and spark reflection...
Lucky. You know what you're doing... I wish I knew that much...

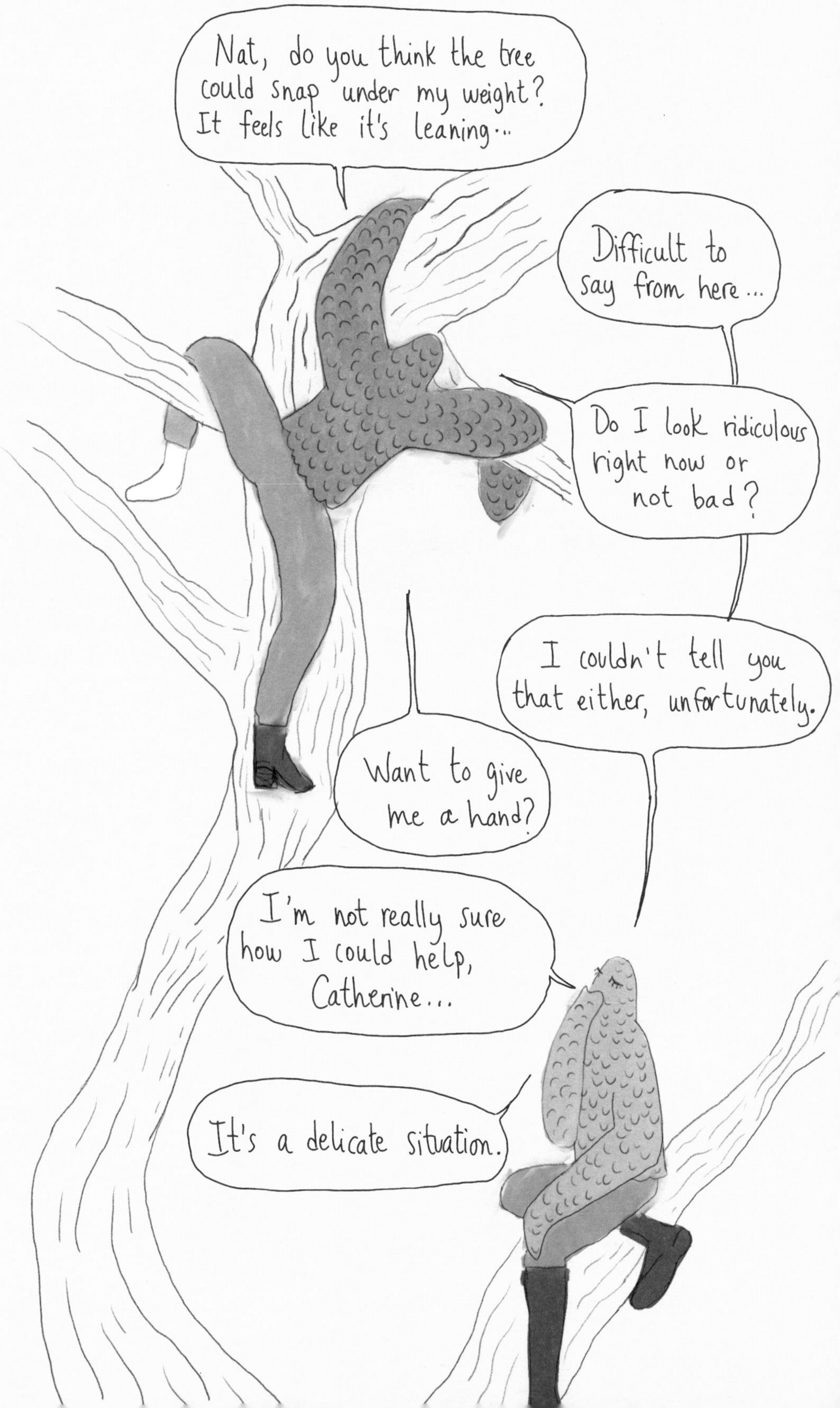
Nat, do you think the tree could snap under my weight? It feels like it's leaning...
Difficult to say from here...
Do I look ridiculous right now or not bad?
I couldn't tell you that either, unfortunately.
Want to give me a hand?
I'm not really sure how I could help, Catherine...
It's a delicate situation.

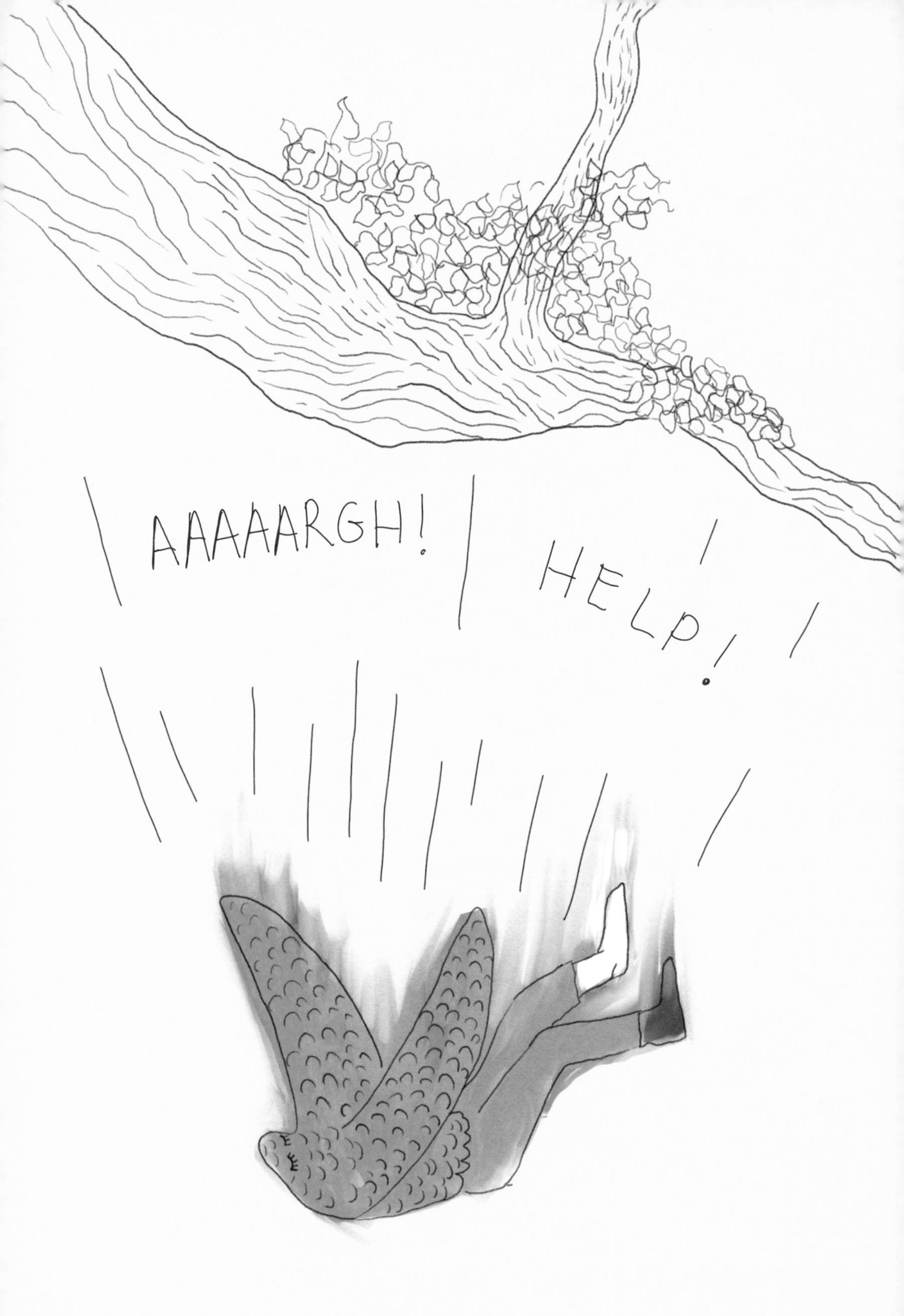
AAAAARGH!
HELP!

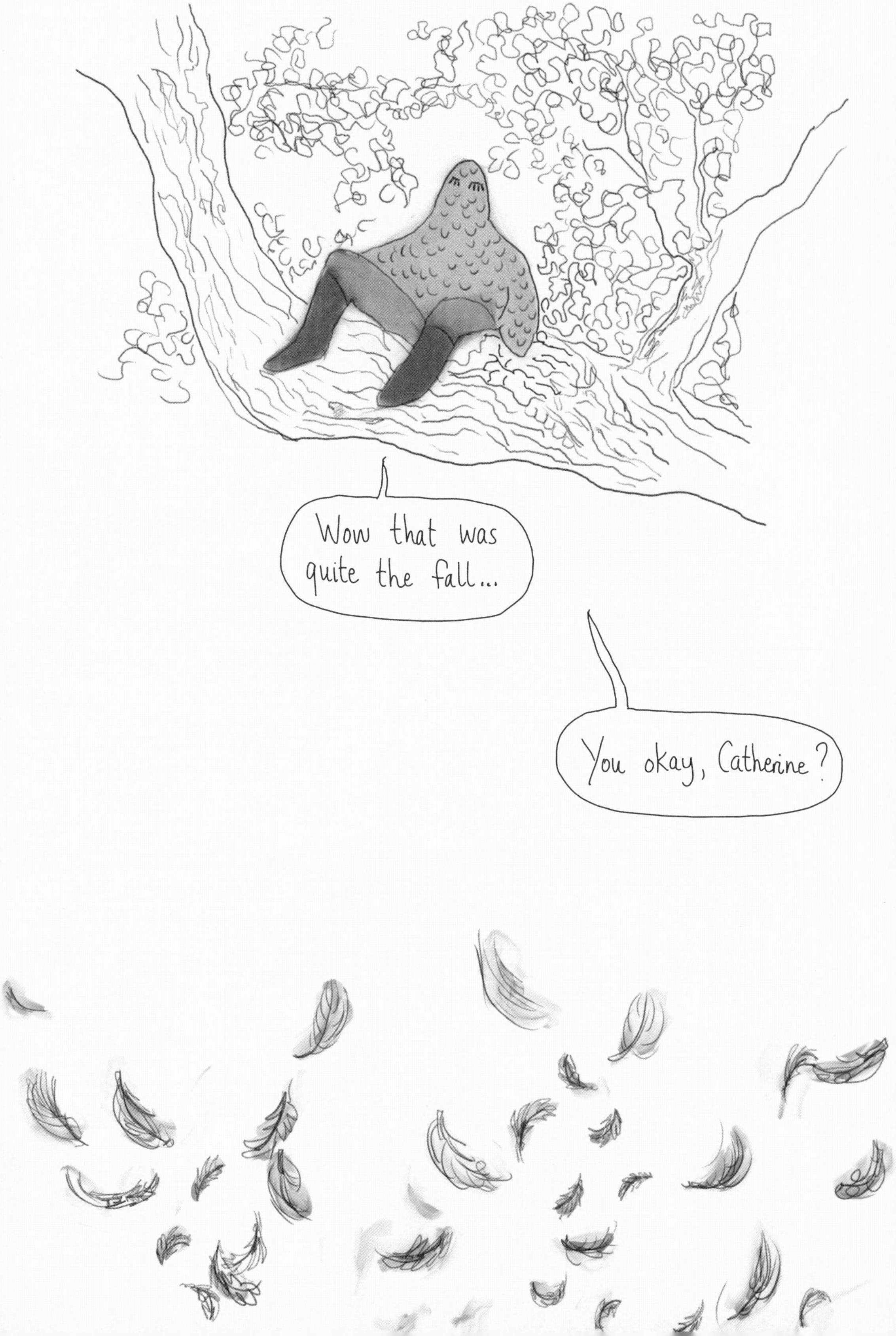
Wow that was quite the fall...
You okay, Catherine?

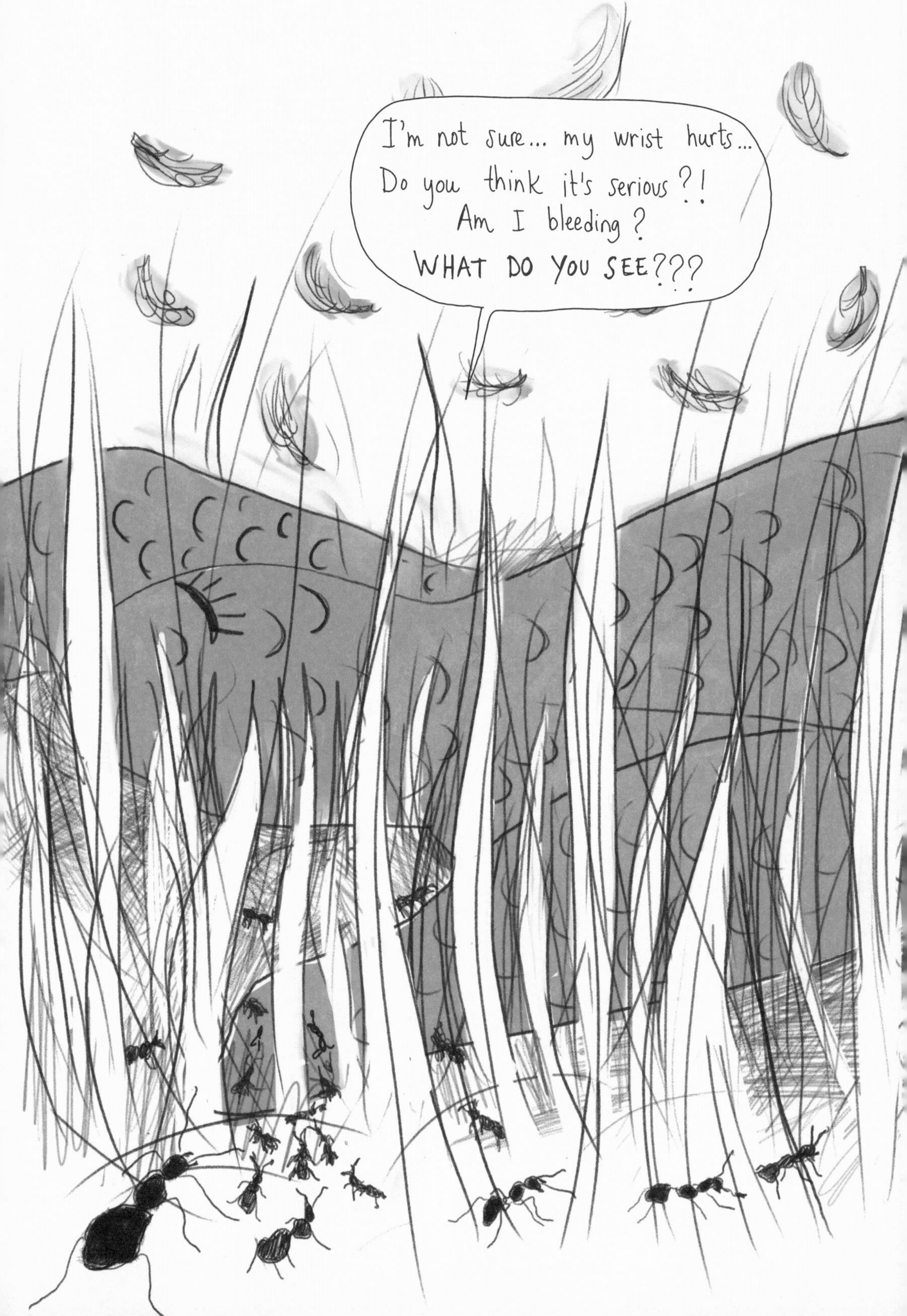
I'm not sure... my wrist hurts... Do you think it's serious?! Am I bleeding? WHAT DO YOU SEE???

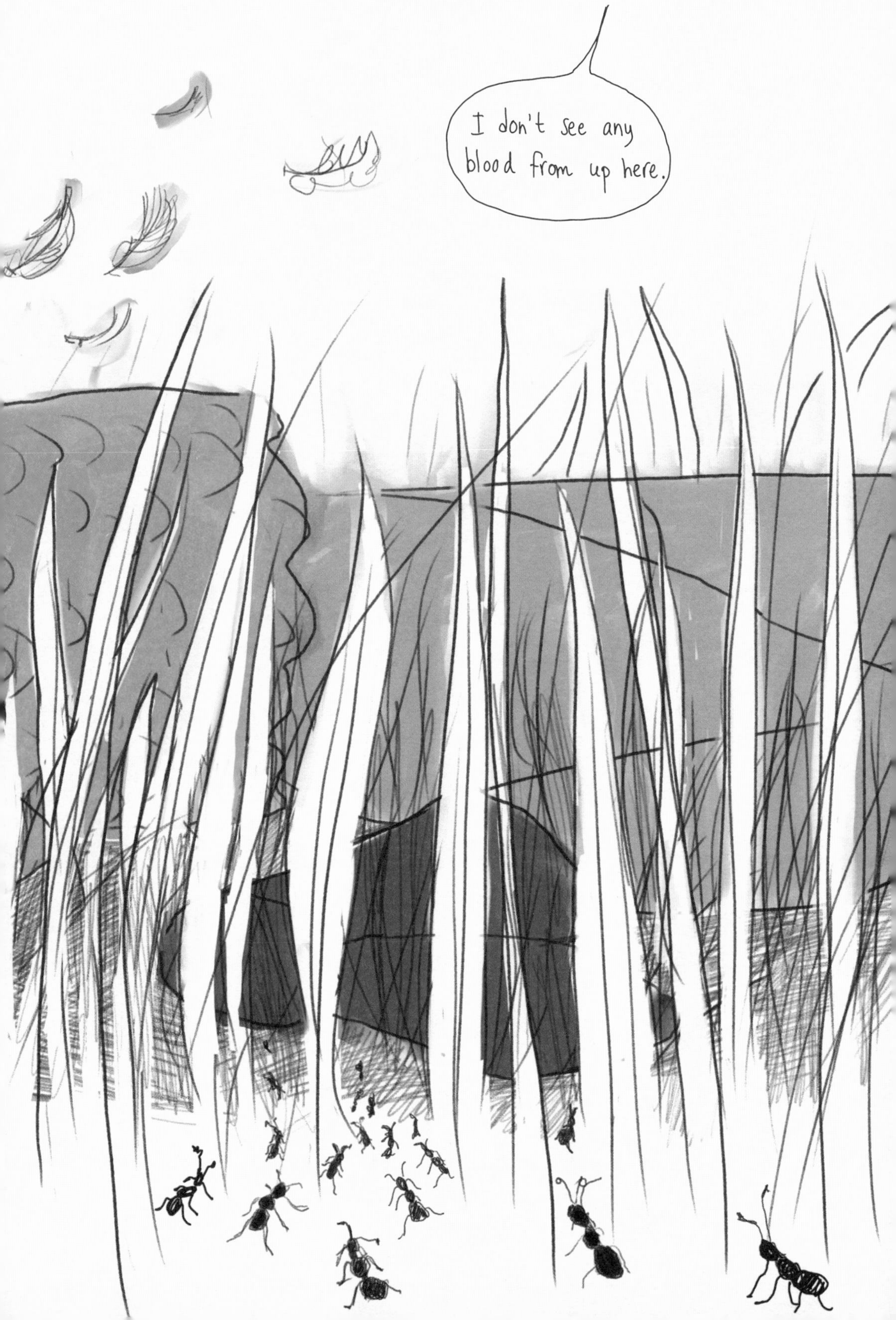
I don't see any blood from up here.

Marie-Claude and Renaud

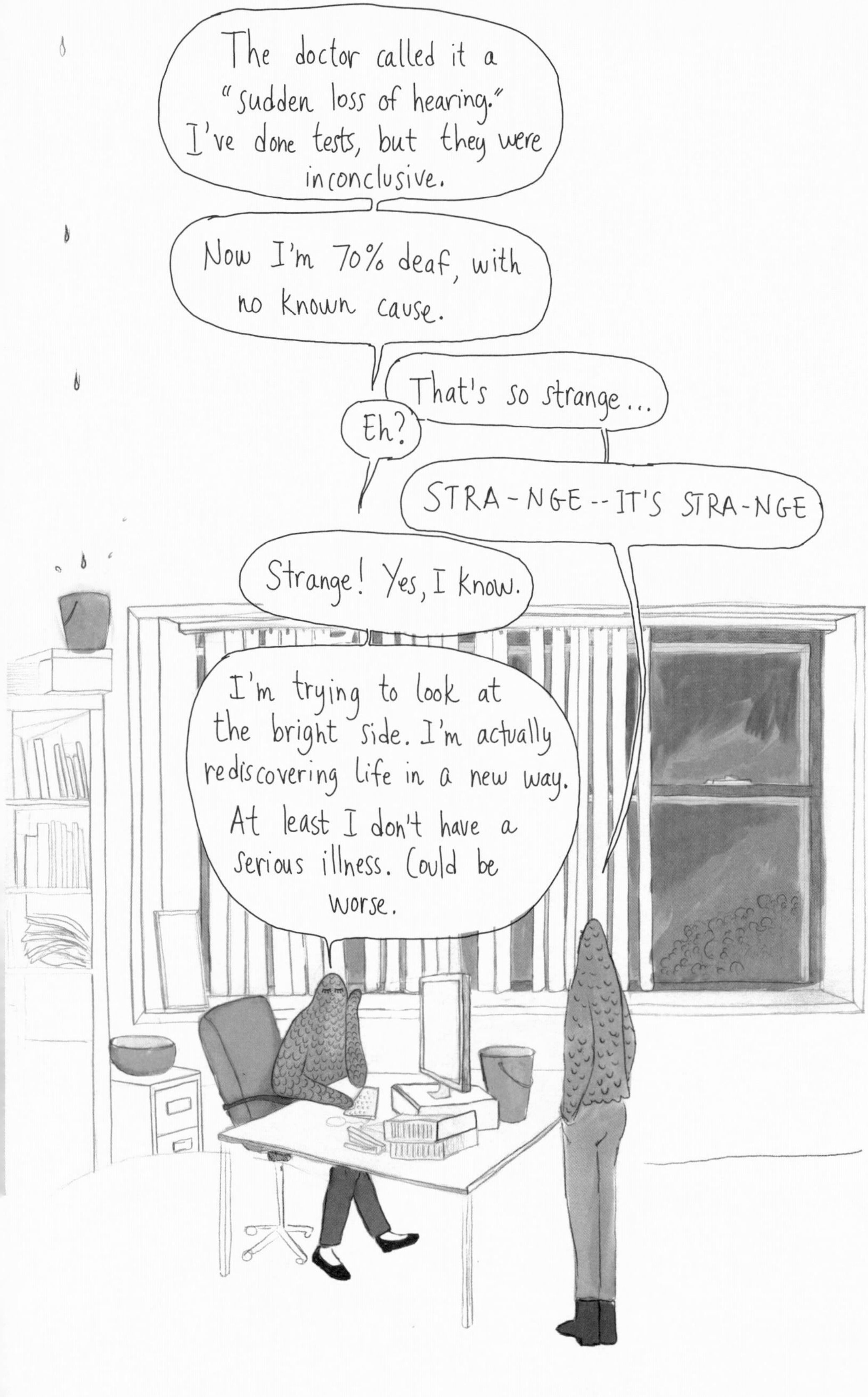
The doctor called it a "sudden loss of hearing." I've done tests, but they were inconclusive.
Now I'm 70% deaf, with no known cause.
That's so strange...
Eh?
STRA-NGE--IT'S STRA-NGE
Strange! Yes, I know.
I'm trying to look at the bright side. I'm actually rediscovering life in a new way.
At least I don't have a serious illness. Could be worse.

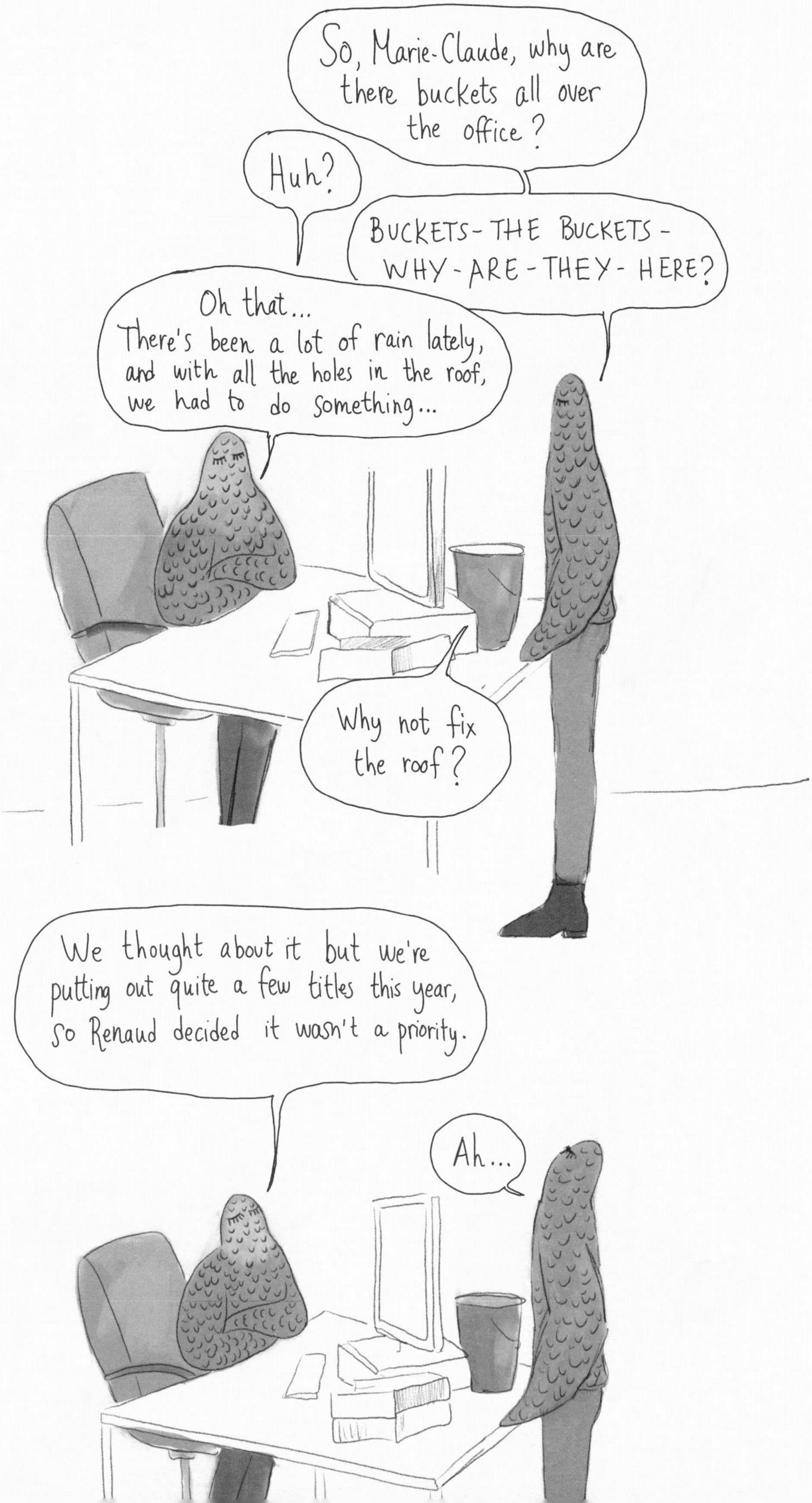
So, Marie-Claude, why are there buckets all over the office?
Huh?
BUCKETS- THE BUCKETS - WHY-ARE-THEY- HERE?
Oh that... There's been a lot of rain lately, and with all the holes in the roof, we had to do something...
Why not fix the roof?
We thought about it but we're putting out quite a few titles this year, so Renaud decided it wasn't a priority.
Ah...

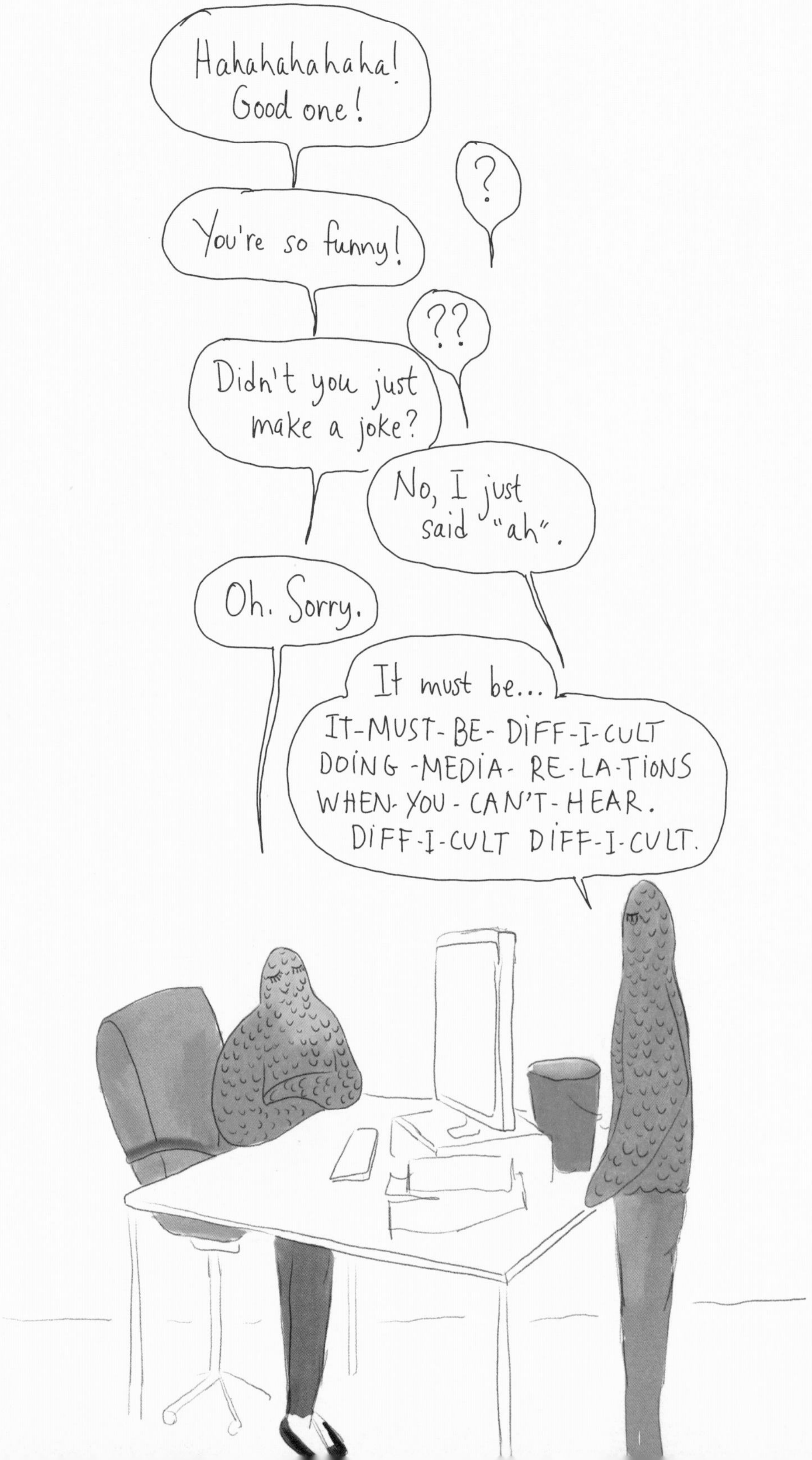
Hahahahahaha! Good one!
You're so funny!
?
??
Didn't you just make a joke?
No, I just said "ah".
Oh. Sorry.
It must be...
IT-MUST-BE-DIFF-I-CULT DOING-MEDIA-RE-LA-TIONS WHEN-YOU-CAN'T-HEAR. DIFF-I-CULT DIFF-I-CULT.

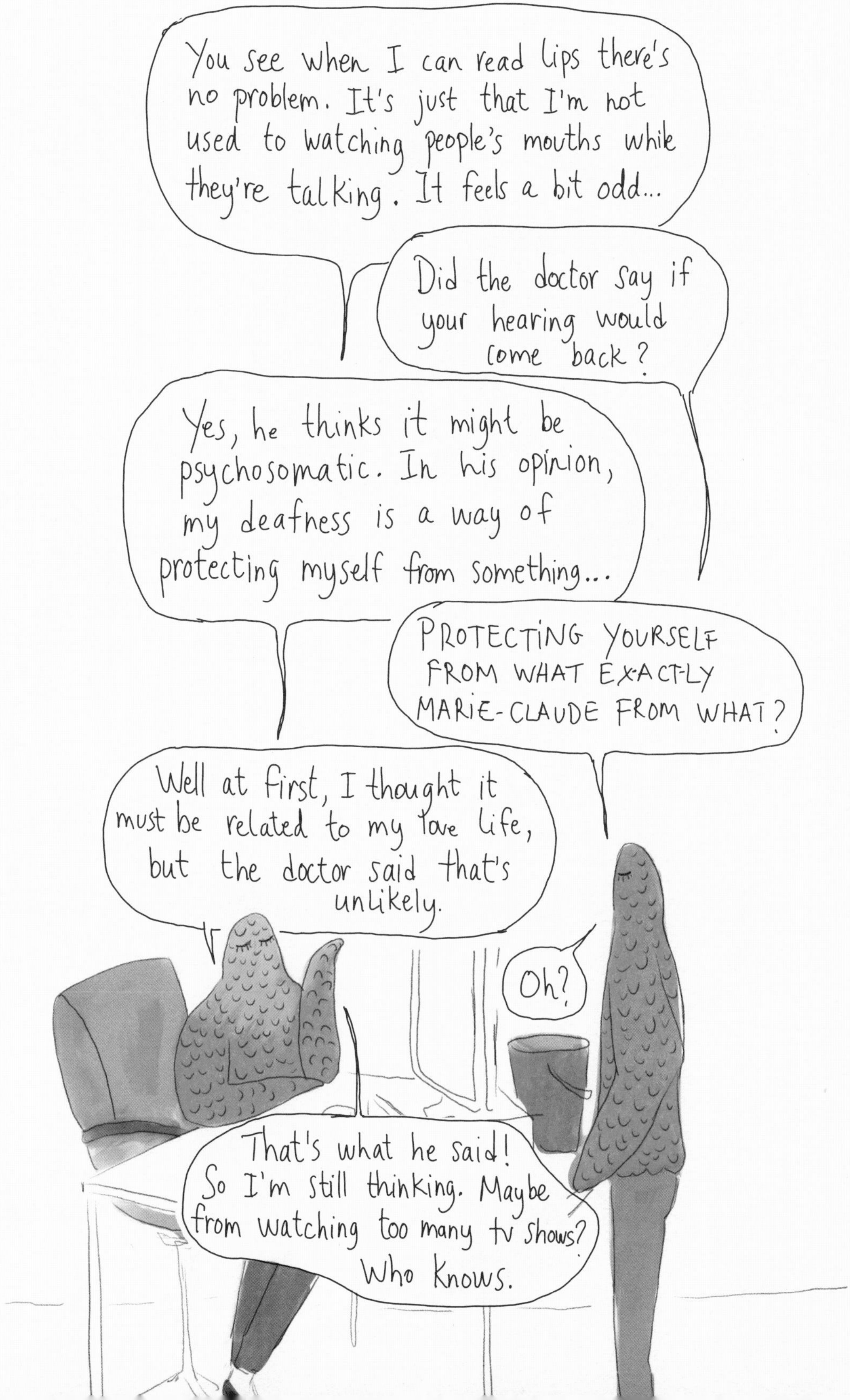
You see when I can read lips there's no problem. It's just that I'm not used to watching people's mouths while they're talking. It feels a bit odd...
Did the doctor say if your hearing would come back?
Yes, he thinks it might be psychosomatic. In his opinion, my deafness is a way of protecting myself from something...
PROTECTING YOURSELF FROM WHAT EXACTLY MARIE-CLAUDE FROM WHAT?
Well at first, I thought it must be related to my love life, but the doctor said that's unlikely.
Oh?
That's what he said! So I'm still thinking. Maybe from watching too many tv shows? Who knows.

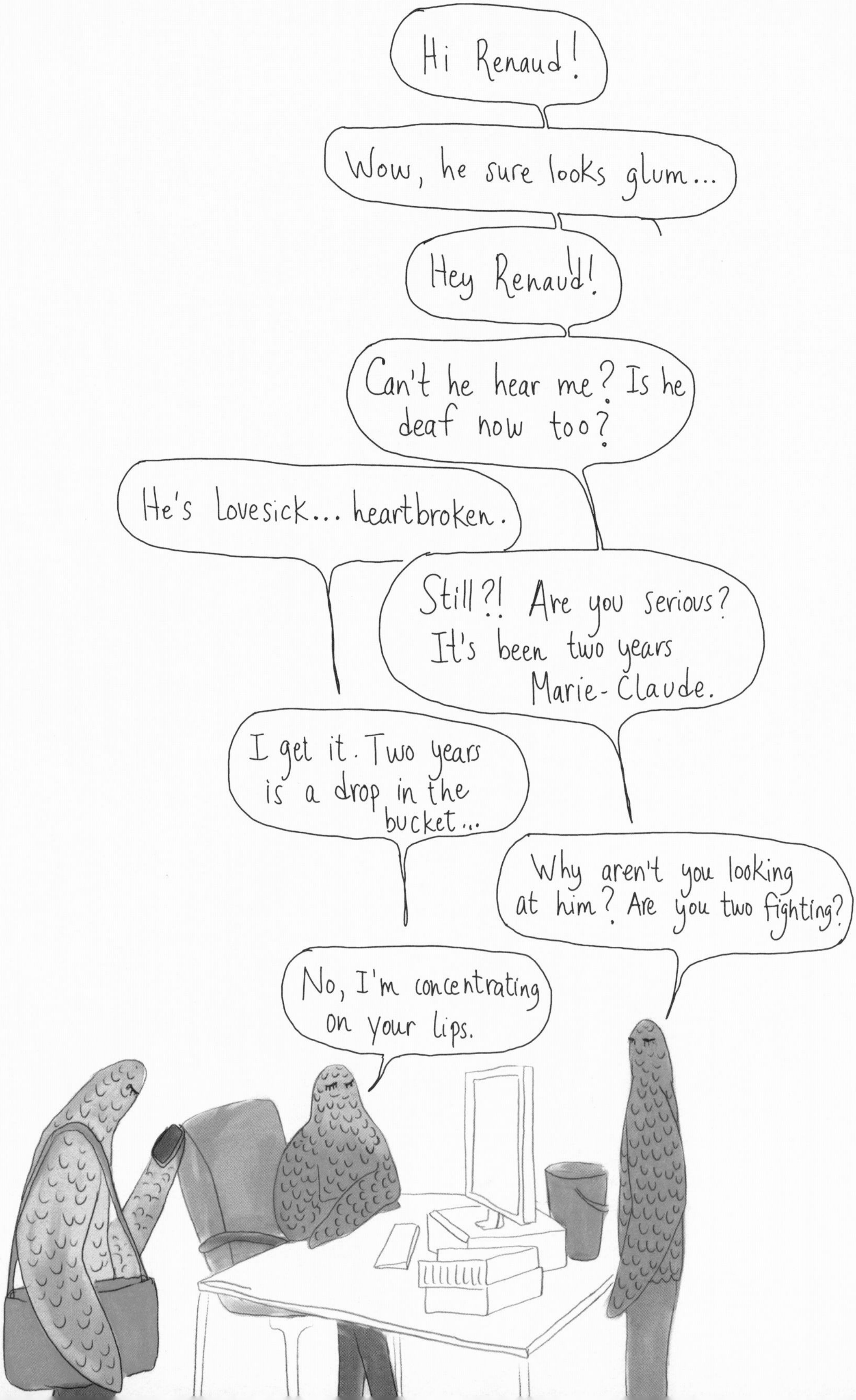
Hi Renaud!
Wow, he sure looks glum...
Hey Renaud!
Can't he hear me? Is he deaf now too?
He's lovesick... heartbroken.
Still?! Are you serious? It's been two years Marie-Claude.
I get it. Two years is a drop in the bucket...
Why aren't you looking at him? Are you two fighting?
No, I'm concentrating on your lips.

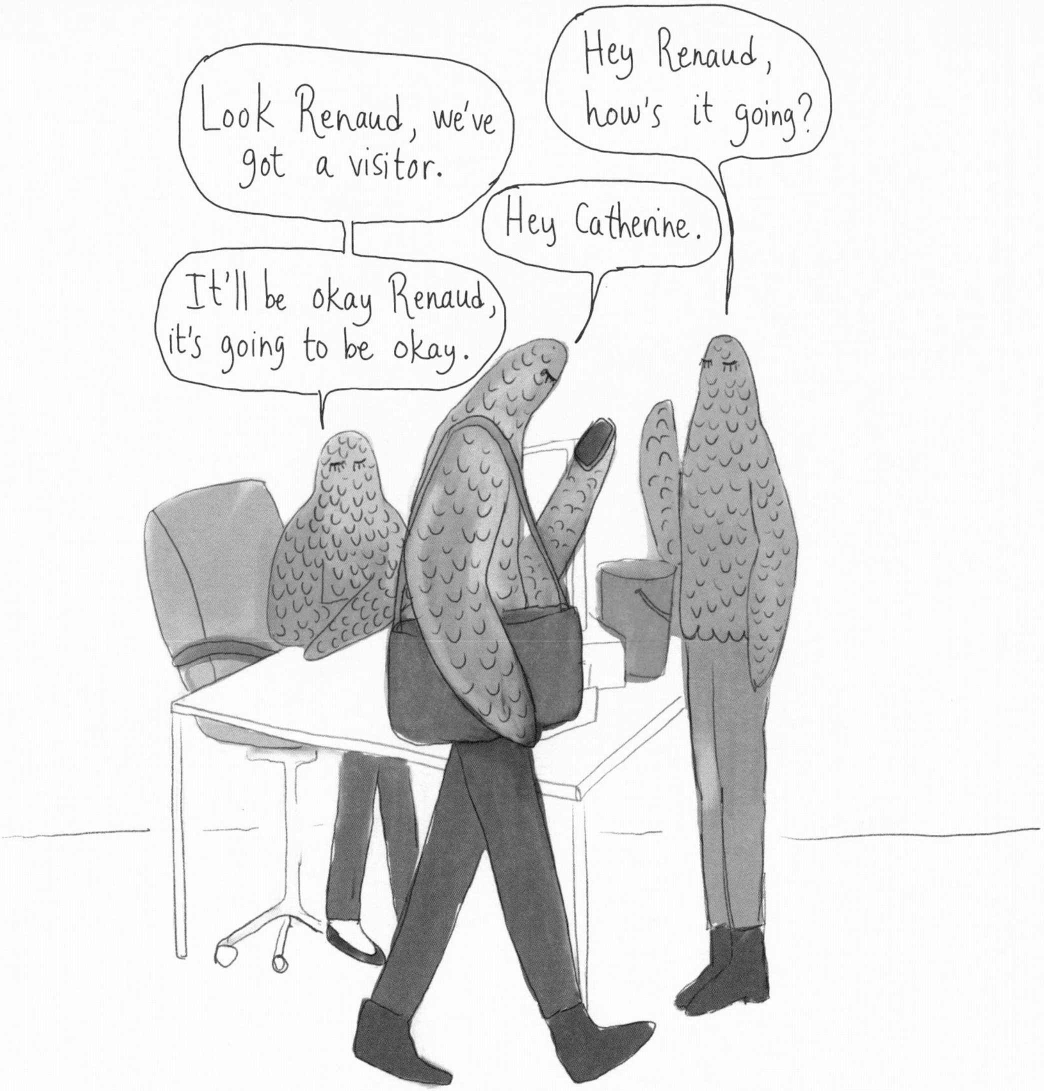
Look Renaud, we've got a visitor.
Hey Renaud, how's it going?
Hey Catherine.
It'll be okay Renaud, it's going to be okay.

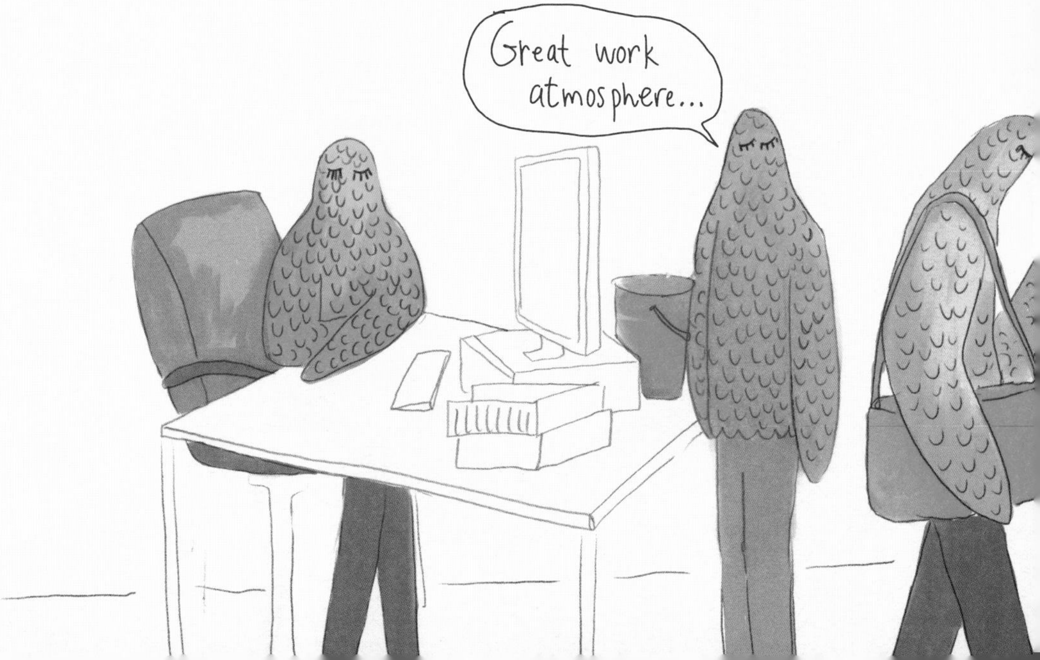
Great work atmosphere...

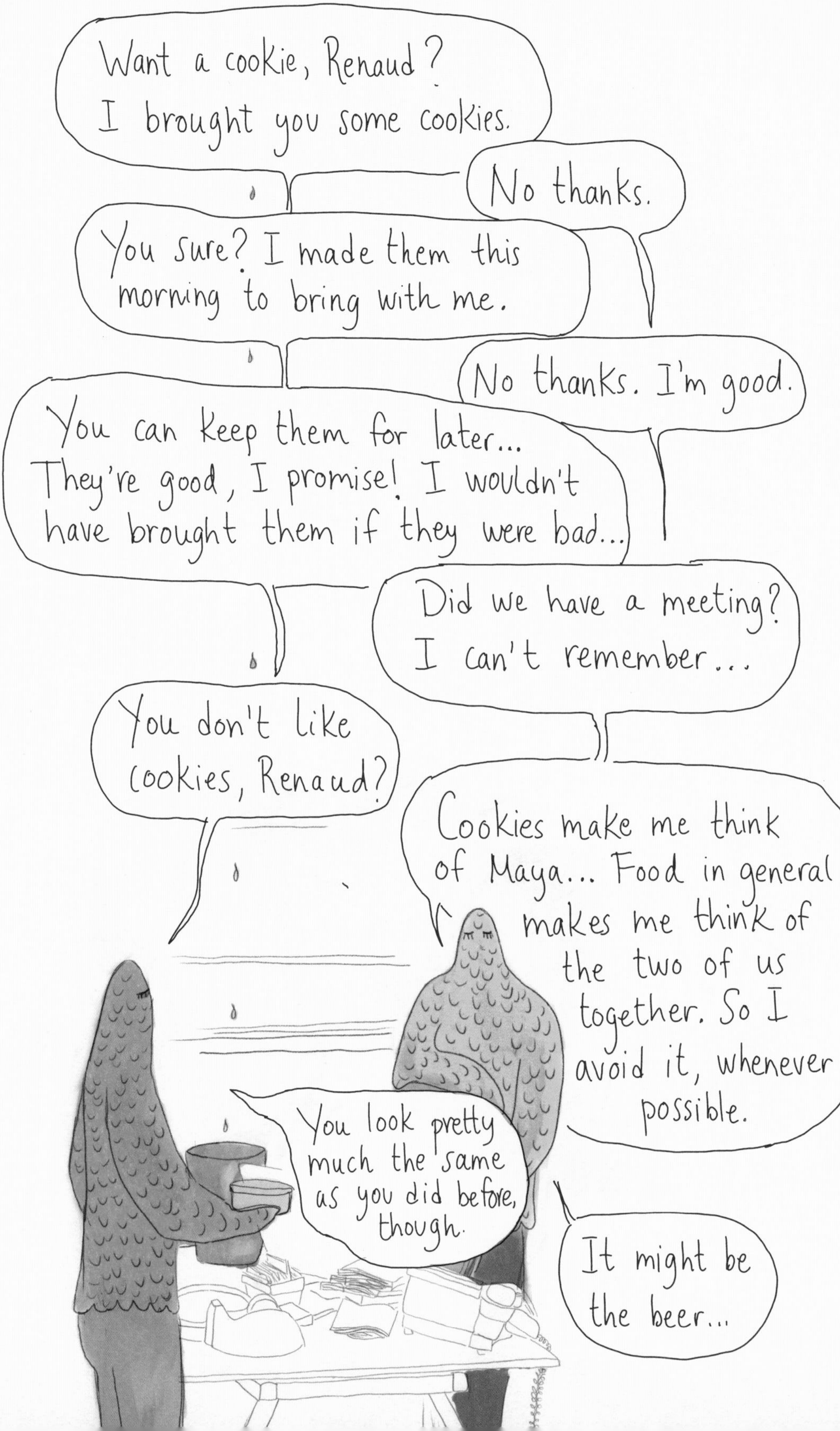
Want a cookie, Renaud? I brought you some cookies.
No thanks.
You sure? I made them this morning to bring with me.
No thanks. I'm good.
You can keep them for later... They're good, I promise! I wouldn't have brought them if they were bad...
Did we have a meeting? I can't remember...
You don't like cookies, Renaud?
Cookies make me think of Maya... Food in general makes me think of the two of us together. So I avoid it, whenever possible.
You look pretty much the same as you did before, though.
It might be the beer...

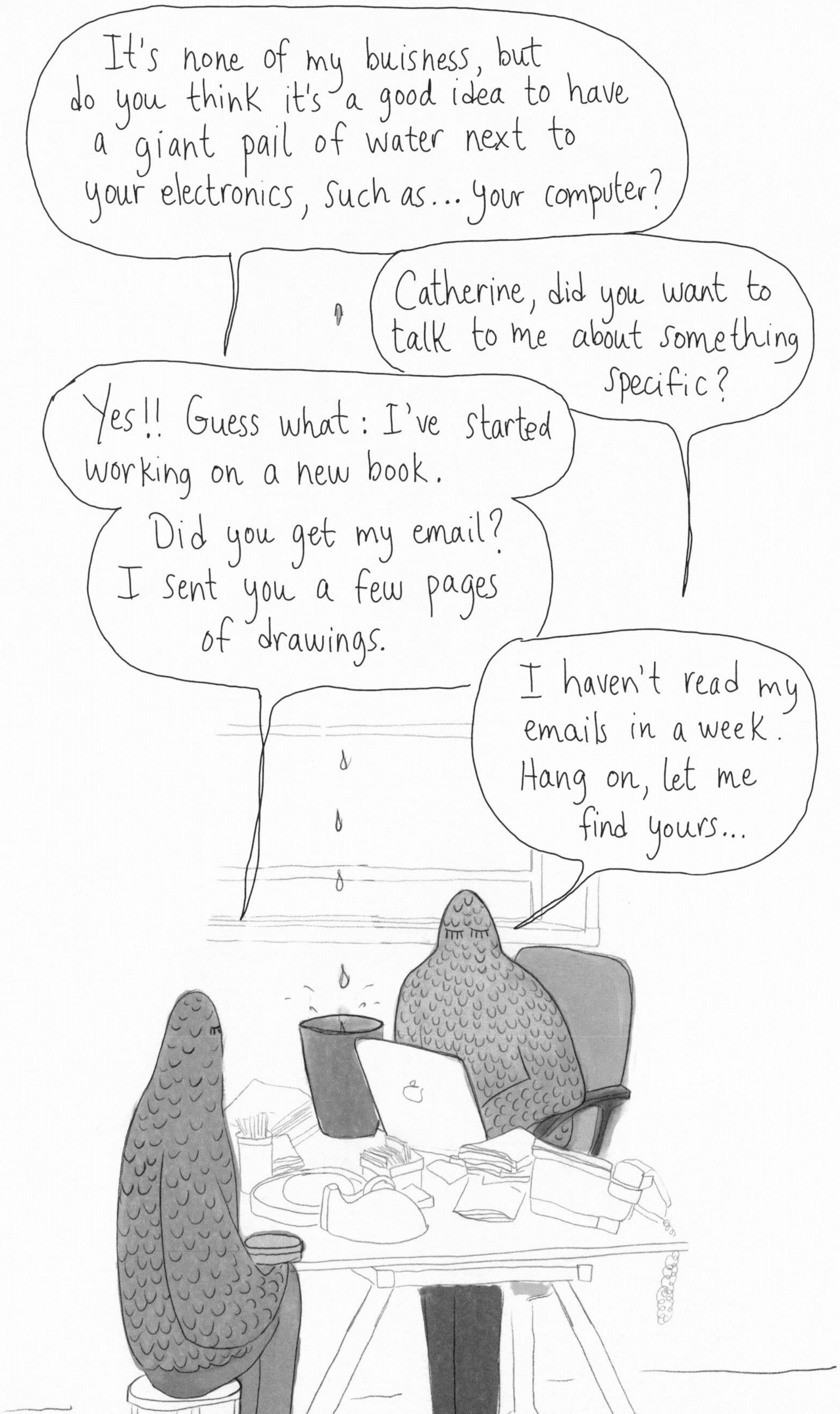
It's none of my buisness, but do you think it's a good idea to have a giant pail of water next to your electronics, such as... your computer?
Catherine, did you want to talk to me about something specific?
Yes!! Guess what: I've started working on a new book.
Did you get my email? I sent you a few pages of drawings.
I haven't read my emails in a week. Hang on, let me find yours...

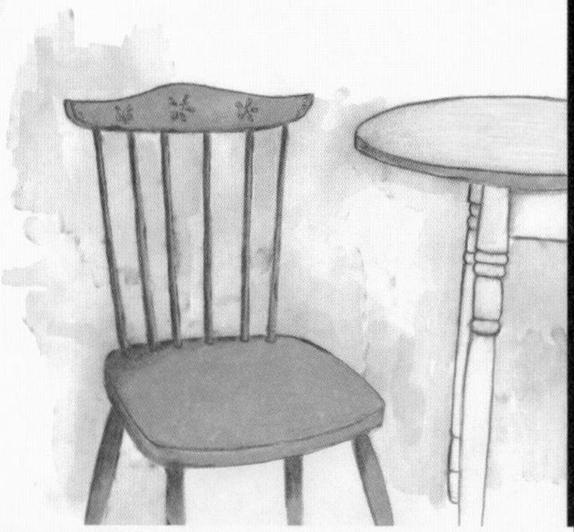

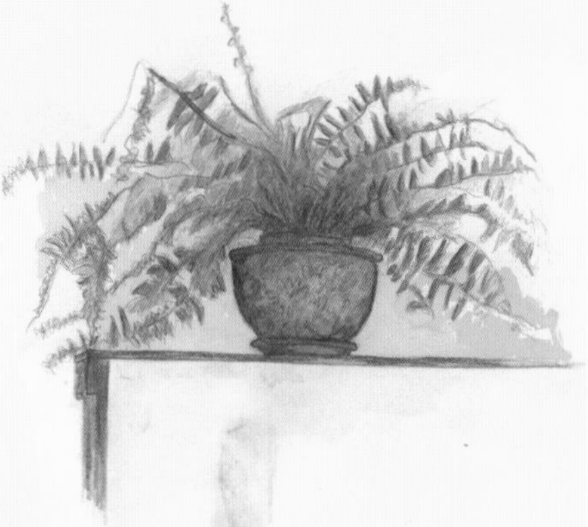

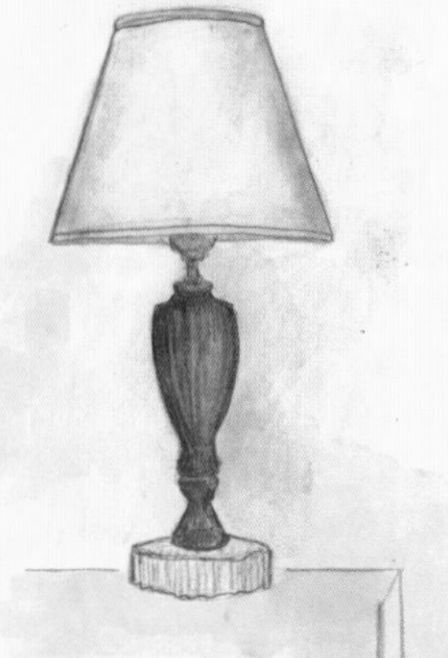

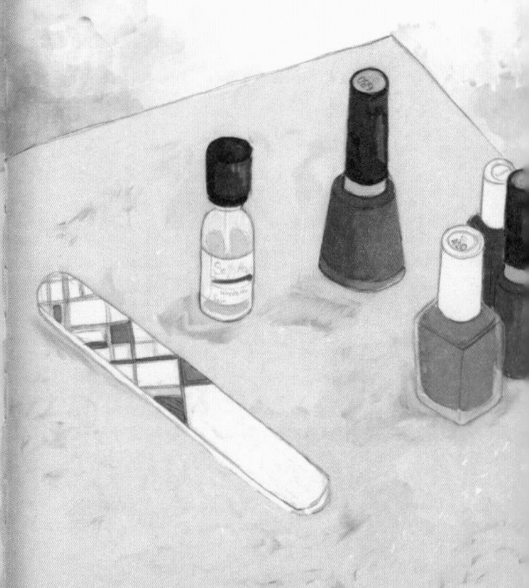

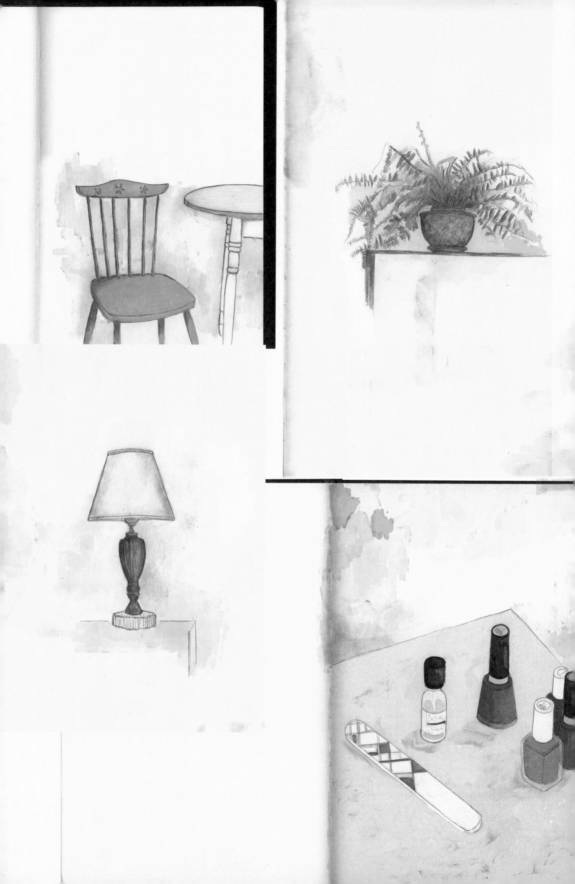

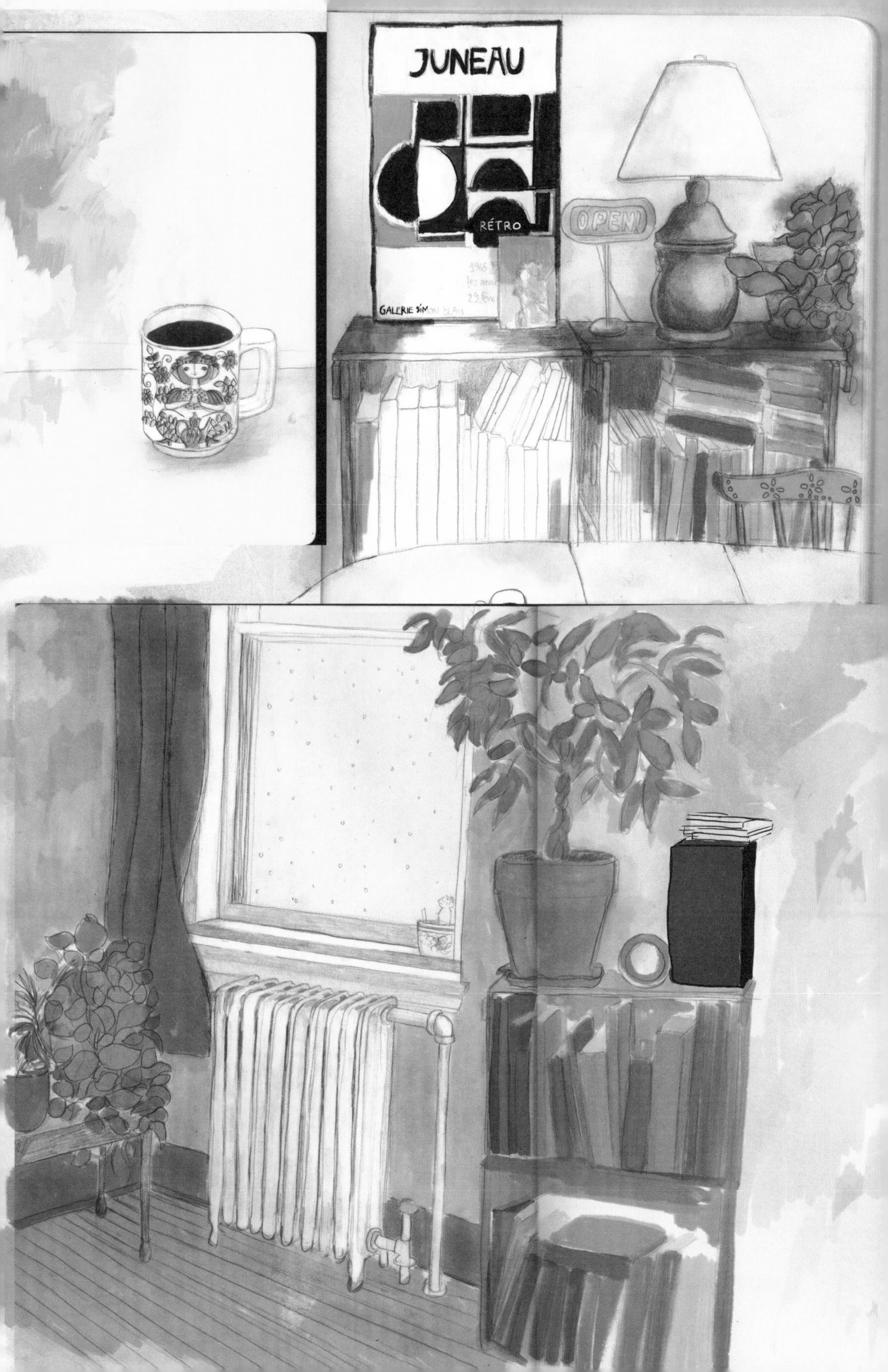
JUNEAU
RÉTRO
GALERIE SIMON BLAIS
OPEN

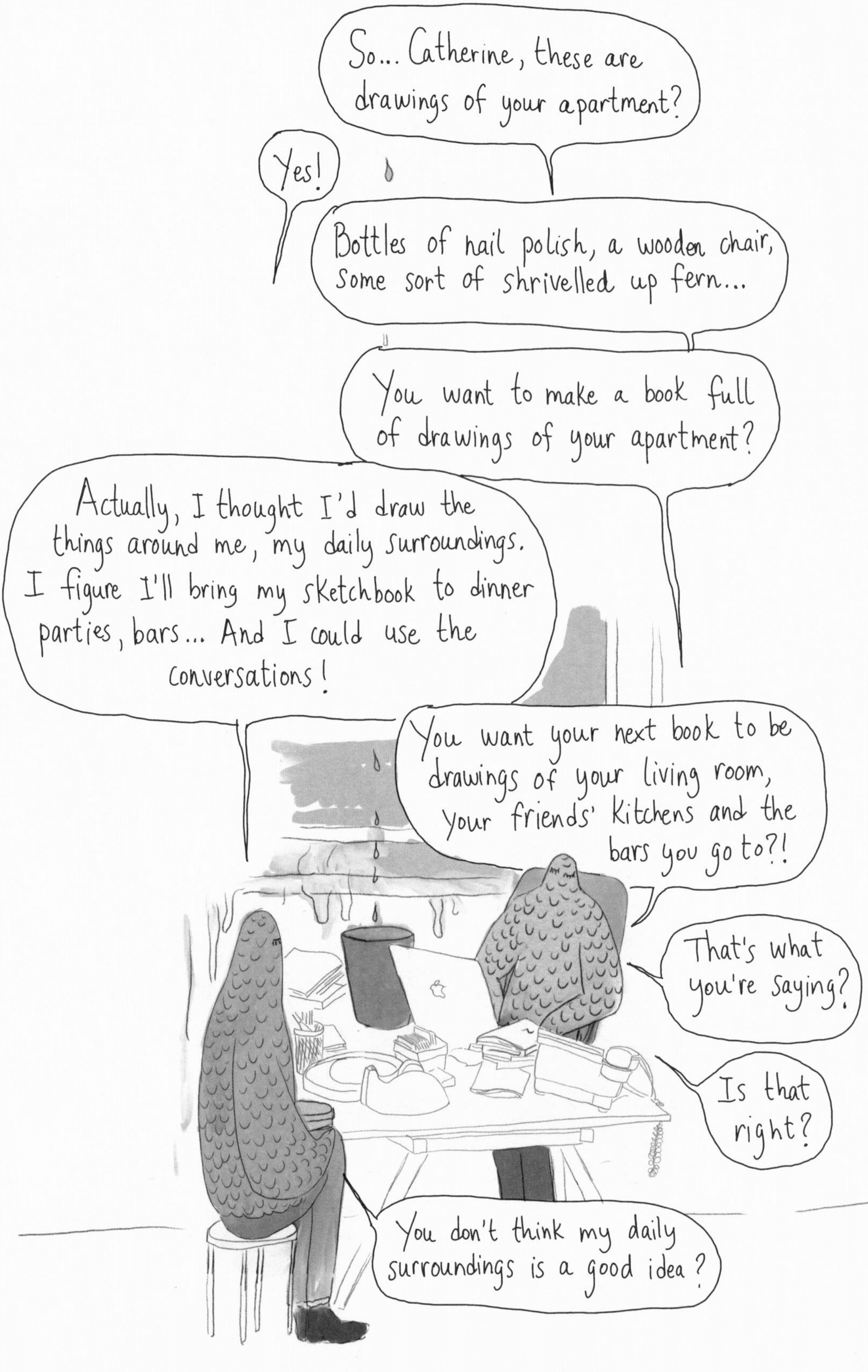
So... Catherine, these are drawings of your apartment?
Yes!
Bottles of nail polish, a wooden chair, some sort of shrivelled up fern...
You want to make a book full of drawings of your apartment?
Actually, I thought I'd draw the things around me, my daily surroundings. I figure I'll bring my sketchbook to dinner parties, bars... And I could use the conversations!
You want your next book to be drawings of your living room, your friends' kitchens and the bars you go to?!
That's what you're saying?
Is that right?
You don't think my daily surroundings is a good idea?

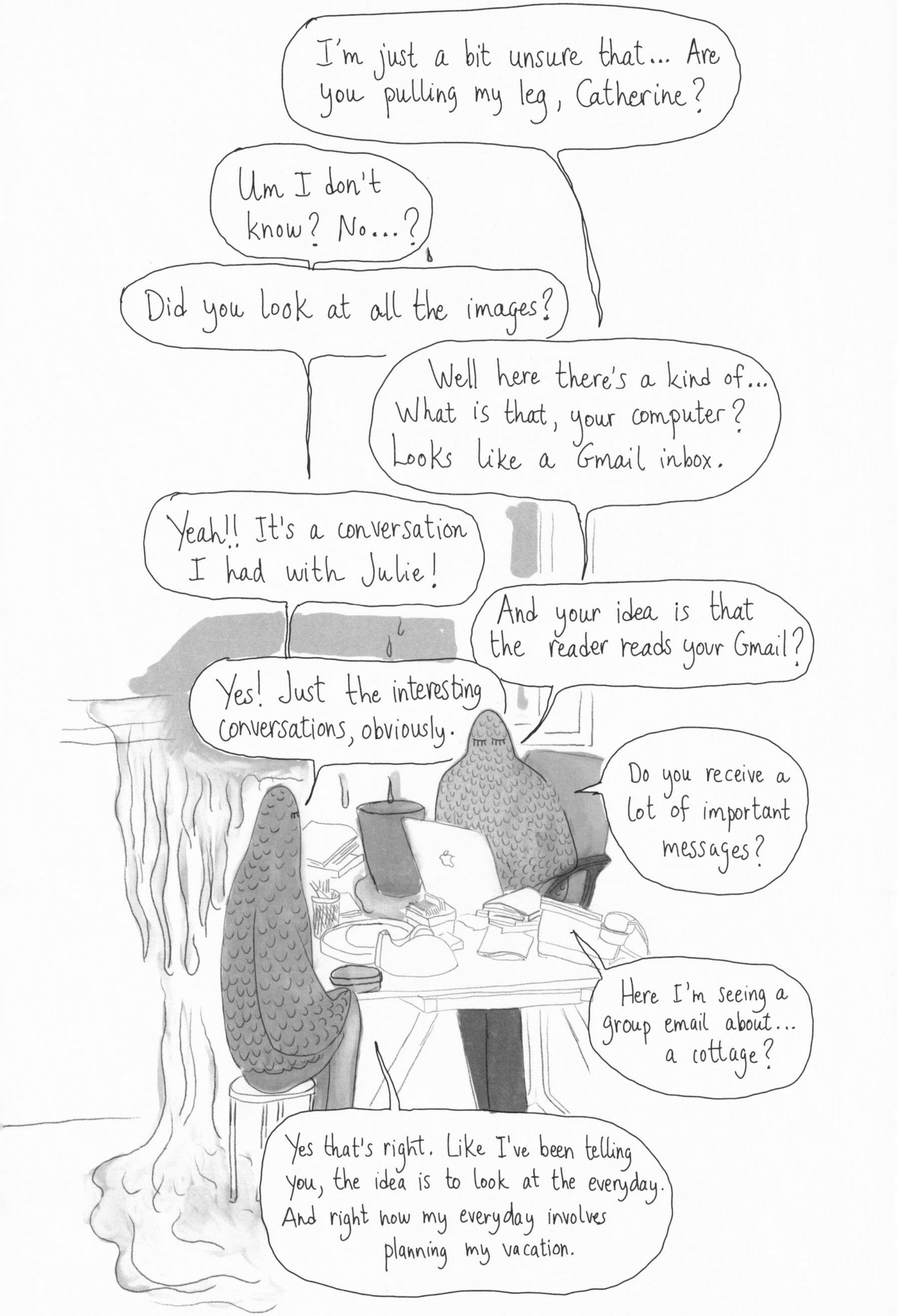
I'm just a bit unsure that... Are you pulling my leg, Catherine?
Um I don't know? No...?
Did you look at all the images?
Well here there's a kind of... What is that, your computer? Looks like a Gmail inbox.
Yeah!! It's a conversation I had with Julie!
And your idea is that the reader reads your Gmail?
Yes! Just the interesting conversations, obviously.
Do you receive a lot of important messages?
Here I'm seeing a group email about... a cottage?
Yes that's right. Like I've been telling you, the idea is to look at the everyday. And right now my everyday involves planning my vacation.

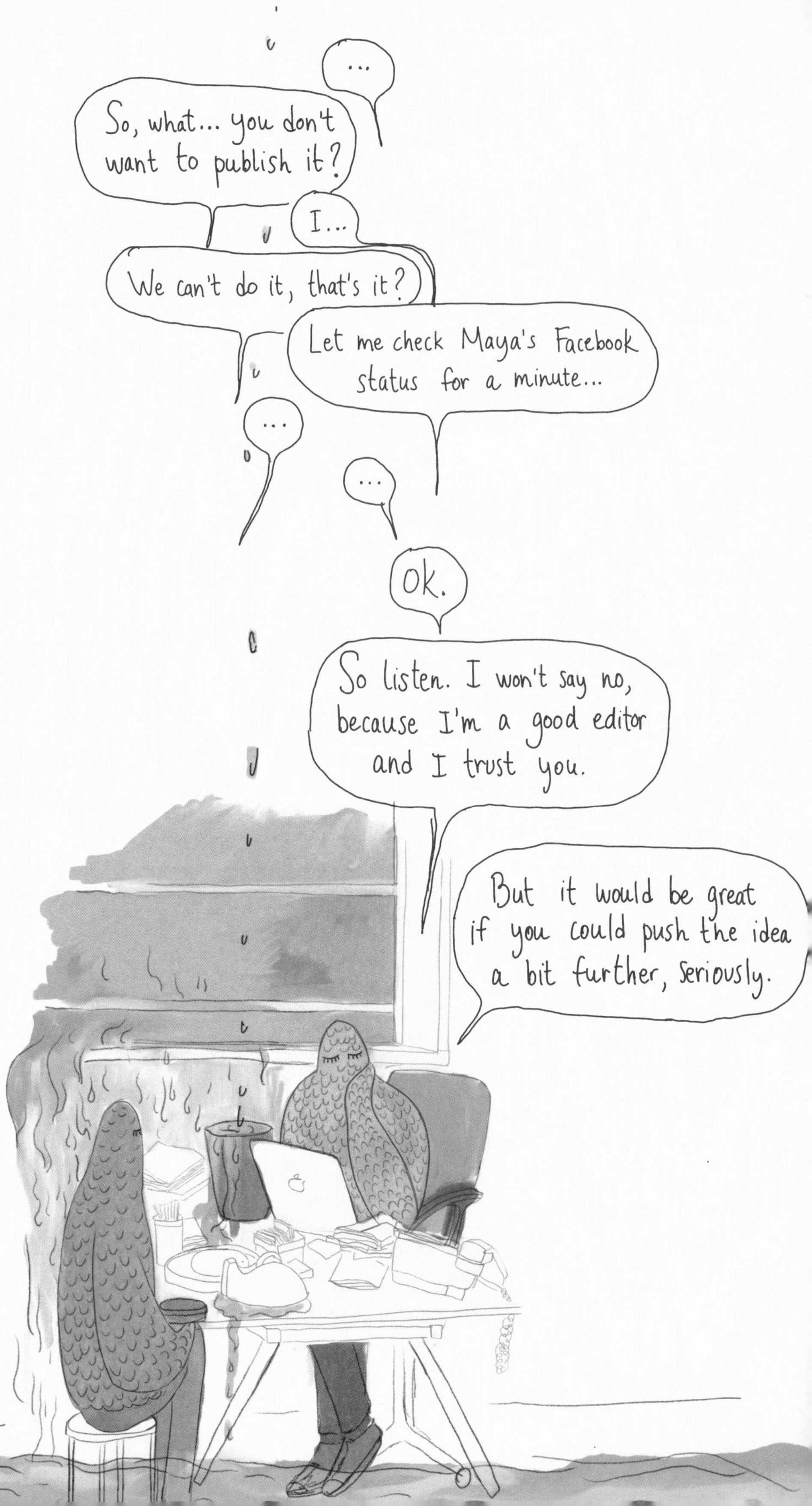
...
So, what... you don't want to publish it?
I...
We can't do it, that's it?
Let me check Maya's Facebook status for a minute...
...
...
Ok.
So listen. I won't say no, because I'm a good editor and I trust you.
But it would be great if you could push the idea a bit further, seriously.

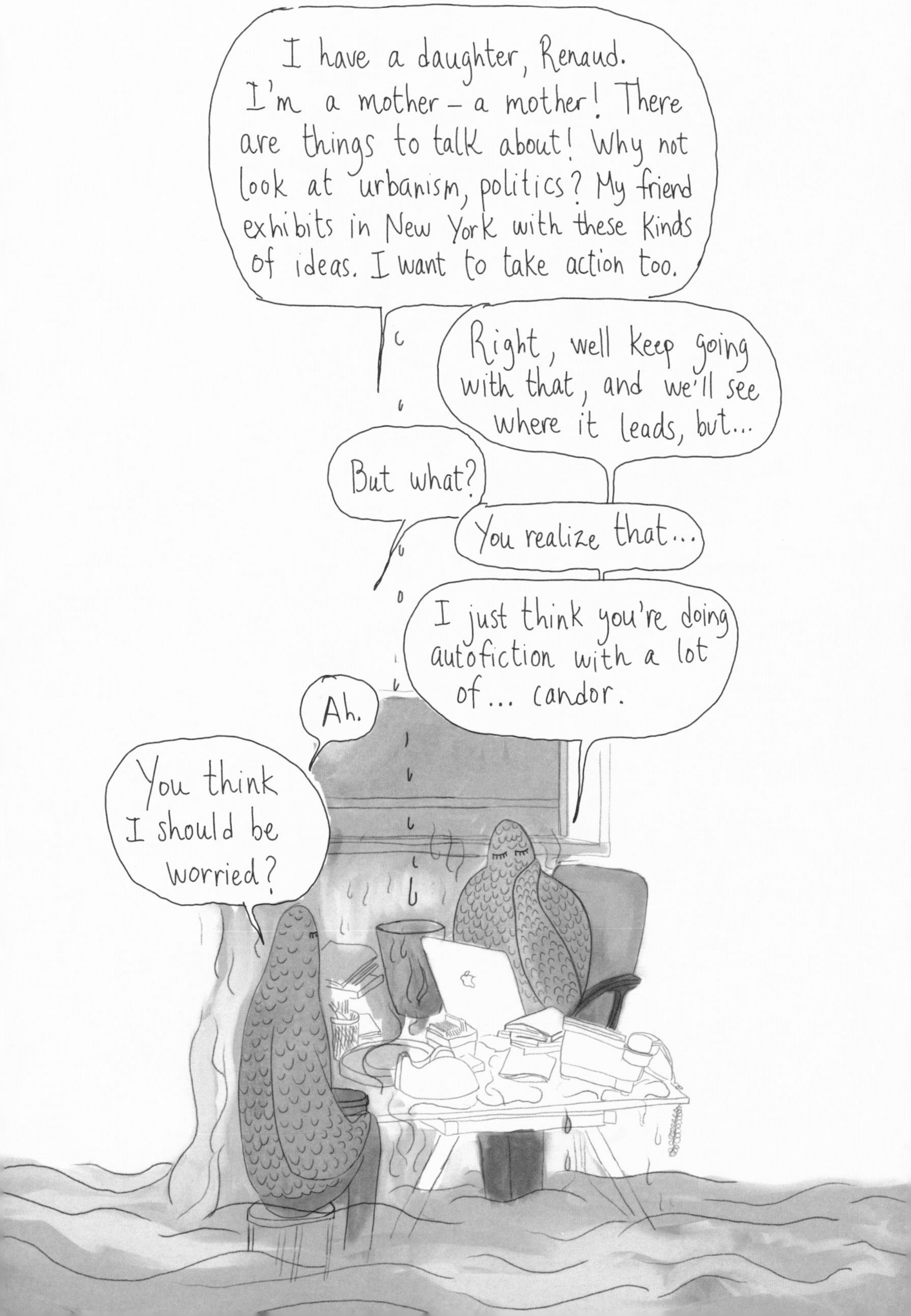
I have a daughter, Renaud. I'm a mother – a mother! There are things to talk about! Why not look at urbanism, politics? My friend exhibits in New York with these kinds of ideas. I want to take action too.
Right, well keep going with that, and we'll see where it leads, but...
But what?
You realize that...
I just think you're doing autofiction with a lot of... candor.
Ah.
You think I should be worried?

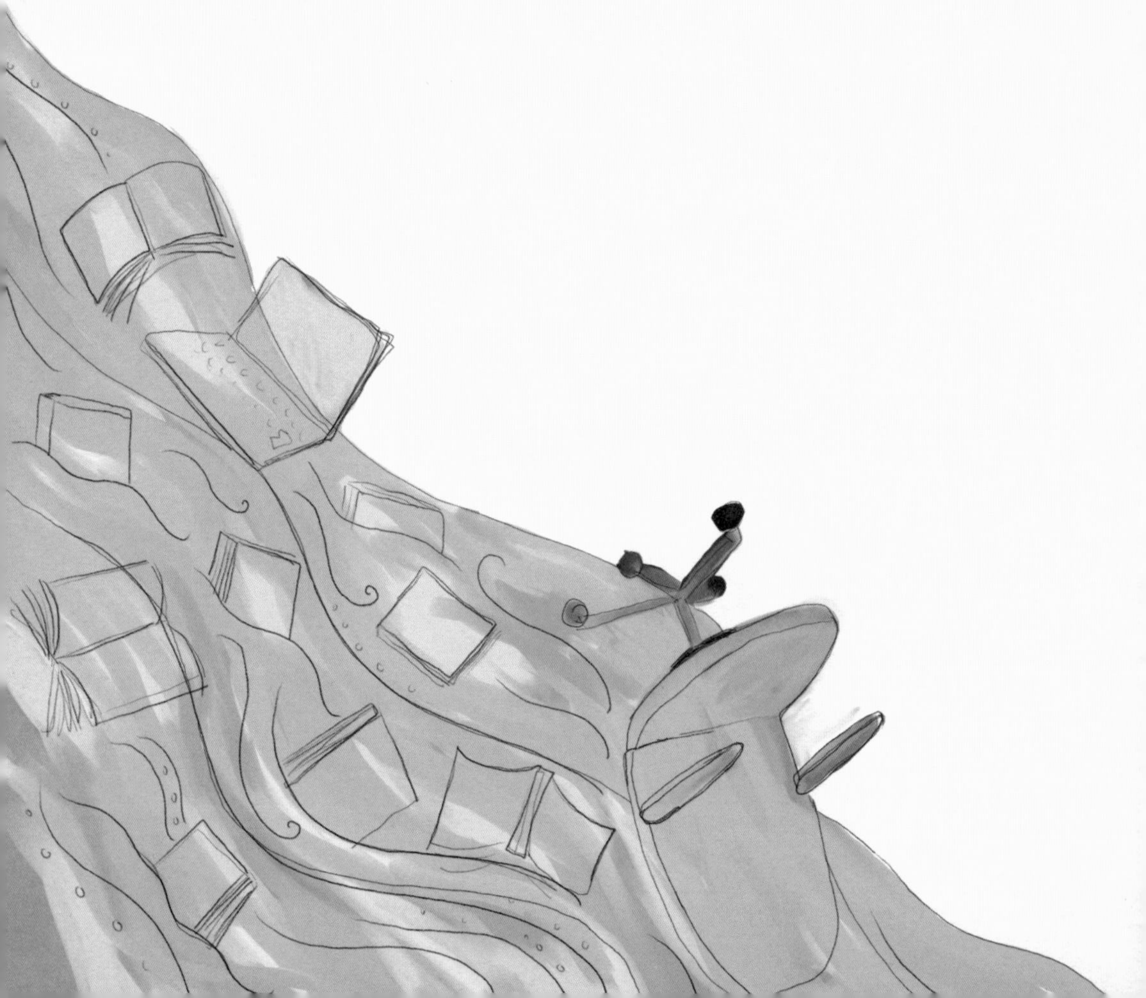

Marcel

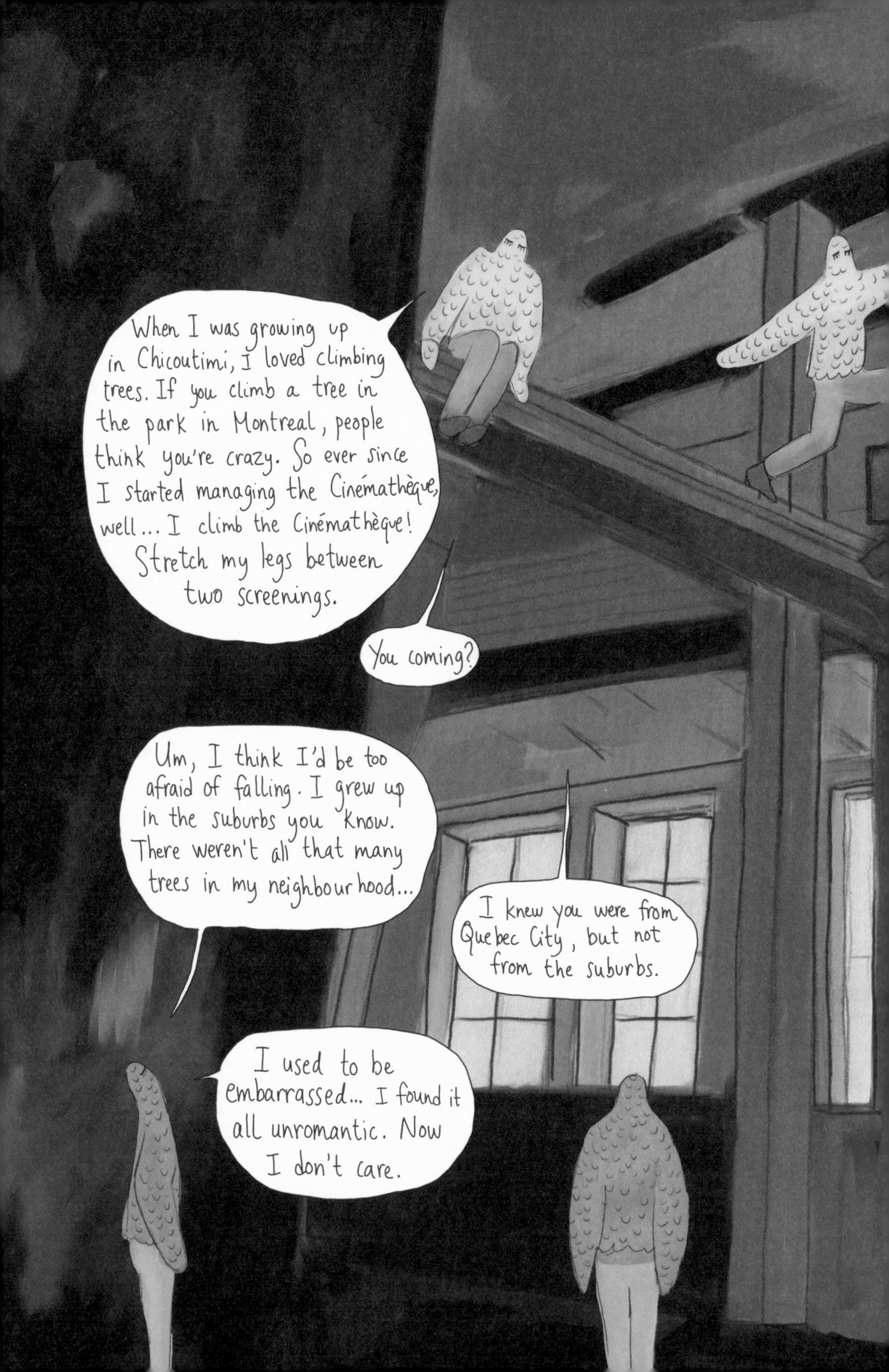
When I was growing up in Chicoutimi, I loved climbing trees. If you climb a tree in the park in Montreal, people think you're crazy. So ever since I started managing the Cinémathèque, well... I climb the Cinémathèque! Stretch my legs between two screenings.
You coming?
Um, I think I'd be too afraid of falling. I grew up in the suburbs you know. There weren't all that many trees in my neighbourhood...
I knew you were from Quebec City, but not from the suburbs.
I used to be embarrassed... I found it all unromantic. Now I don't care.

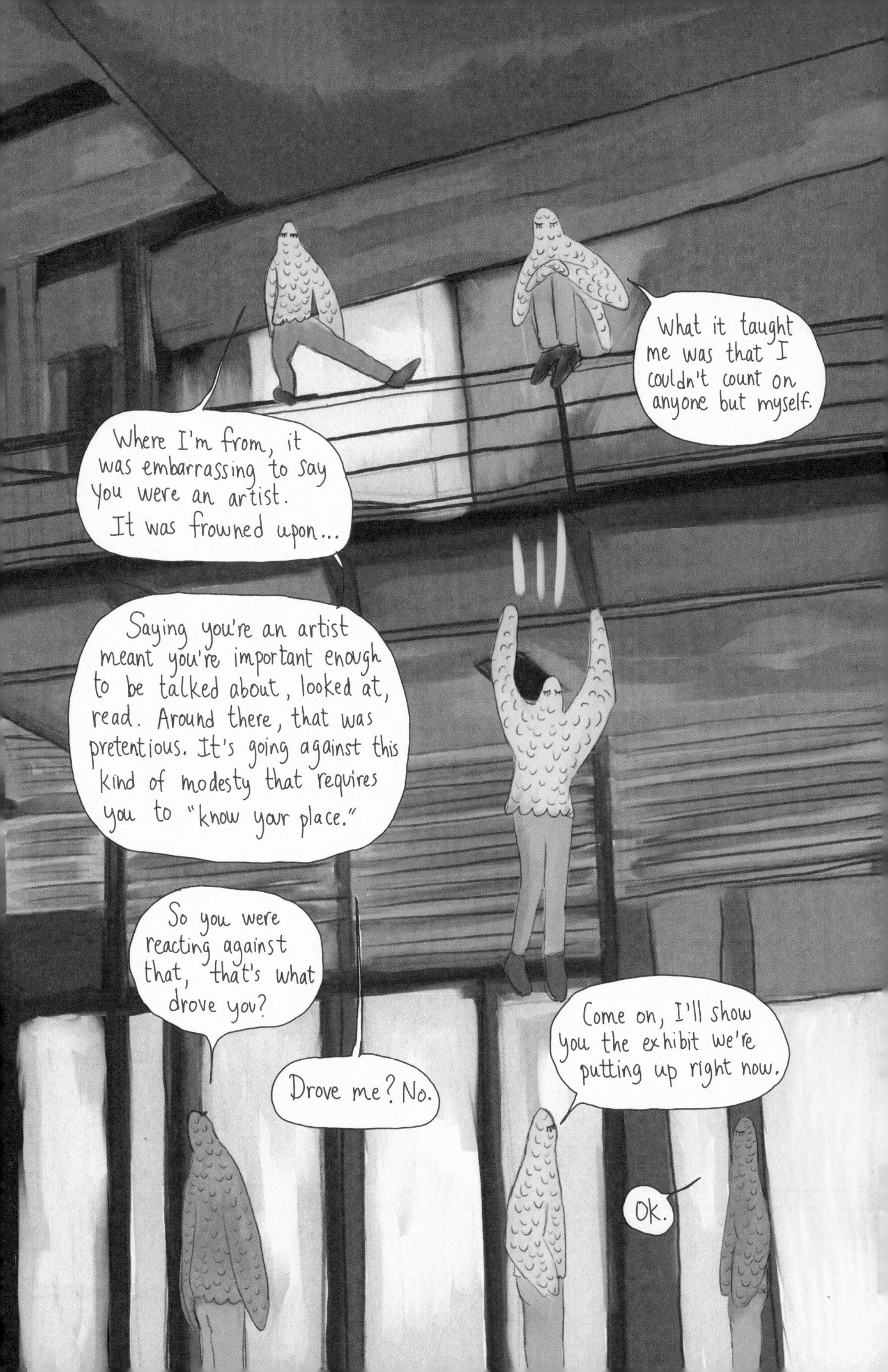
Where I'm from, it was embarrassing to say you were an artist. It was frowned upon...
What it taught me was that I couldn't count on anyone but myself.
Saying you're an artist meant you're important enough to be talked about, looked at, read. Around there, that was pretentious. It's going against this kind of modesty that requires you to "know your place."
So you were reacting against that, that's what drove you?
Drove me? No.
Come on, I'll show you the exhibit we're putting up right now.
Ok.

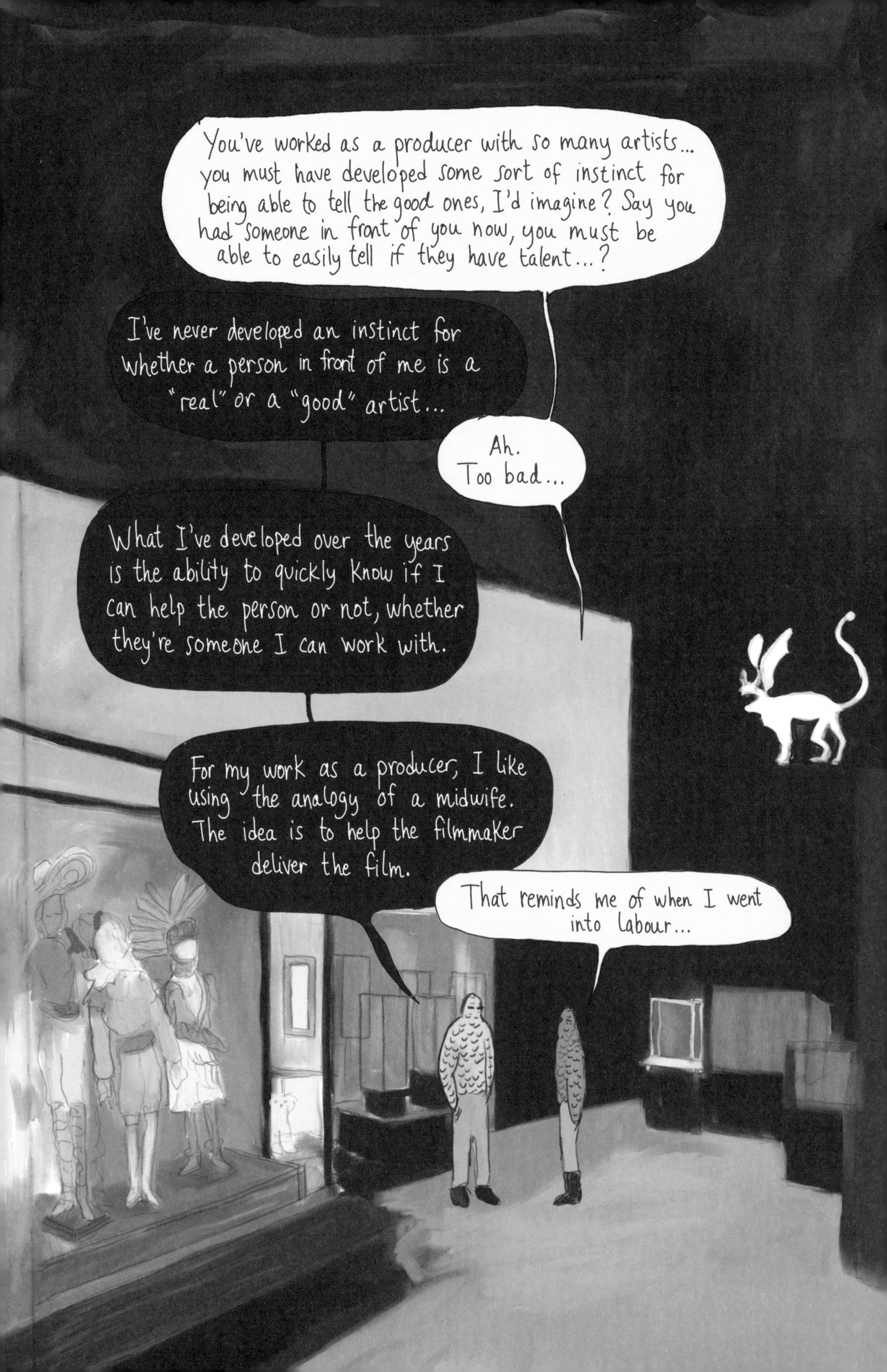
You've worked as a producer with so many artists... you must have developed some sort of instinct for being able to tell the good ones, I'd imagine? Say you had someone in front of you now, you must be able to easily tell if they have talent...?
I've never developed an instinct for whether a person in front of me is a "real" or a "good" artist...
Ah. Too bad...
What I've developed over the years is the ability to quickly know if I can help the person or not, whether they're someone I can work with.
For my work as a producer, I like using the analogy of a midwife. The idea is to help the filmmaker deliver the film.
That reminds me of when I went into labour...

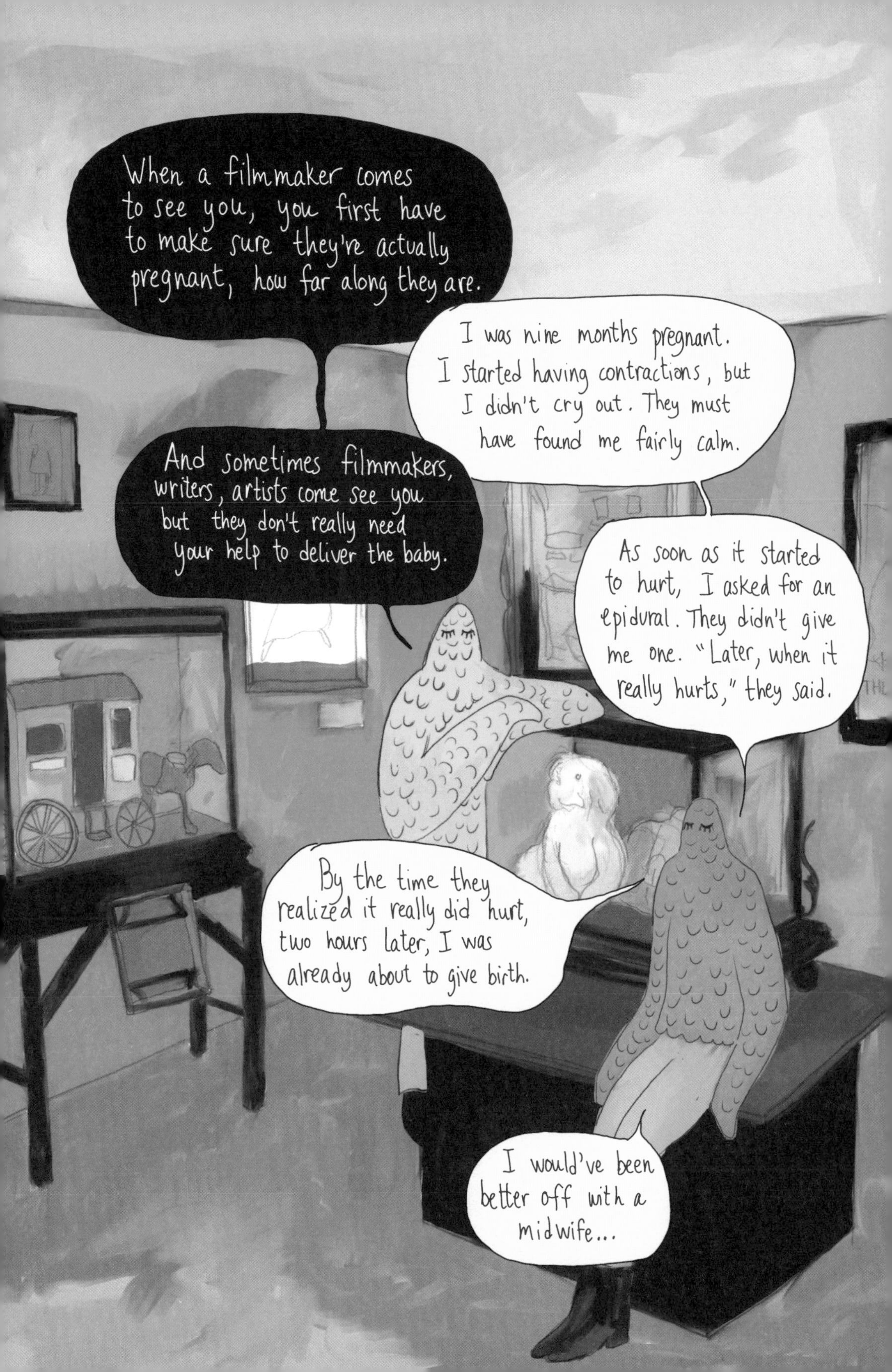
When a filmmaker comes to see you, you first have to make sure they're actually pregnant, how far along they are.
And sometimes filmmakers, writers, artists come see you but they don't really need your help to deliver the baby.
I was nine months pregnant. I started having contractions, but I didn't cry out. They must have found me fairly calm.
As soon as it started to hurt, I asked for an epidural. They didn't give me one. "Later, when it really hurts," they said.
By the time they realized it really did hurt, two hours later, I was already about to give birth.
I would've been better off with a midwife...

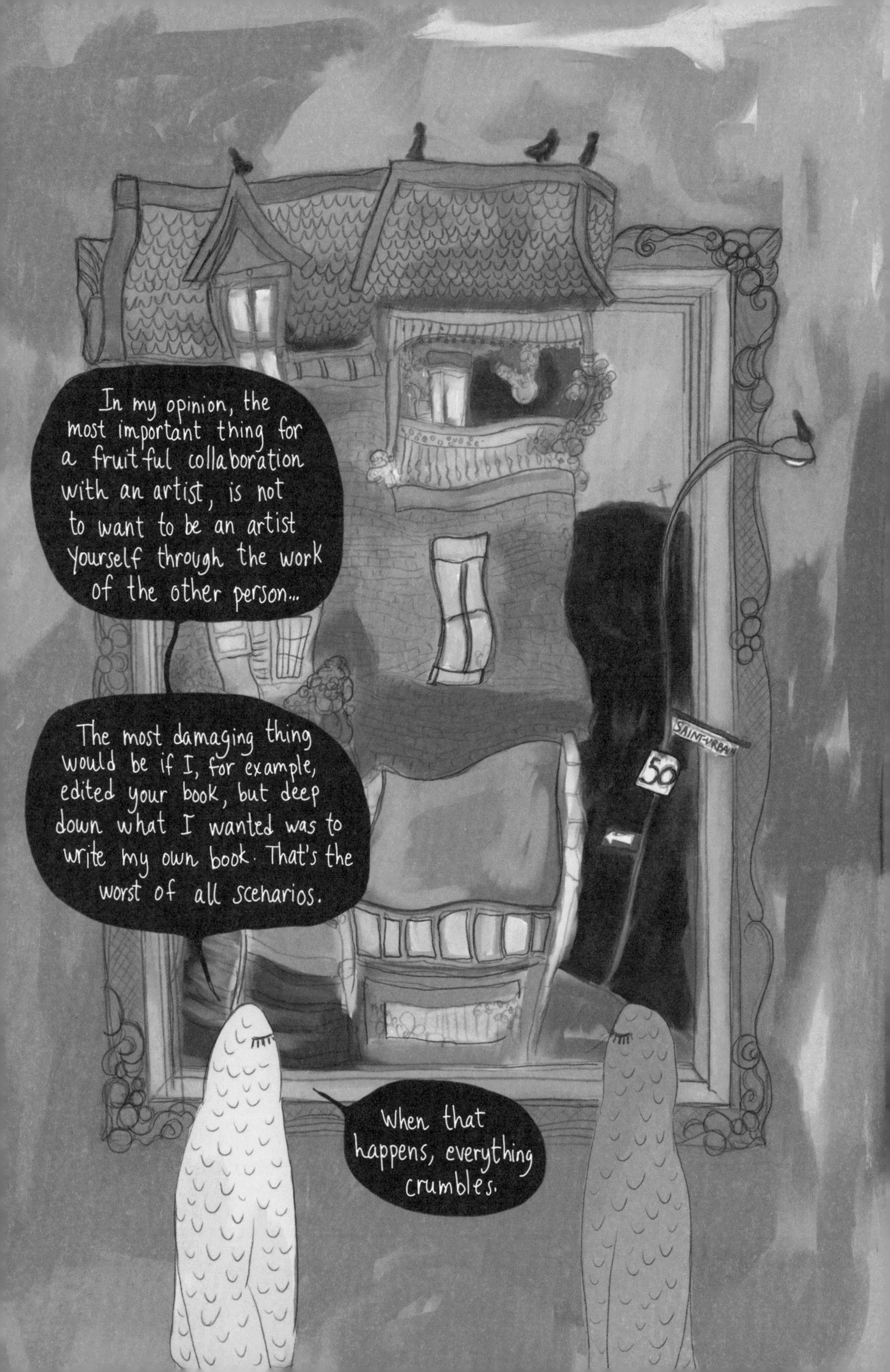
In my opinion, the most important thing for a fruitful collaboration with an artist, is not to want to be an artist yourself through the work of the other person...
The most damaging thing would be if I, for example, edited your book, but deep down what I wanted was to write my own book. That's the worst of all scenarios.
SAINT-URBAIN
50
When that happens, everything crumbles.

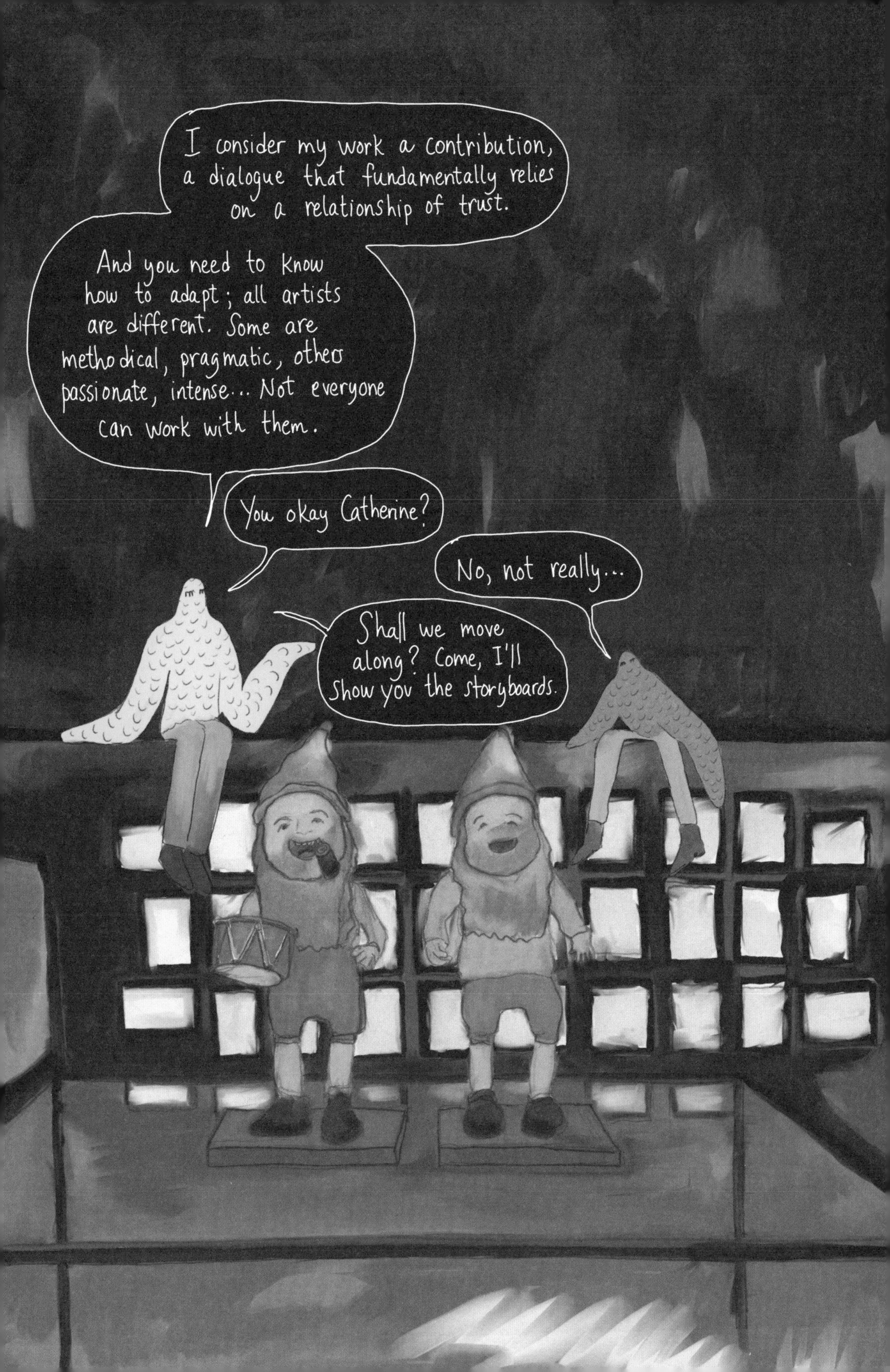
I consider my work a contribution, a dialogue that fundamentally relies on a relationship of trust.
And you need to know how to adapt; all artists are different. Some are methodical, pragmatic, others passionate, intense... Not everyone can work with them.
You okay Catherine?
No, not really...
Shall we move along? Come, I'll show you the storyboards.

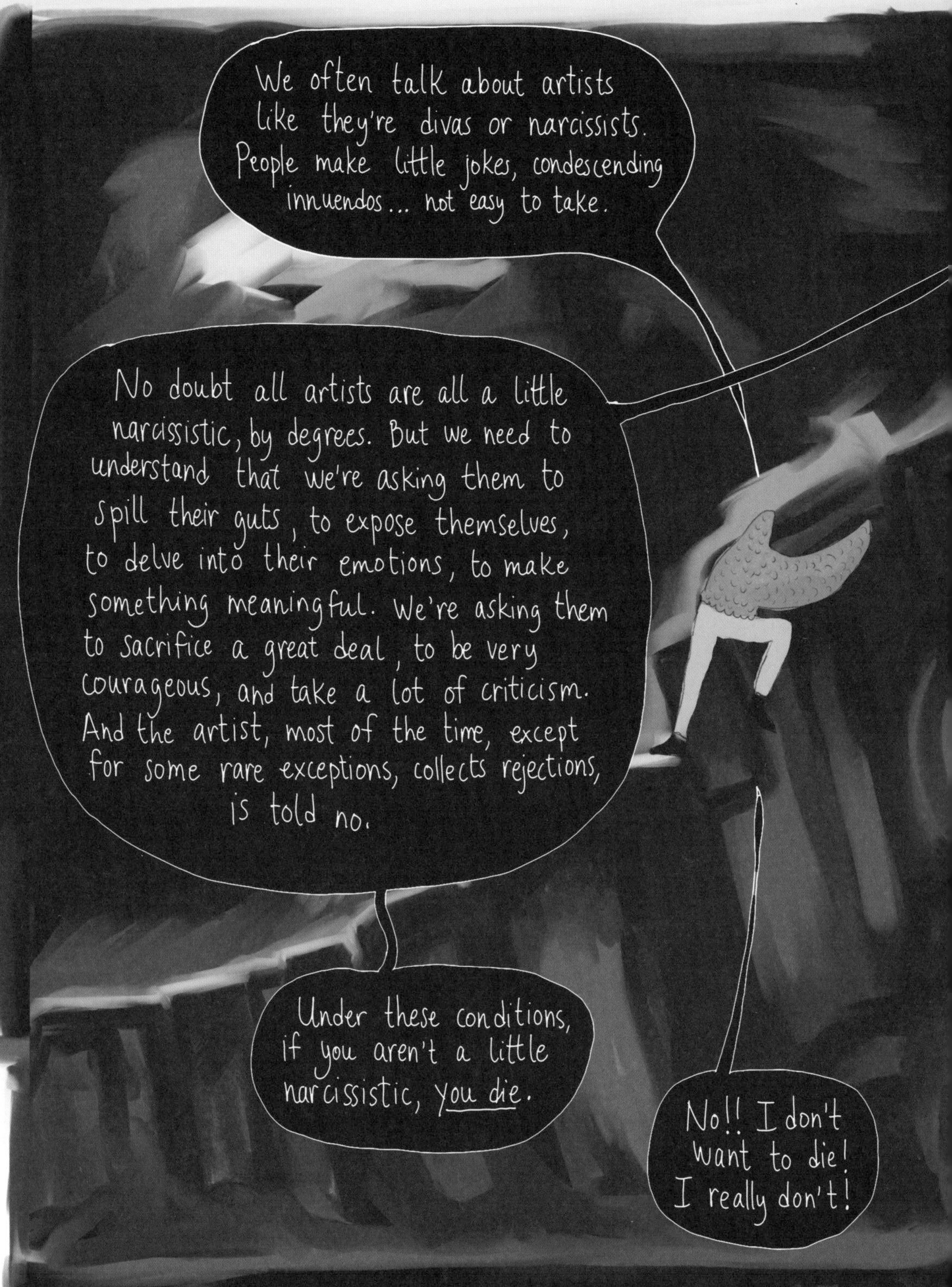
We often talk about artists like they're divas or narcissists. People make little jokes, condescending innuendos... not easy to take.
No doubt all artists are all a little narcissistic, by degrees. But we need to understand that we're asking them to spill their guts, to expose themselves, to delve into their emotions, to make something meaningful. We're asking them to sacrifice a great deal, to be very courageous, and take a lot of criticism. And the artist, most of the time, except for some rare exceptions, collects rejections, is told no.
Under these conditions, if you aren't a little narcissistic, you die.
No!! I don't want to die! I really don't!

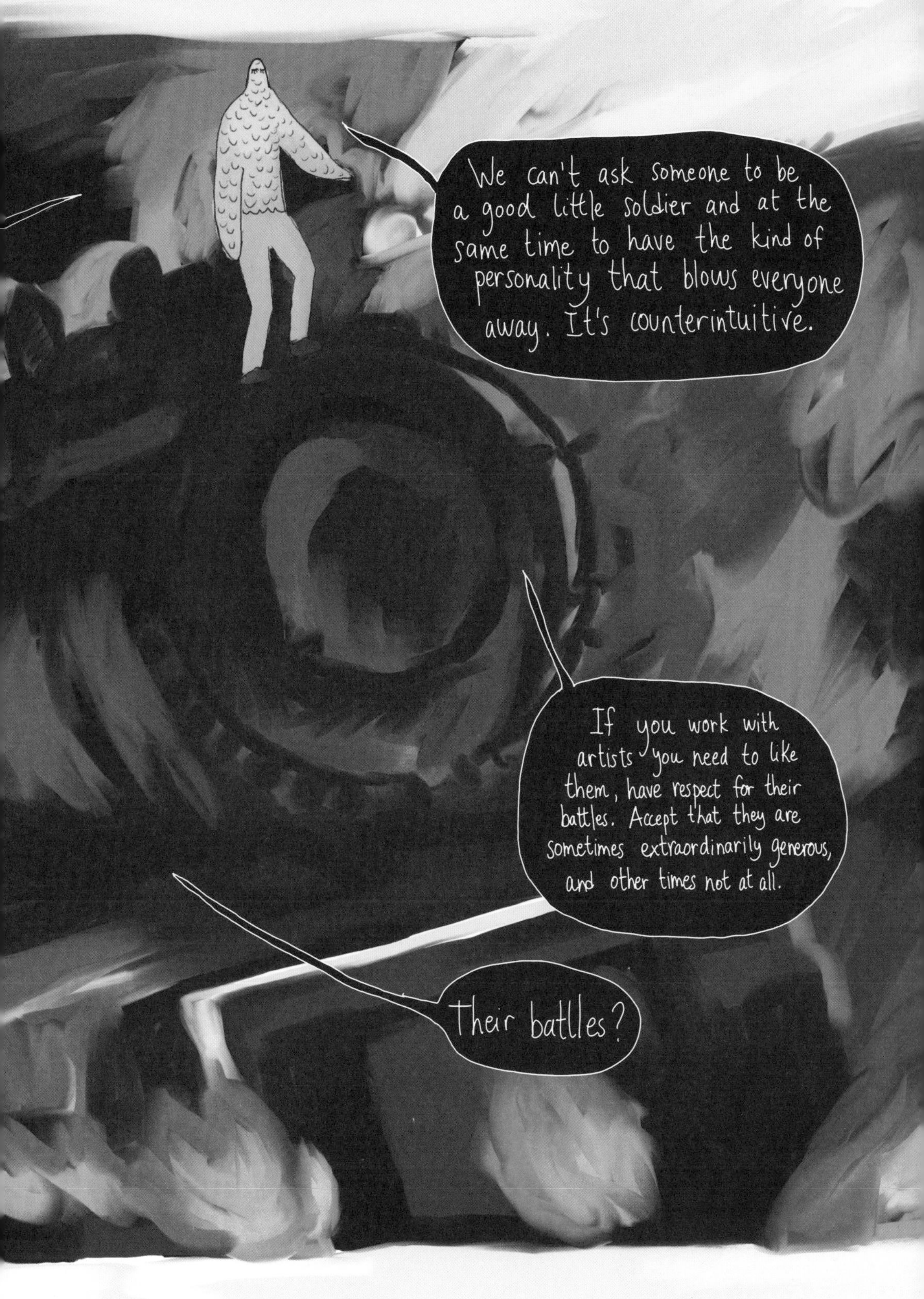
We can't ask someone to be a good little soldier and at the same time to have the kind of personality that blows everyone away. It's counterintuitive.
If you work with artists you need to like them, have respect for their battles. Accept that they are sometimes extraordinarily generous, and other times not at all.
Their battles?

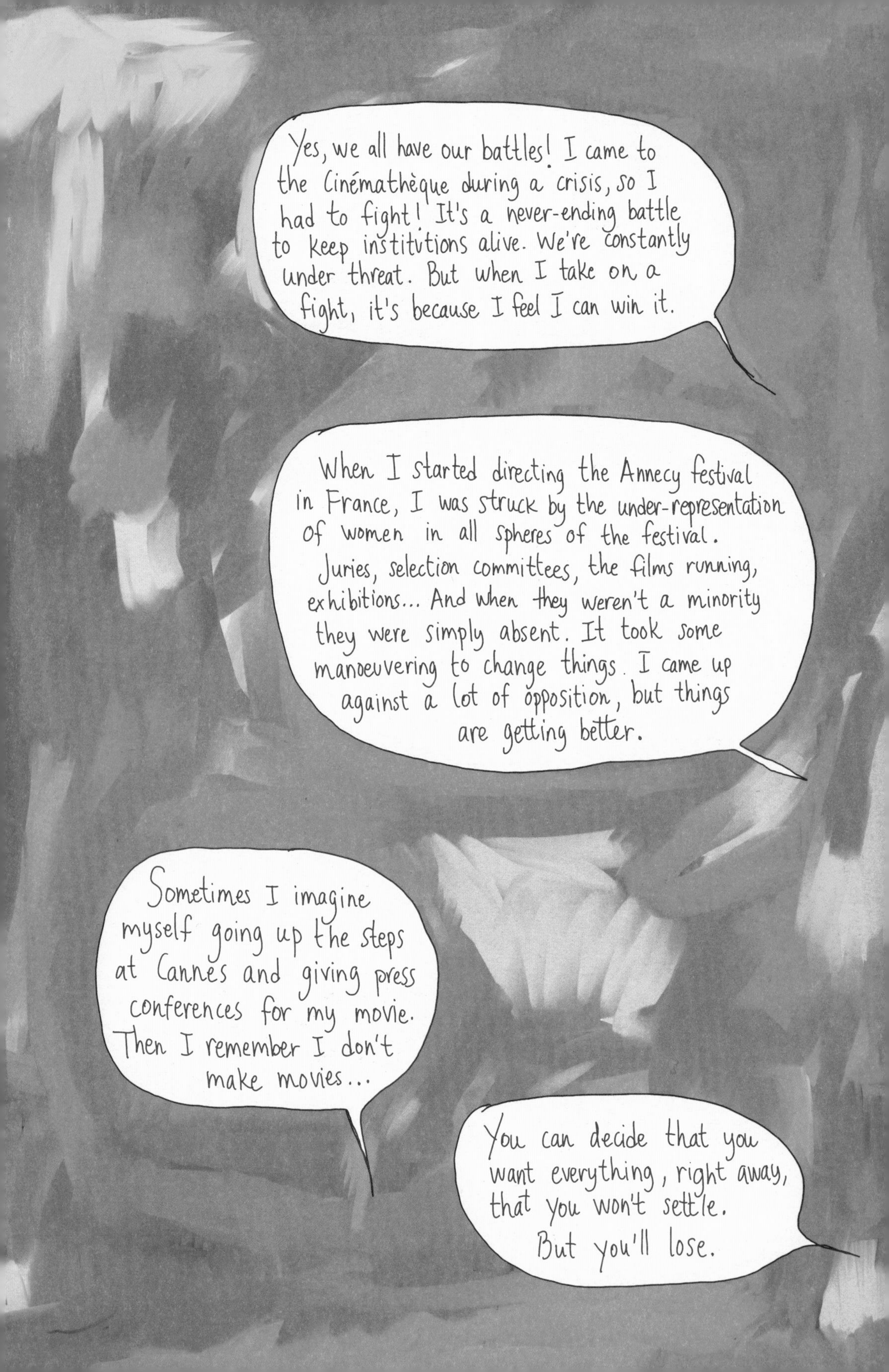
Yes, we all have our battles! I came to the Cinémathèque during a crisis, so I had to fight! It's a never-ending battle to keep institutions alive. We're constantly under threat. But when I take on a fight, it's because I feel I can win it.
When I started directing the Annecy festival in France, I was struck by the under-representation of women in all spheres of the festival. Juries, selection committees, the films running, exhibitions... And when they weren't a minority they were simply absent. It took some manoeuvering to change things. I came up against a lot of opposition, but things are getting better.
Sometimes I imagine myself going up the steps at Cannes and giving press conferences for my movie. Then I remember I don't make movies...
You can decide that you want everything, right away, that you won't settle. But you'll lose.

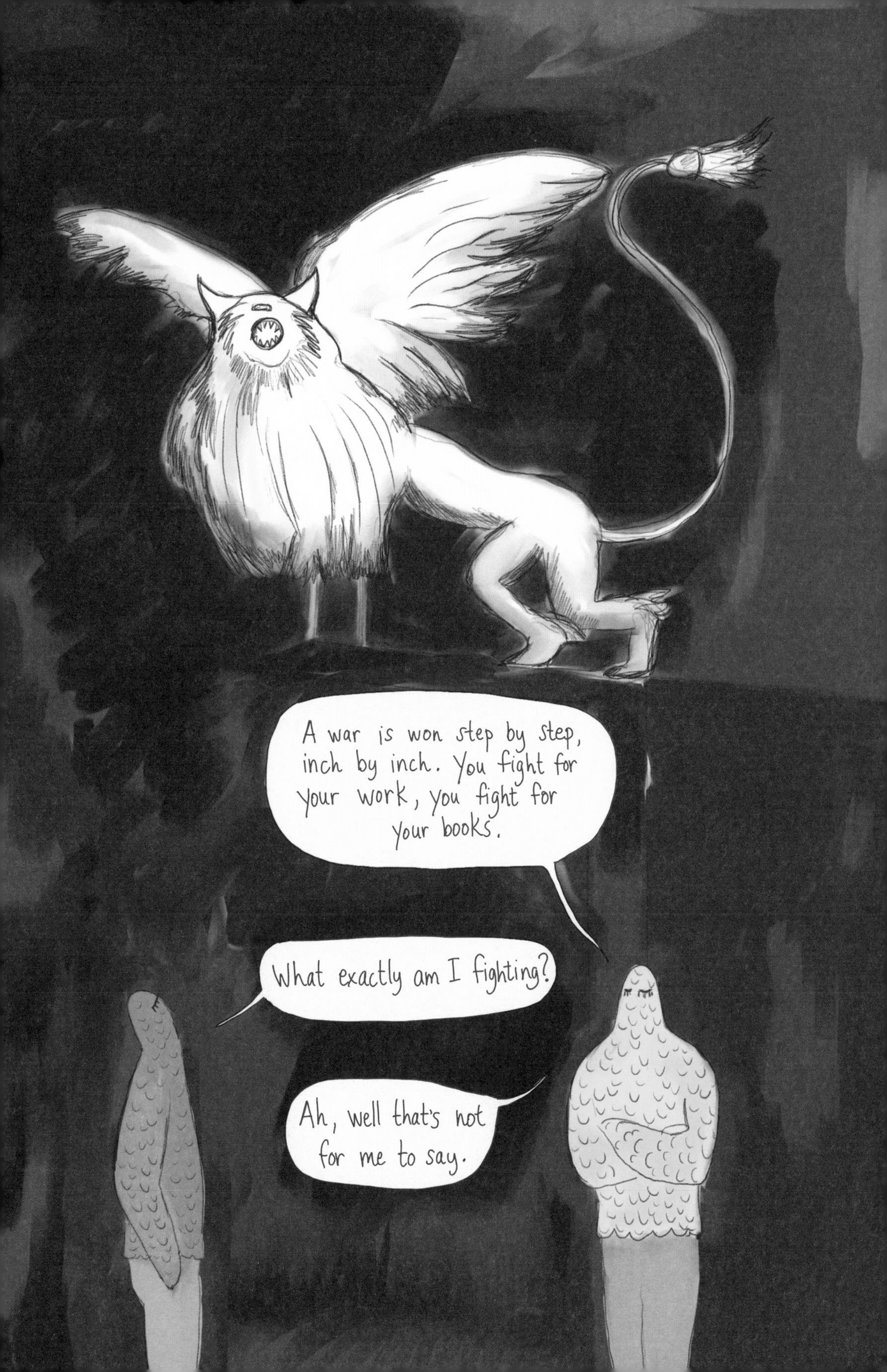
A war is won step by step, inch by inch. You fight for your work, you fight for your books.
What exactly am I fighting?
Ah, well that's not for me to say.

Daphné and Julie

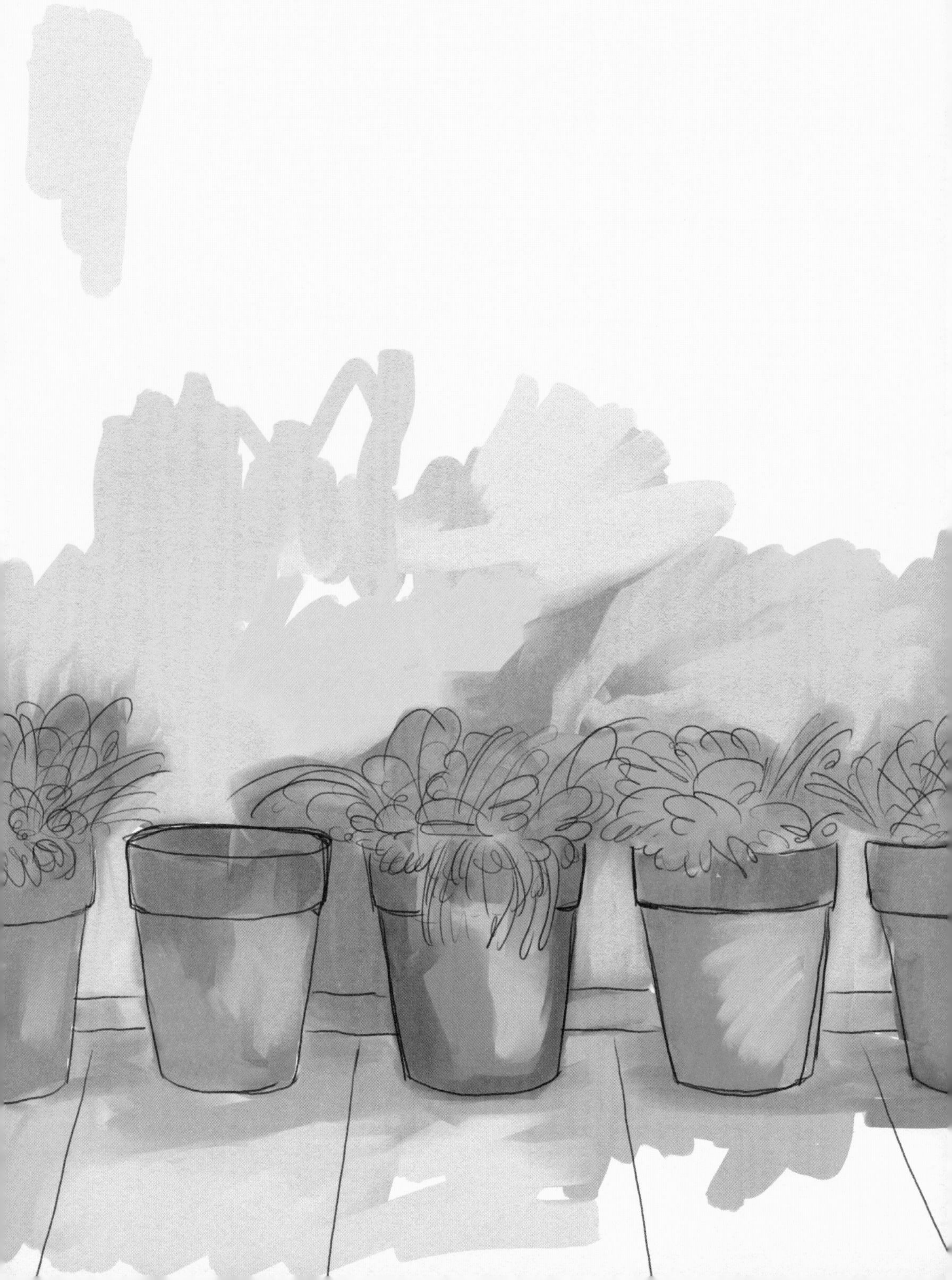

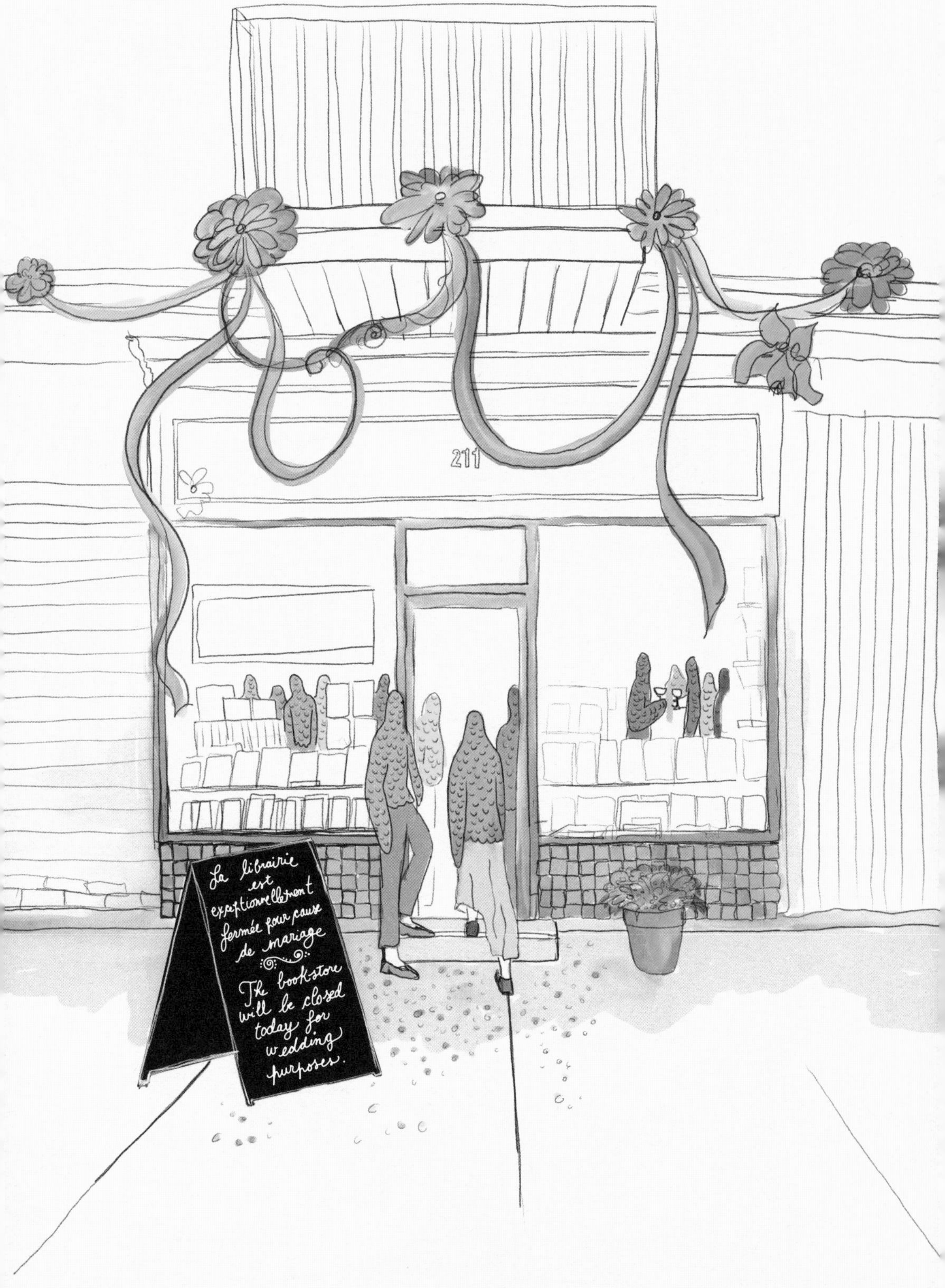
211
La librairie est exceptionnellement fermée pour cause de mariage
The bookstore will be closed today for wedding purposes.

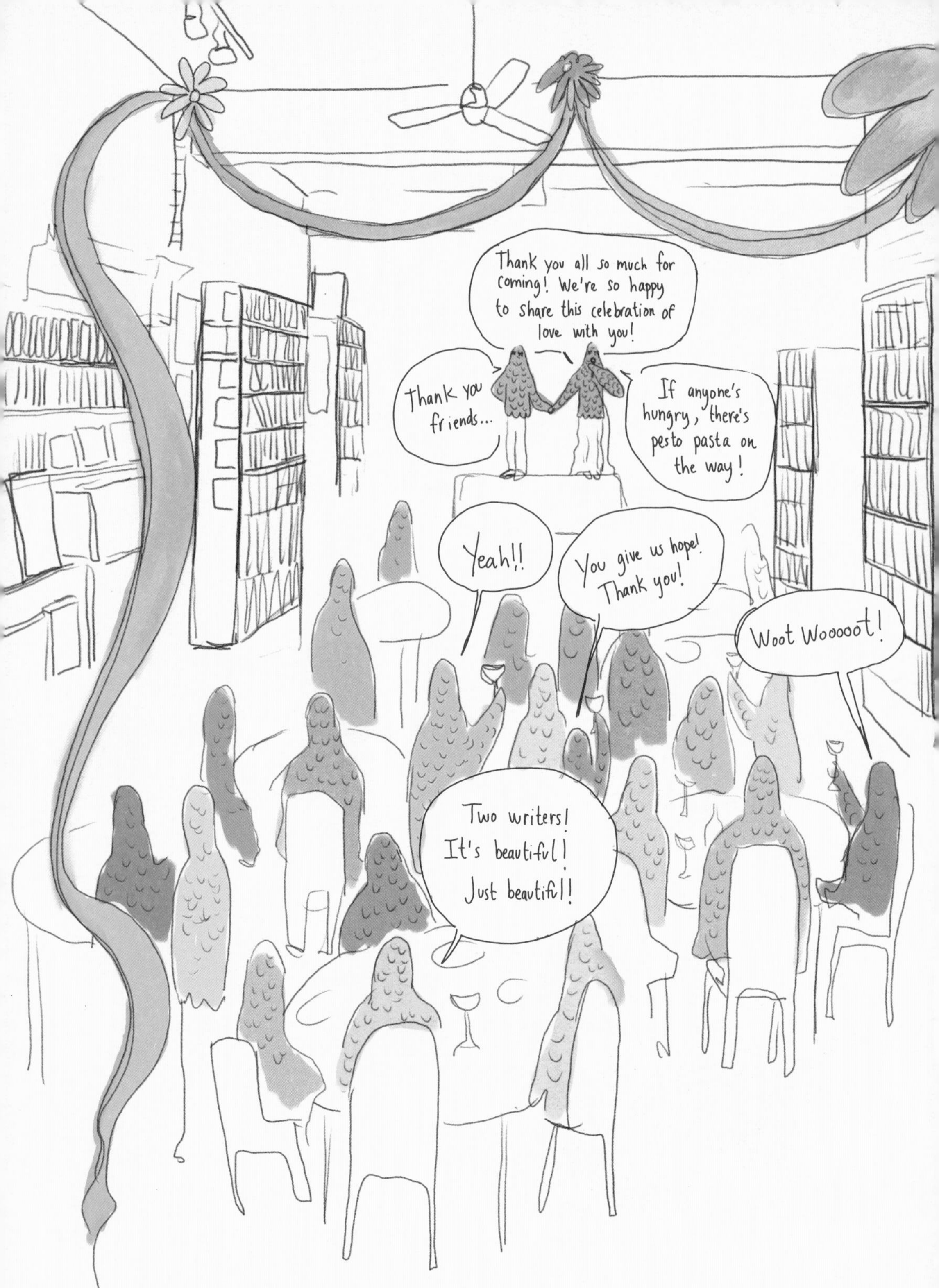
Thank you all so much for coming! We're so happy to share this celebration of love with you!
Thank you friends...
If anyone's hungry, there's pesto pasta on the way!
Yeah!!
You give us hope! Thank you!
Woot Wooooot!
Two writers! It's beautiful! Just beautiful!

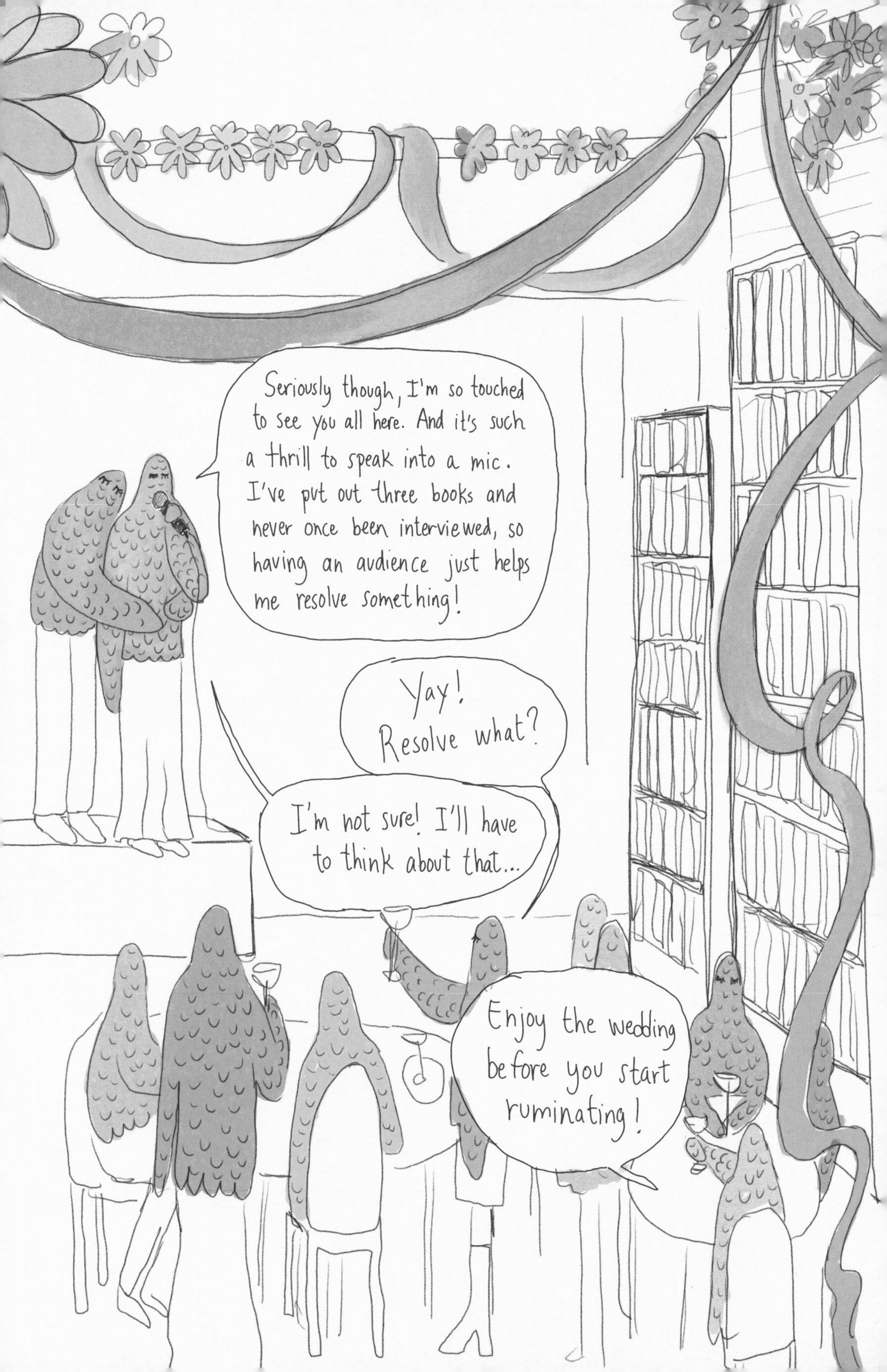
Seriously though, I'm so touched to see you all here. And it's such a thrill to speak into a mic. I've put out three books and never once been interviewed, so having an audience just helps me resolve something!
Yay! Resolve what?
I'm not sure! I'll have to think about that...
Enjoy the wedding before you start ruminating!

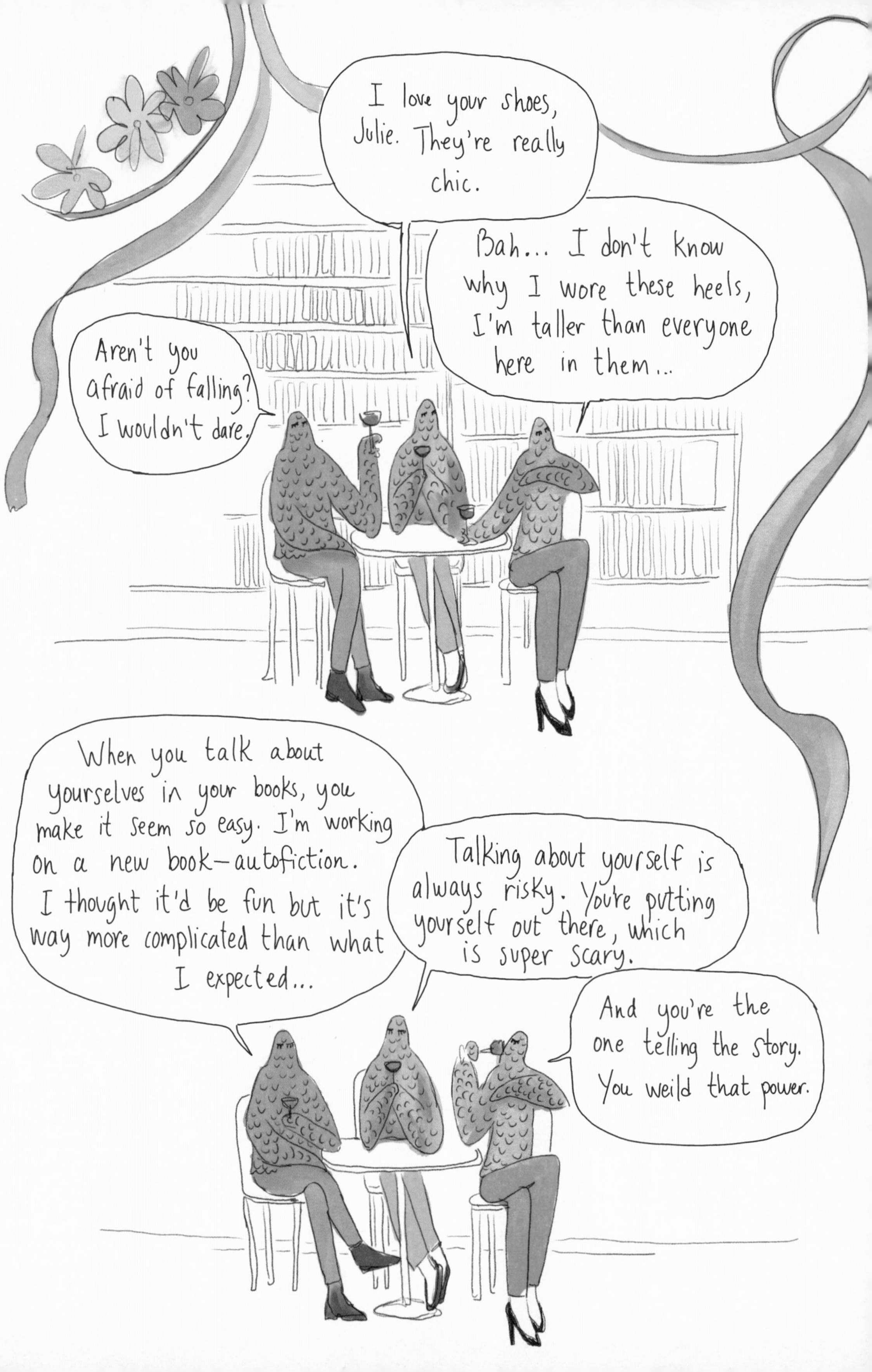
I love your shoes, Julie. They're really chic.
Bah... I don't know why I wore these heels, I'm taller than everyone here in them...
Aren't you afraid of falling? I wouldn't dare.
When you talk about yourselves in your books, you make it seem so easy. I'm working on a new book—autofiction. I thought it'd be fun but it's way more complicated than what I expected...
Talking about yourself is always risky. You're putting yourself out there, which is super scary.
And you're the one telling the story. You weild that power.

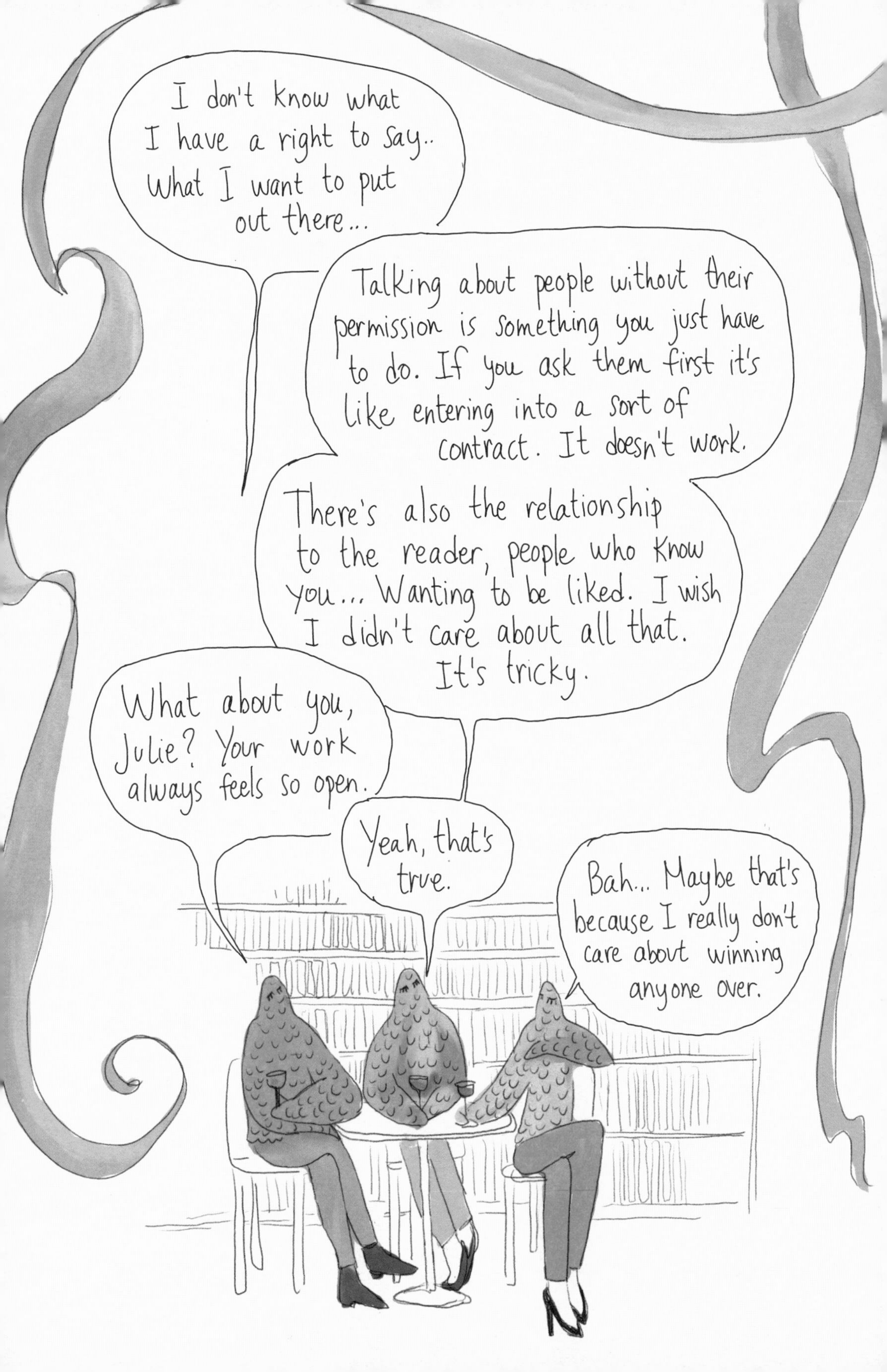
I don't know what I have a right to say.. What I want to put out there...
Talking about people without their permission is something you just have to do. If you ask them first it's like entering into a sort of contract. It doesn't work.
There's also the relationship to the reader, people who know you... Wanting to be liked. I wish I didn't care about all that. It's tricky.
What about you, Julie? Your work always feels so open.
Yeah, that's true.
Bah... Maybe that's because I really don't care about winning anyone over.

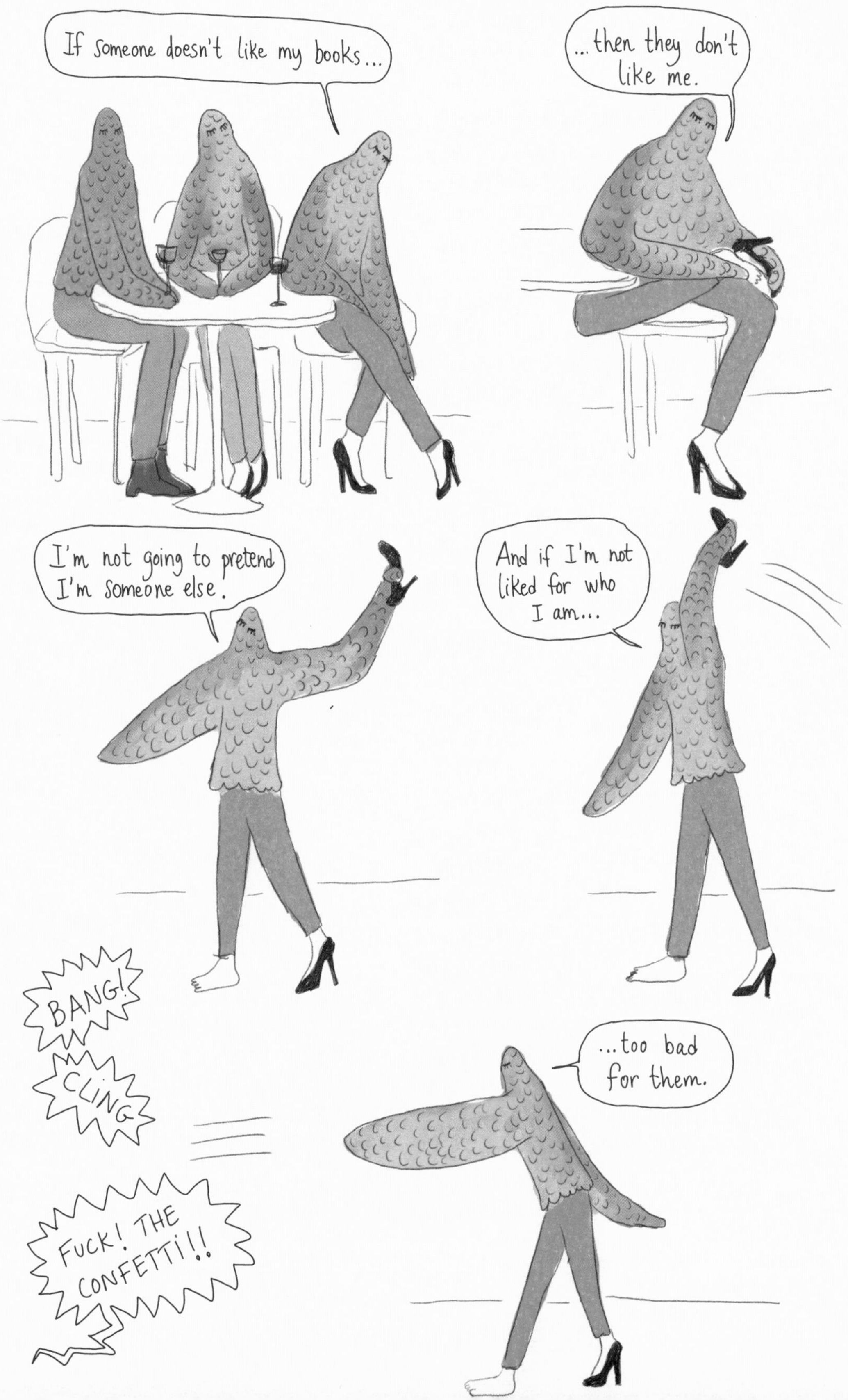

If someone doesn't like my books...
...then they don't like me.
I'm not going to pretend I'm someone else.
And if I'm not liked for who I am...
BANG!
CLING
...too bad for them.
FUCK! THE CONFETTI!!

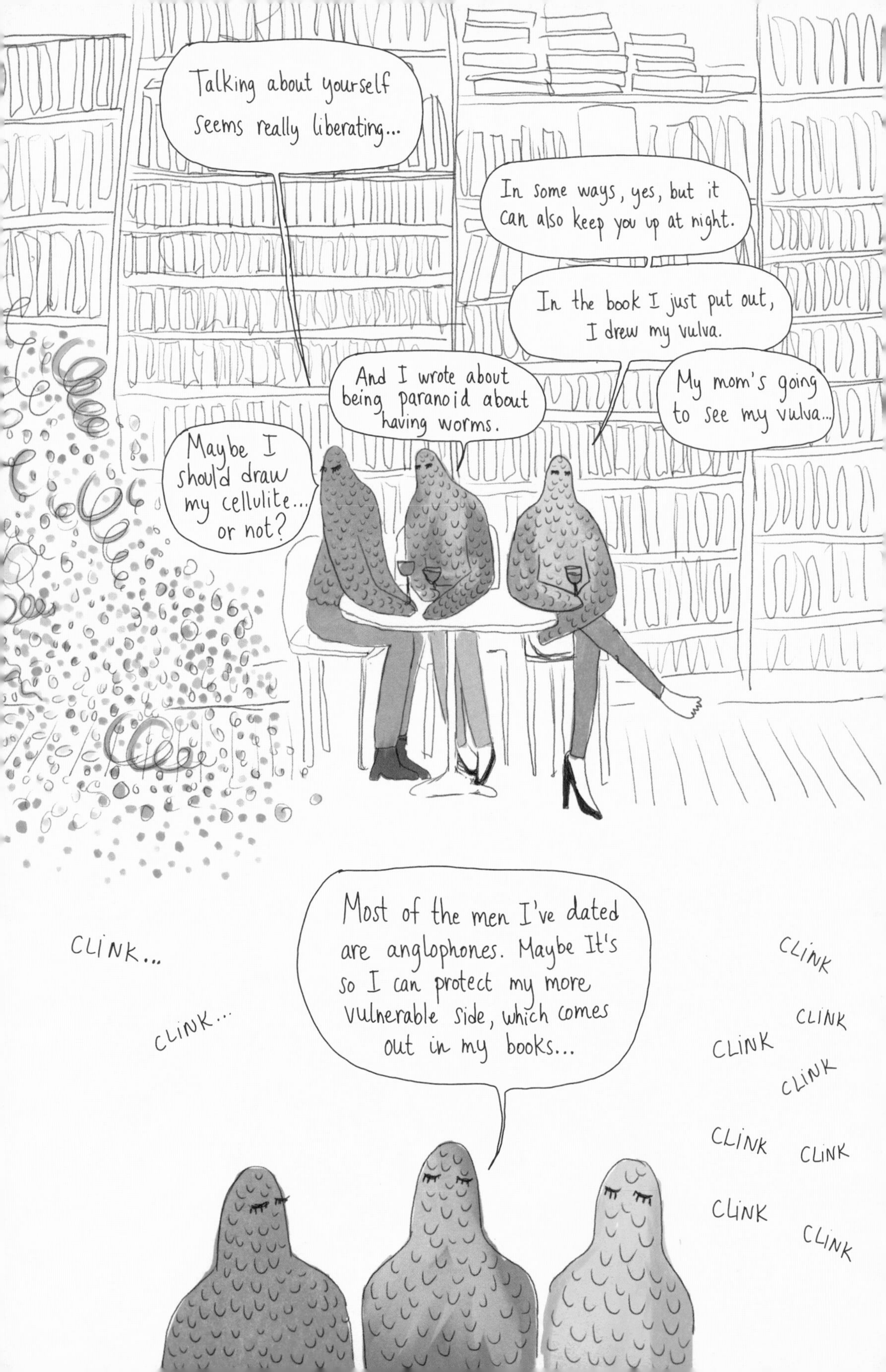
Talking about yourself seems really liberating...
In some ways, yes, but it can also keep you up at night.
In the book I just put out, I drew my vulva.
My mom's going to see my vulva...
And I wrote about being paranoid about having worms.
Maybe I should draw my cellulite... or not?
CLINK...
CLINK...
Most of the men I've dated are anglophones. Maybe It's so I can protect my more vulnerable side, which comes out in my books...
CLINK
CLINK
CLINK
CLINK
CLINK
CLINK
CLINK
CLINK

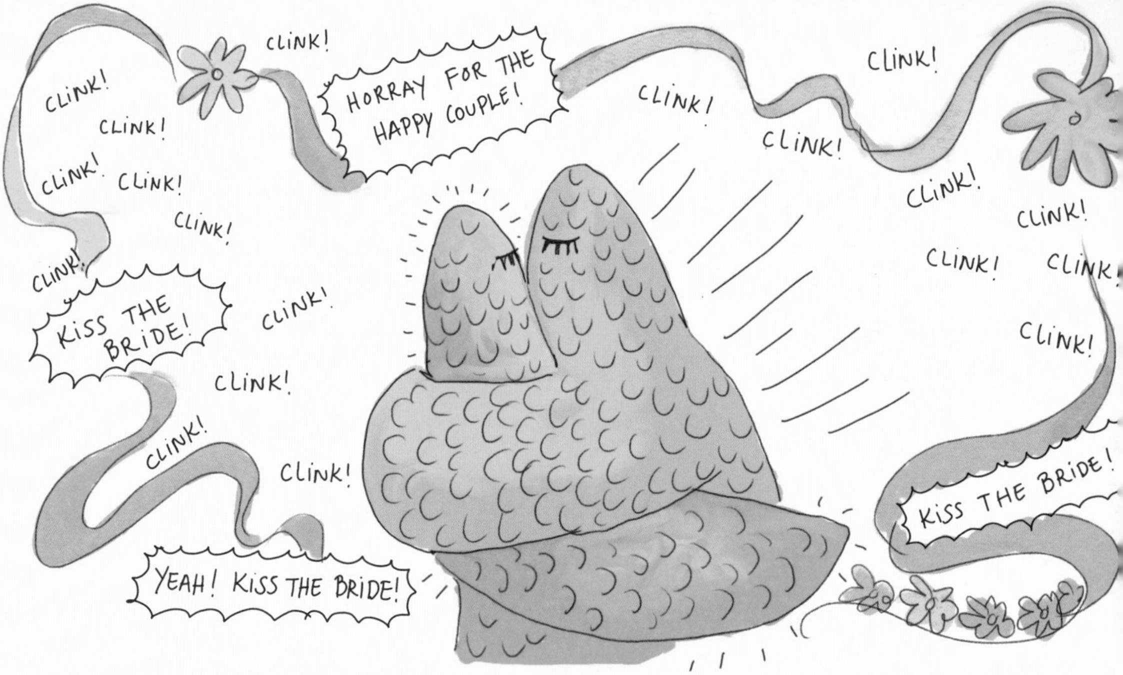
CLINK!
CLINK!
CLINK!
CLINK!
CLINK!
CLINK!
CLINK!
HORRAY FOR THE HAPPY COUPLE!
KISS THE BRIDE!
CLINK!
CLINK!
CLINK!
CLINK!
YEAH! KISS THE BRIDE!
CLINK!
CLINK!
CLINK!
CLINK!
CLINK!
CLINK!
CLINK!
CLINK!
KISS THE BRIDE!

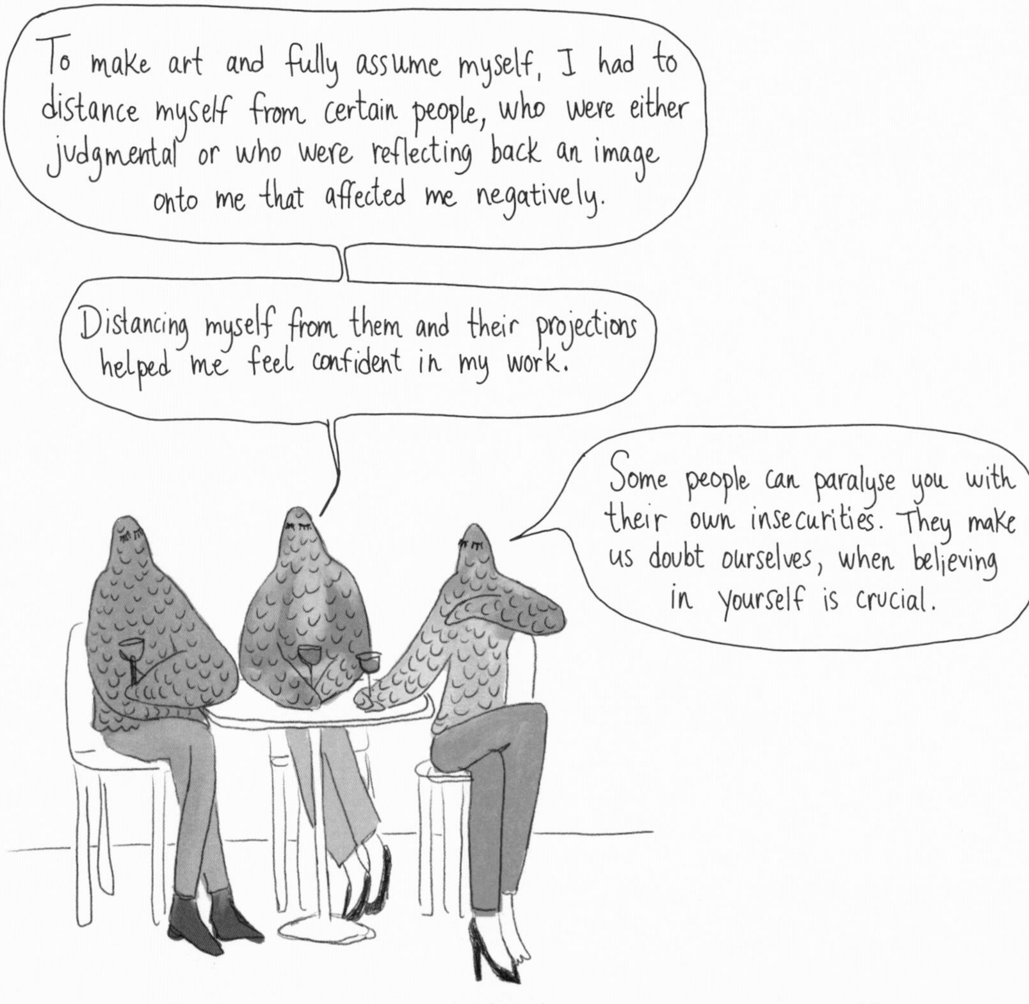
To make art and fully assume myself, I had to distance myself from certain people, who were either judgmental or who were reflecting back an image onto me that affected me negatively.
Distancing myself from them and their projections helped me feel confident in my work.
Some people can paralyse you with their own insecurities. They make us doubt ourselves, when believing in yourself is crucial.

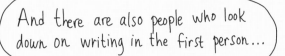

And there are also people who look down on writing in the first person...

It doesn't make sense to me to invent a fictional character that vaguely resembles me...

Pffff. You can make a porn film with a good cinematographer and they'll call it great Art.

But tell your birth story or talk about sadness, tears or cellulite, and that's "personal," implying that it's not art, at least not serious art.

All I have to say to that is...

... the personal...

...is political.

POW

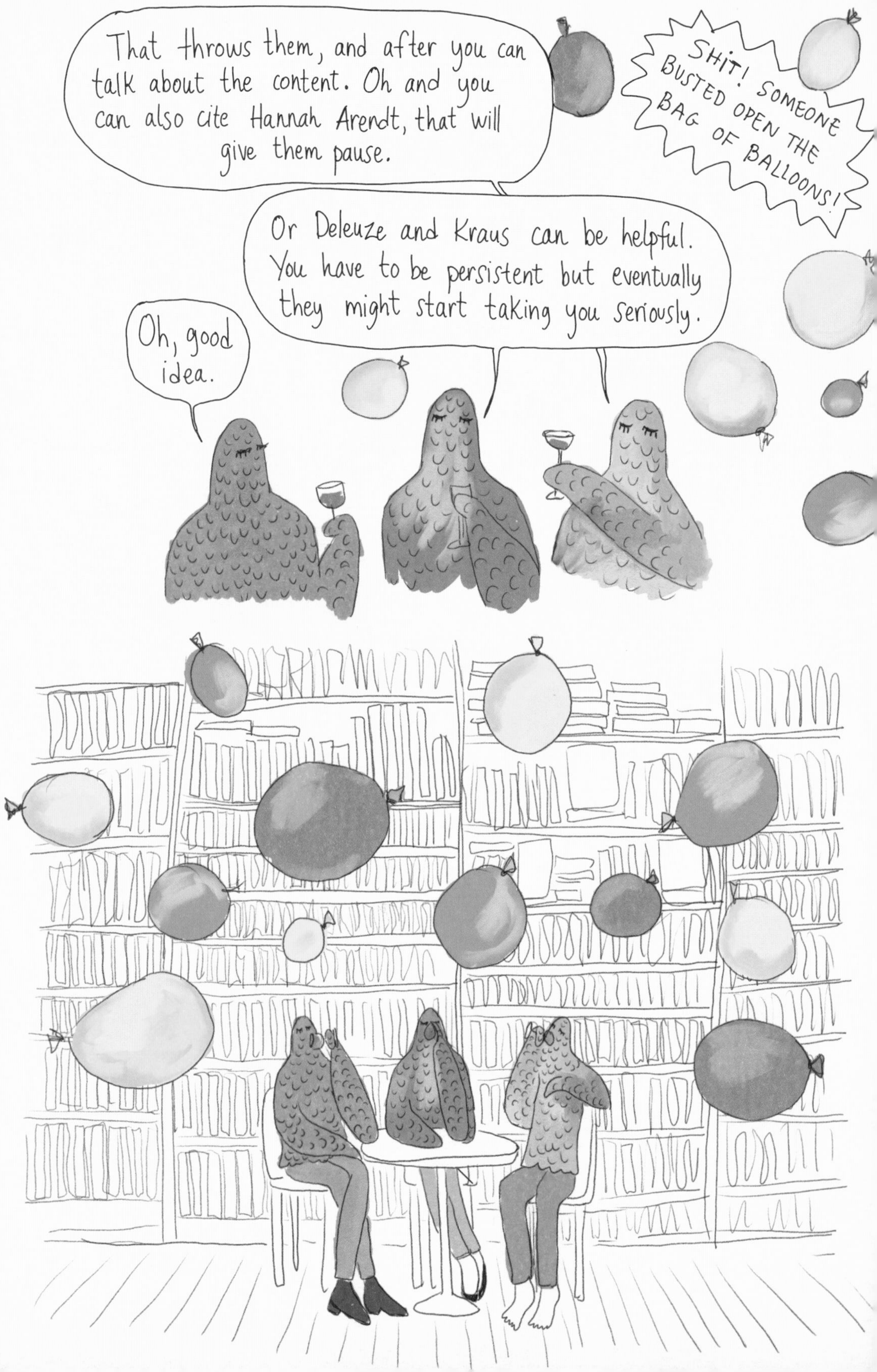
That throws them, and after you can talk about the content. Oh and you can also cite Hannah Arendt, that will give them pause.
SHIT! SOMEONE BUSTED OPEN THE BAG OF BALLOONS!
Or Deleuze and Kraus can be helpful. You have to be persistent but eventually they might start taking you seriously.
Oh, good idea.

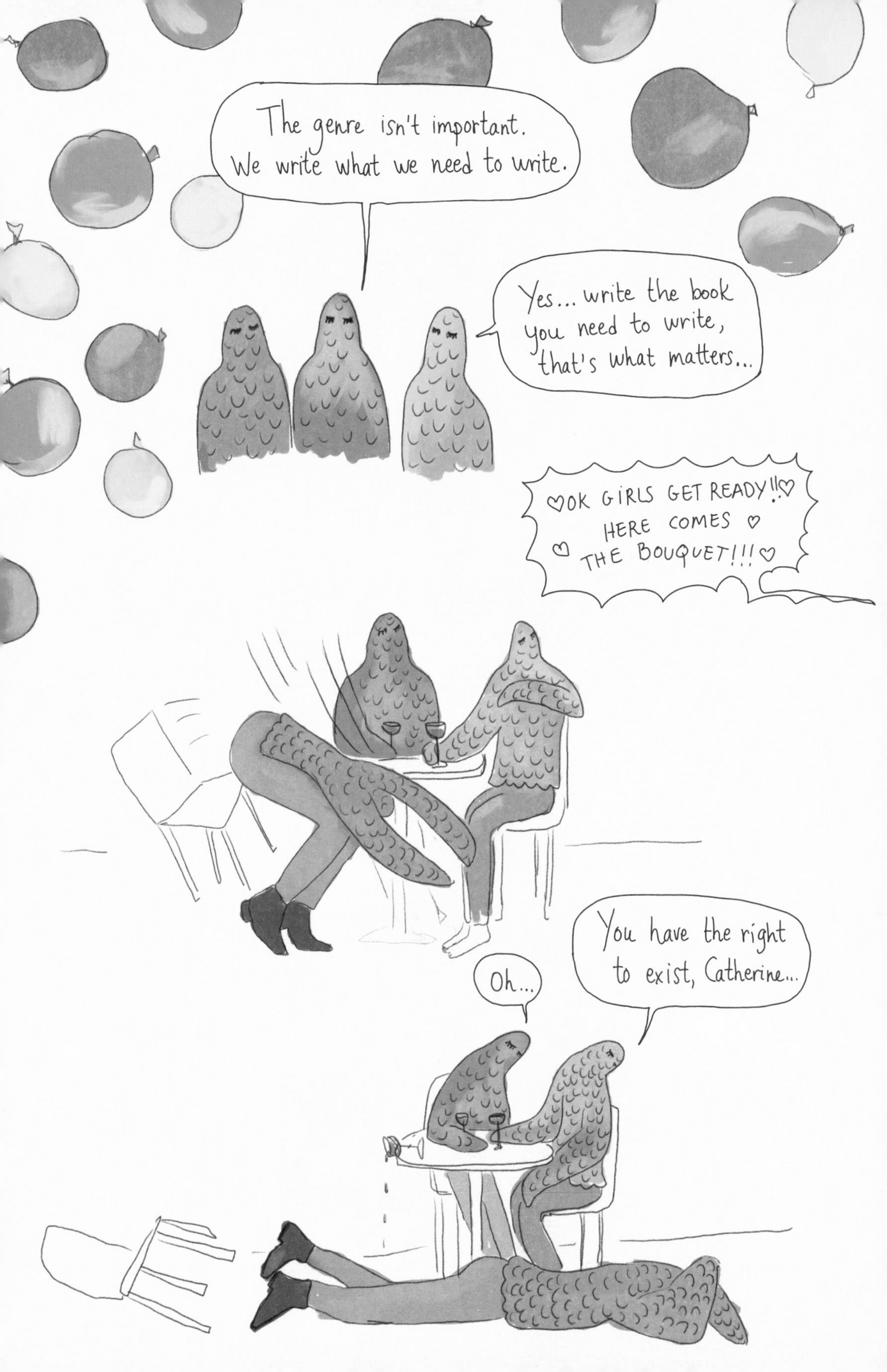
The genre isn't important. We write what we need to write.
Yes... write the book you need to write, that's what matters...
OK GIRLS GET READY!! HERE COMES THE BOUQUET!!!
Oh...
You have the right to exist, Catherine...

Kiki, Louise, Philippe, Iris, Stéphanie,
Nathalie, Marguerite, Martin, etc.

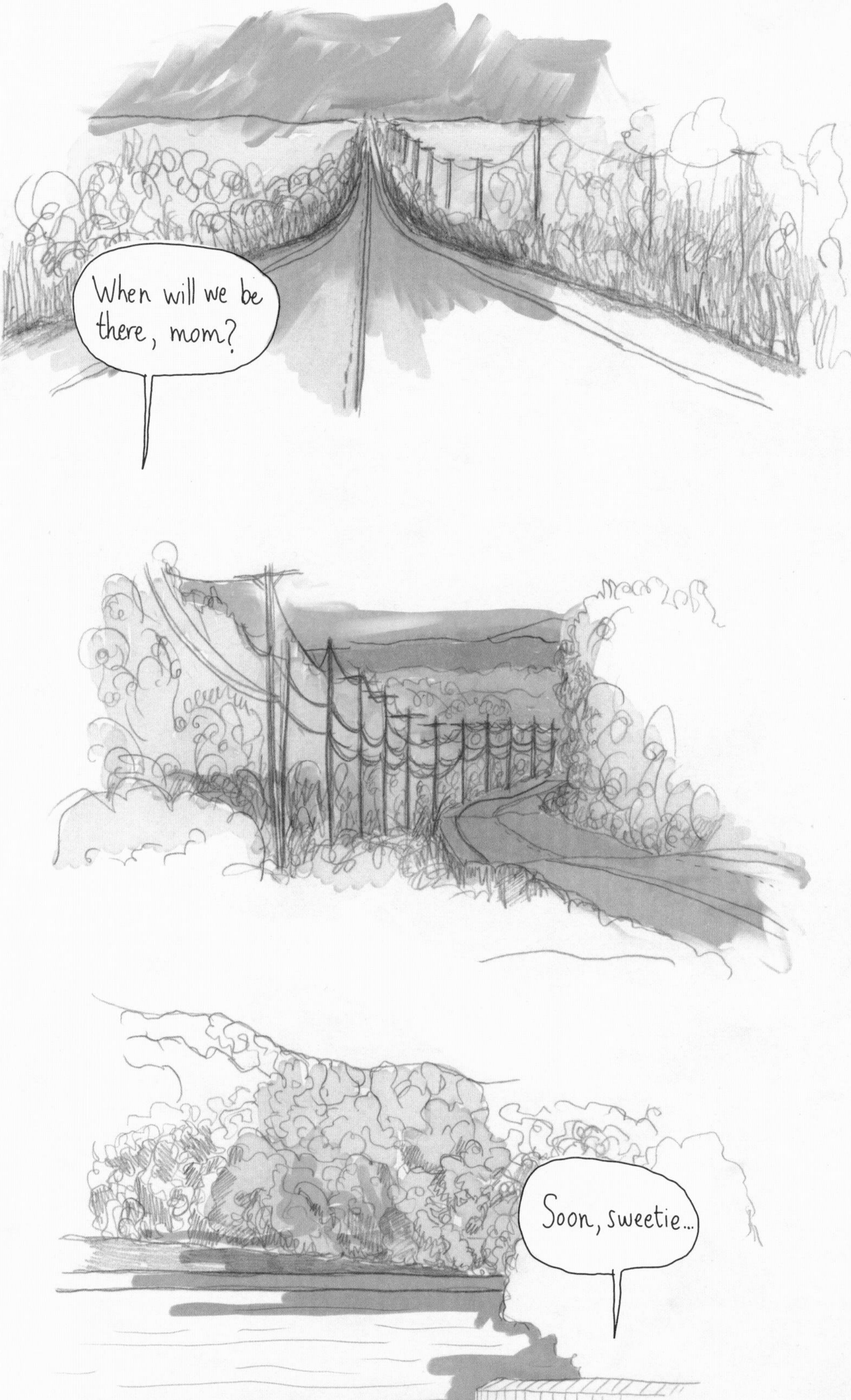
When will we be there, mom?
Soon, sweetie...

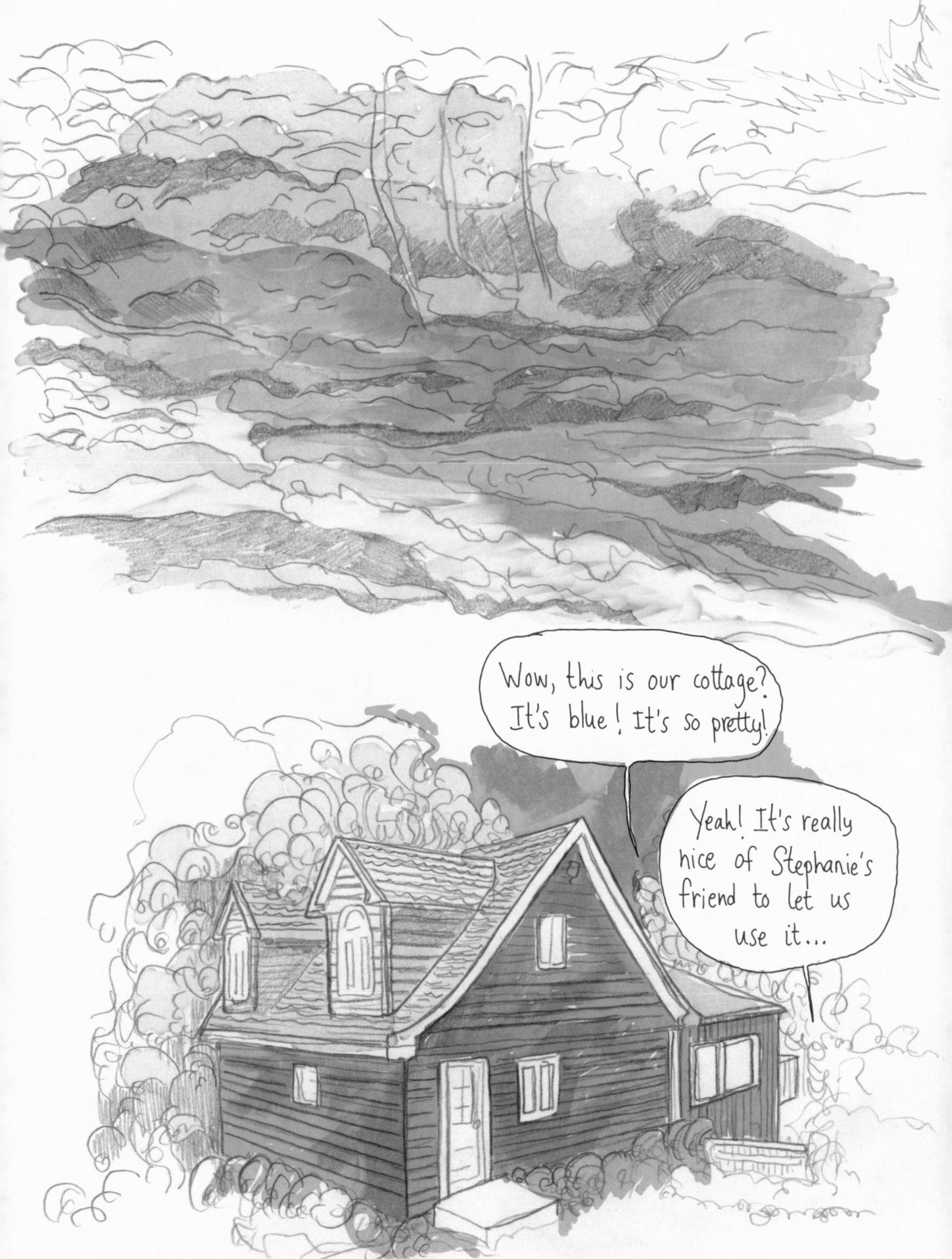
Wow, this is our cottage? It's blue! It's so pretty!
Yeah! It's really nice of Stephanie's friend to let us use it...

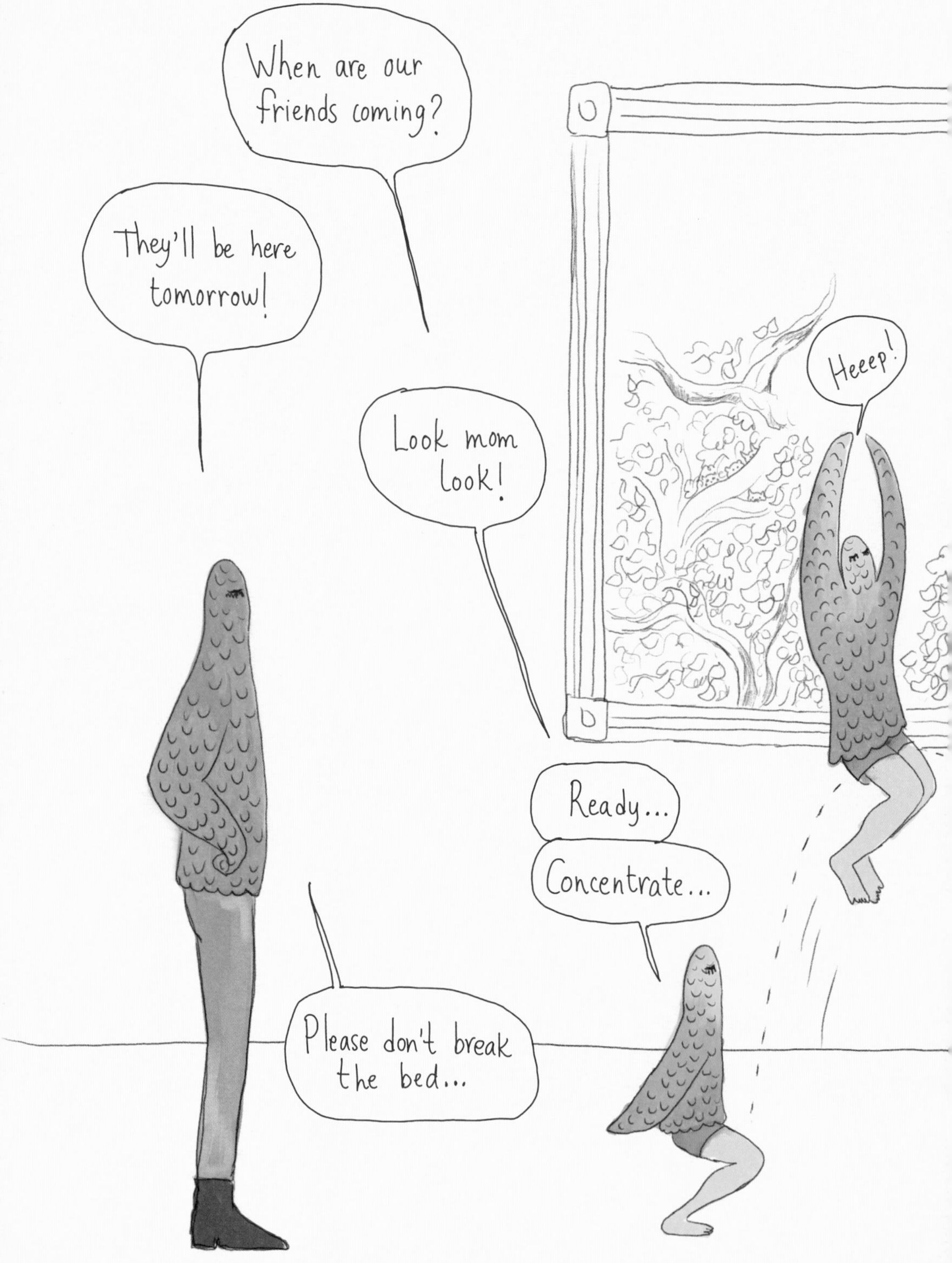
When are our friends coming?
They'll be here tomorrow!
Look mom look!
Heeep!
Ready...
Concentrate...
Please don't break the bed...

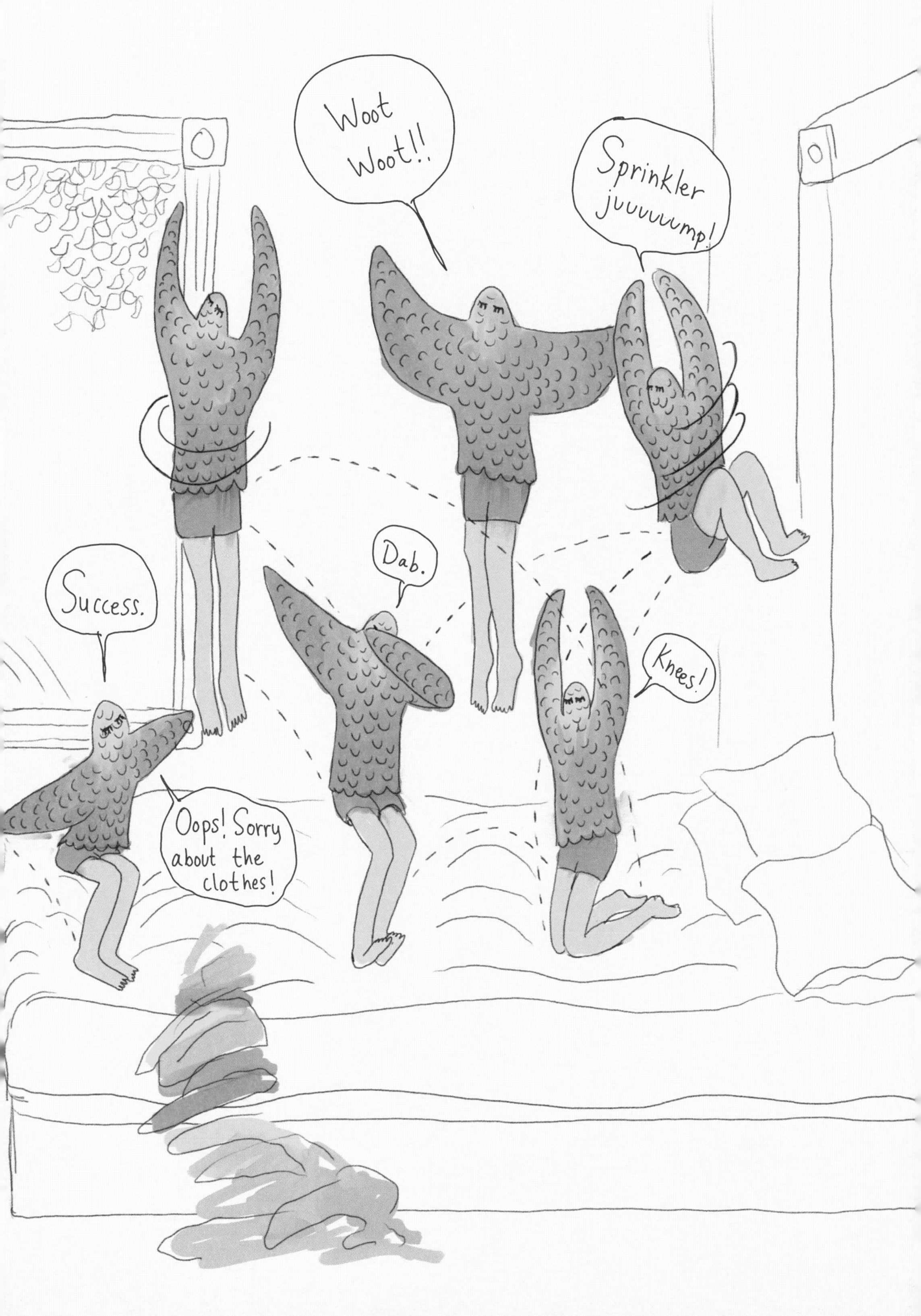

Woot Woot!!
Sprinkler juuuuuump!
Success.
Dab.
Knees!
Oops! Sorry about the clothes!

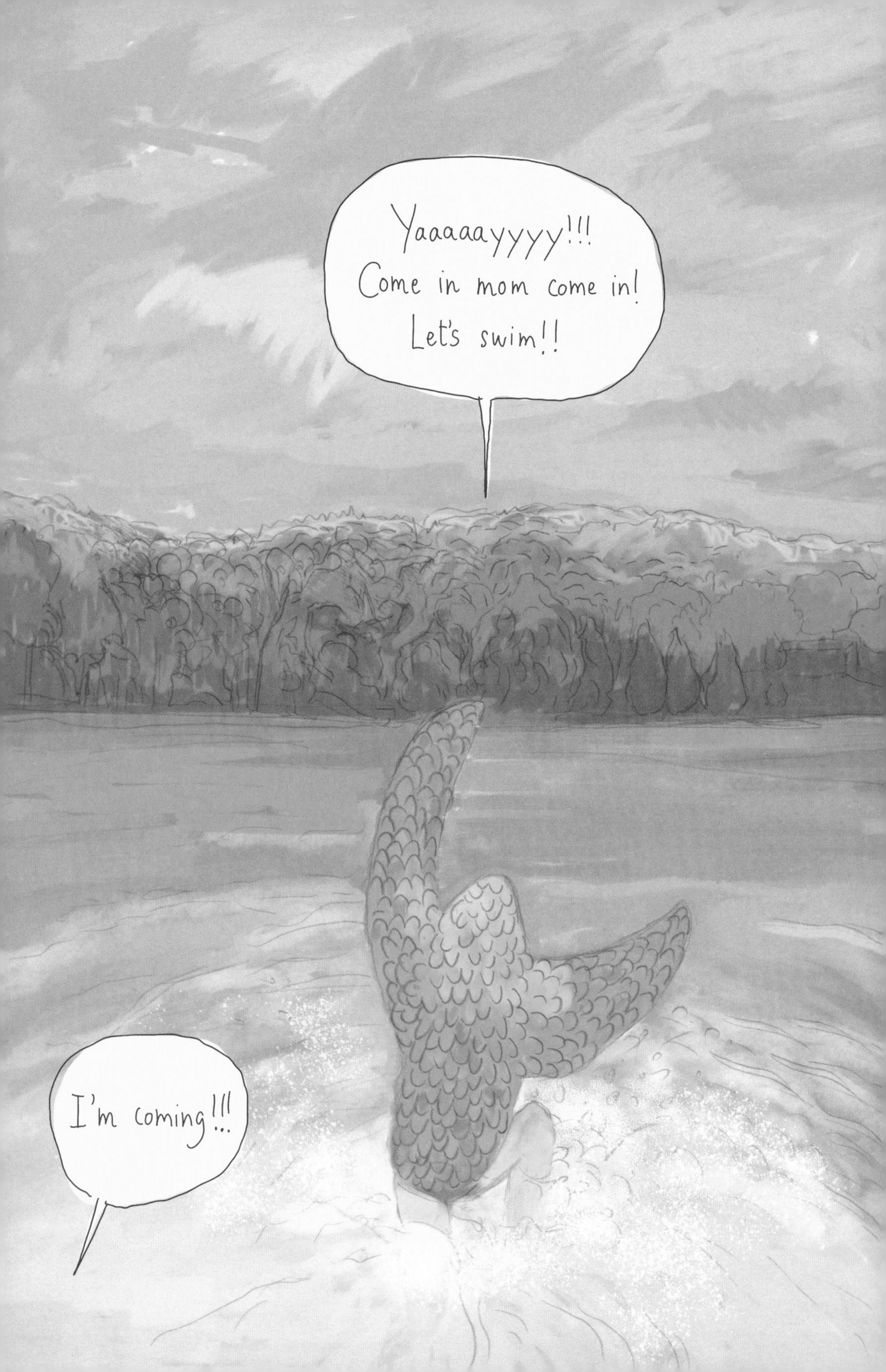
Yaaaaayyyy!!! Come in mom come in! Let's swim!!
I'm coming!!!...

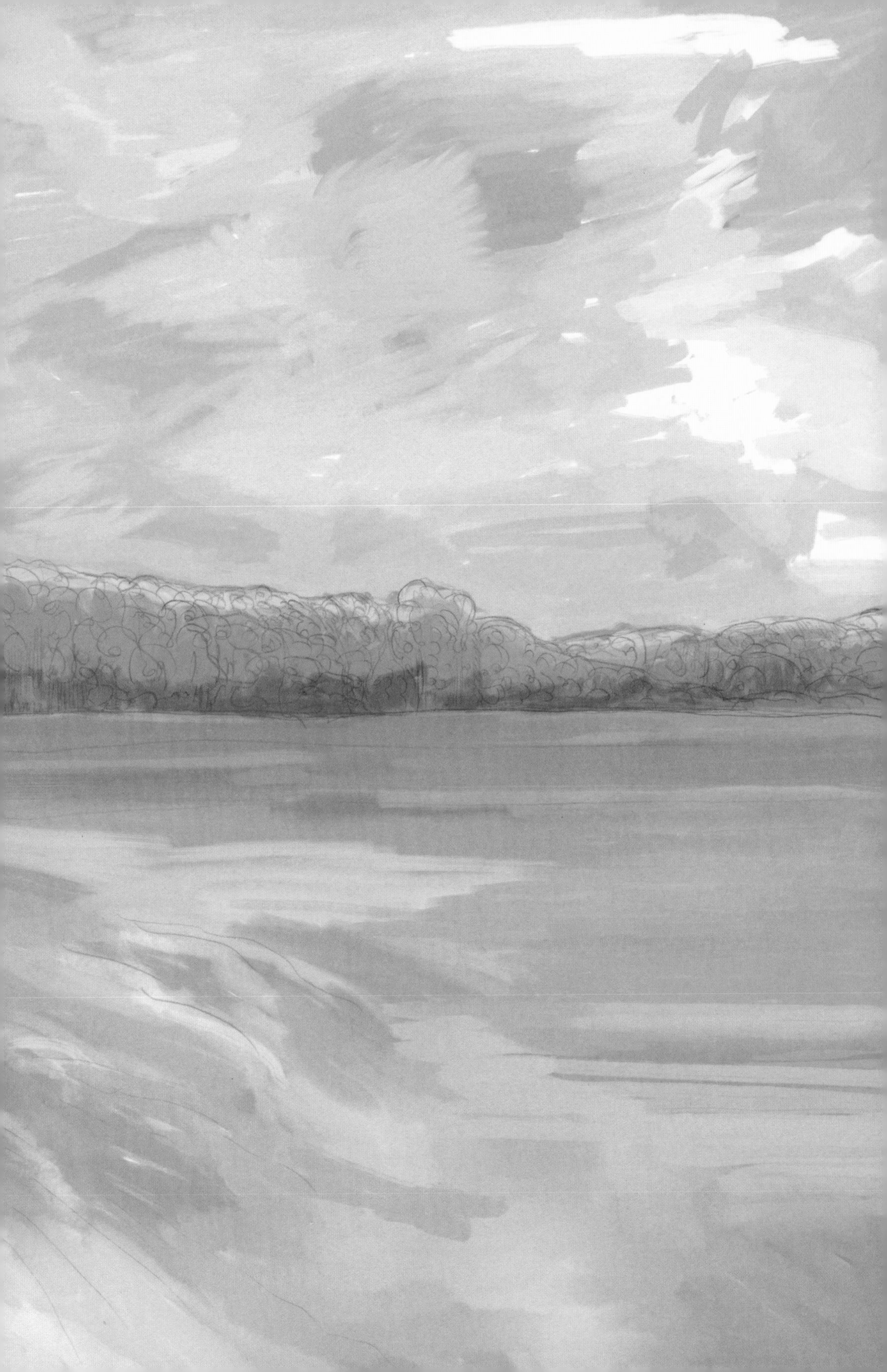

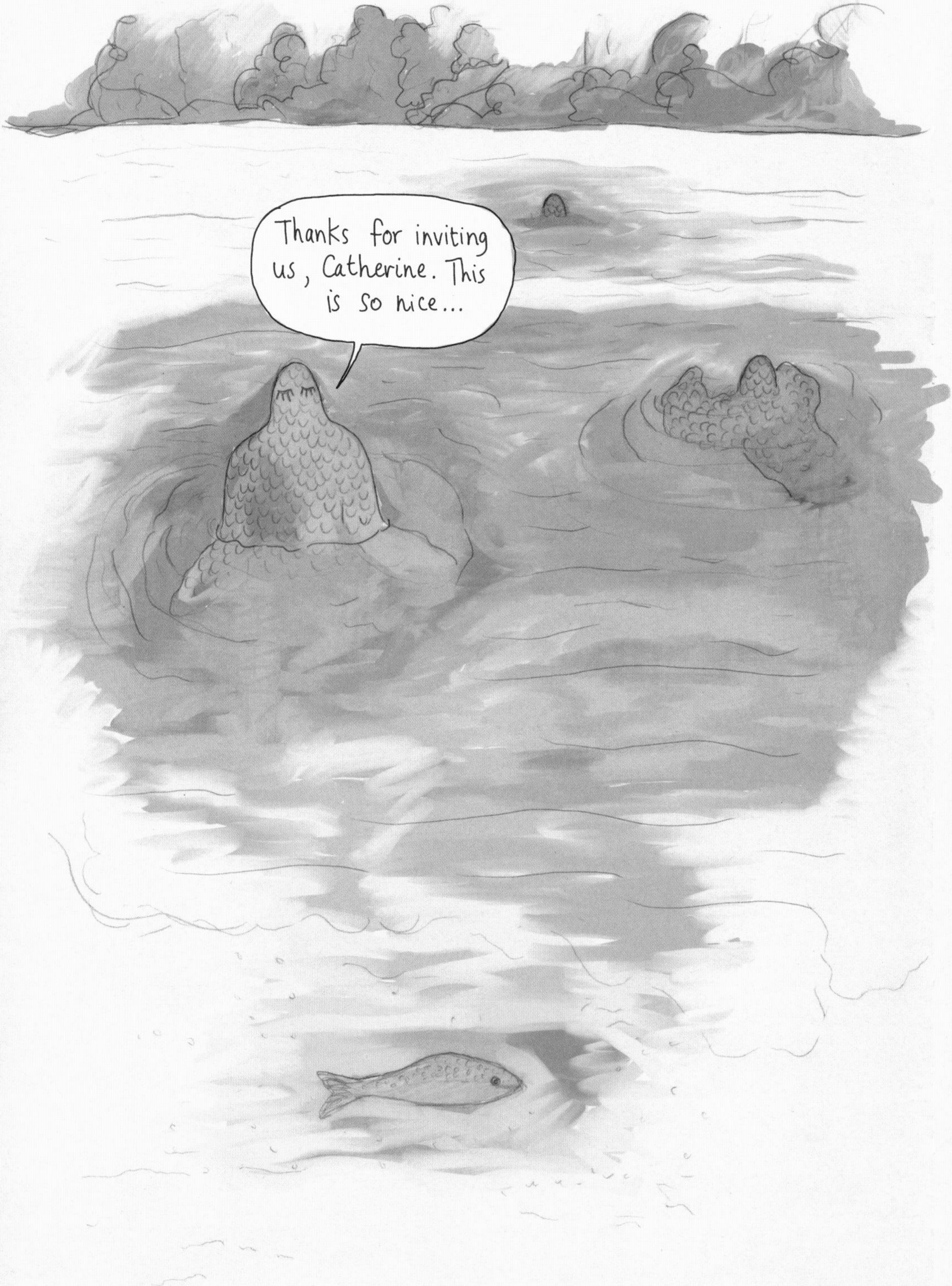
Thanks for inviting us, Catherine. This is so nice...

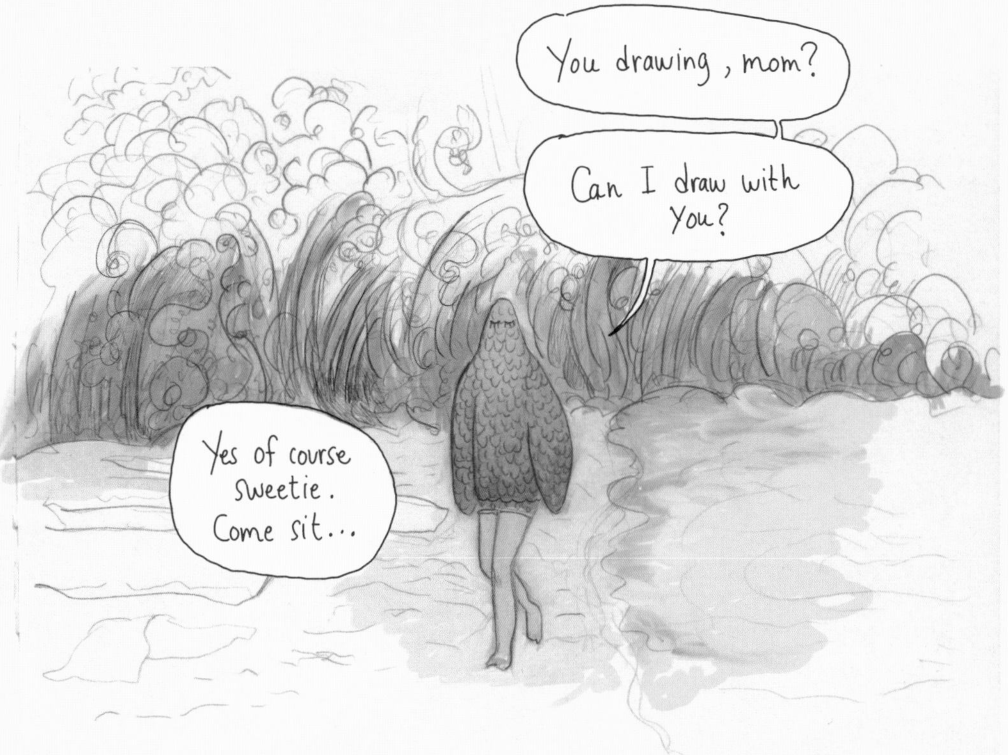
You drawing, mom?
Can I draw with you?
Yes of course sweetie. Come sit...

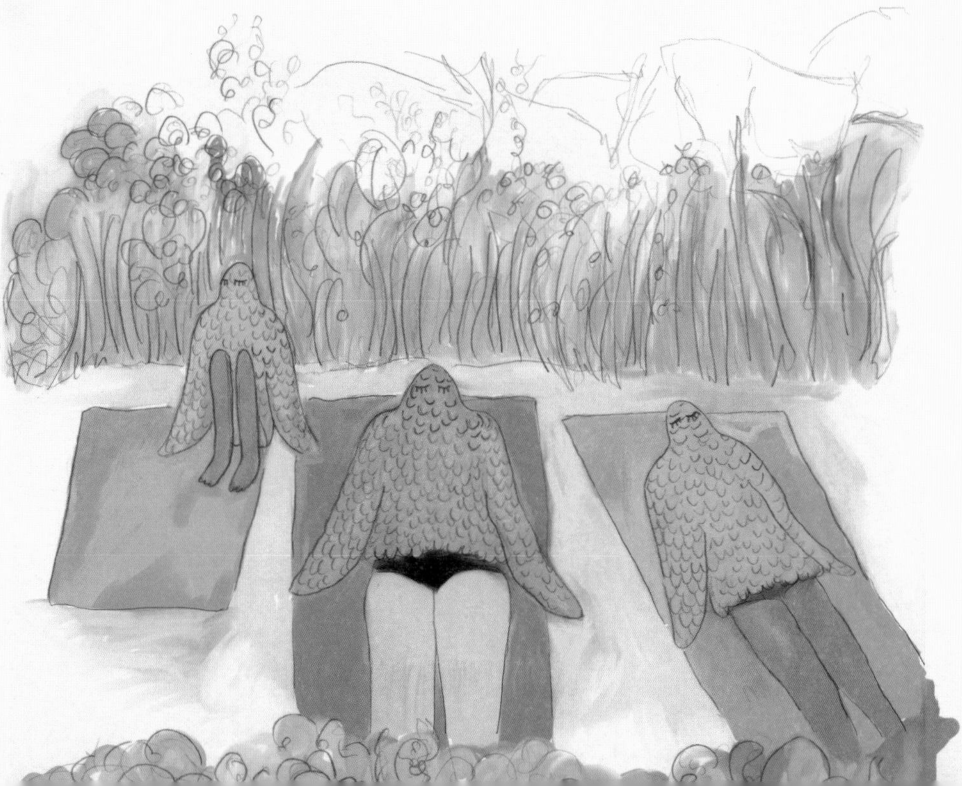

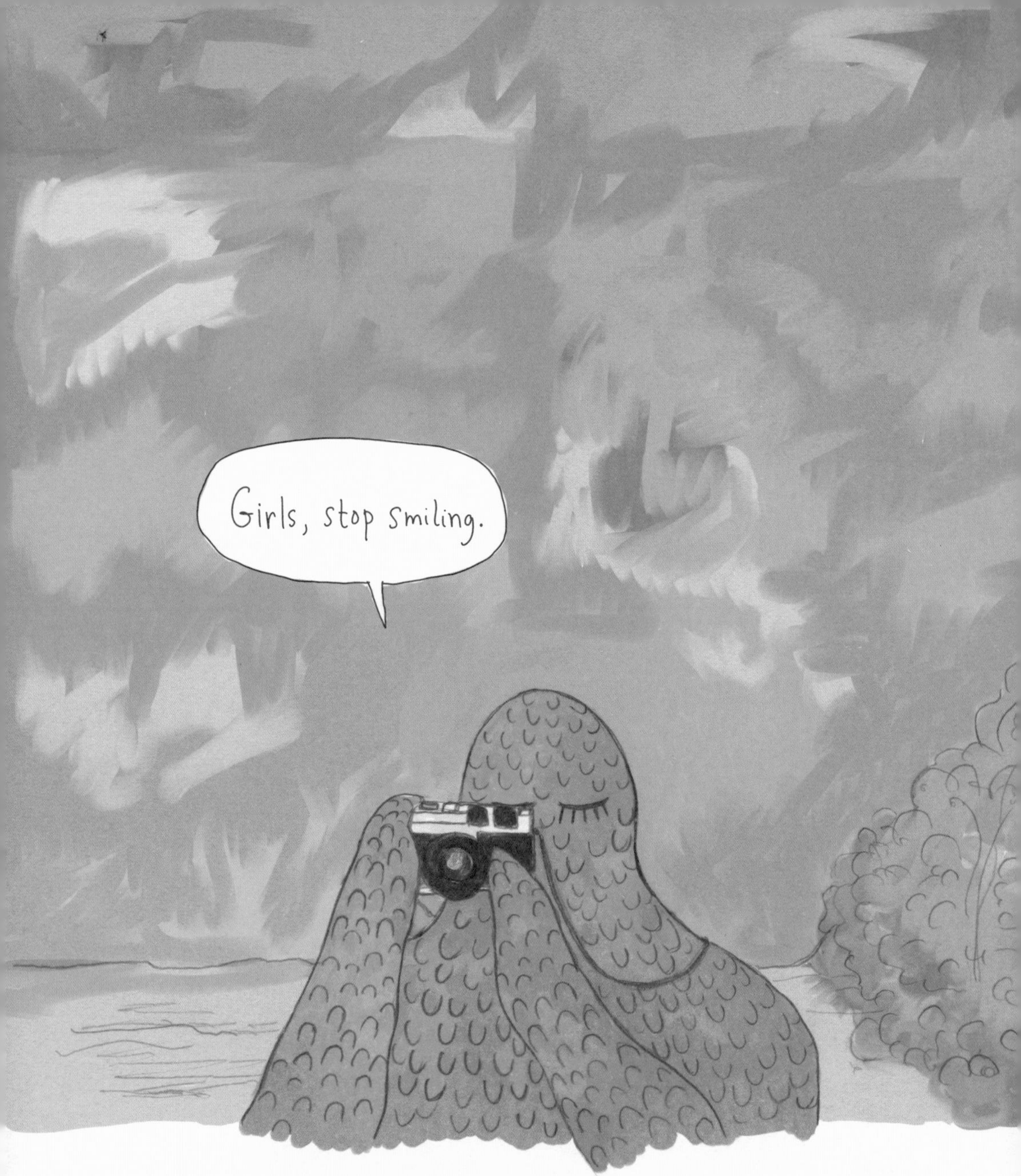
Girls, stop smiling.

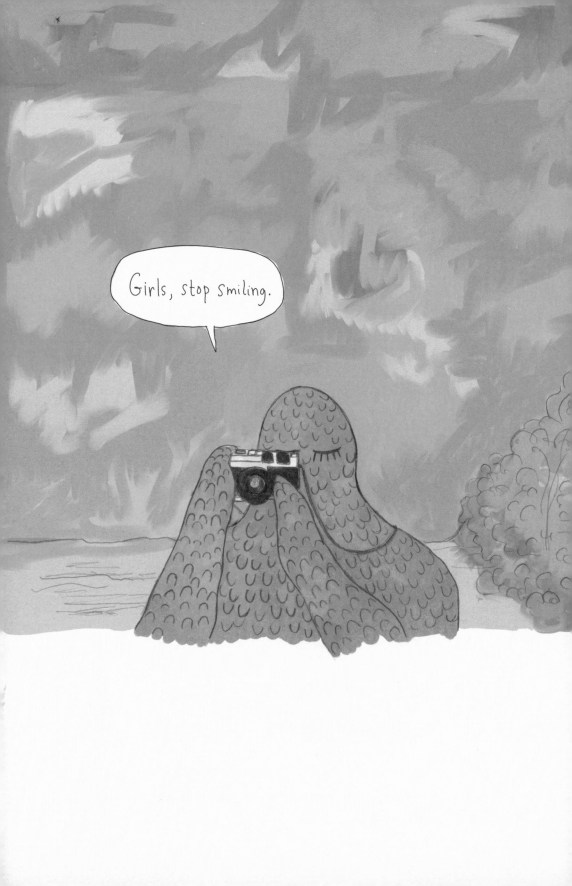

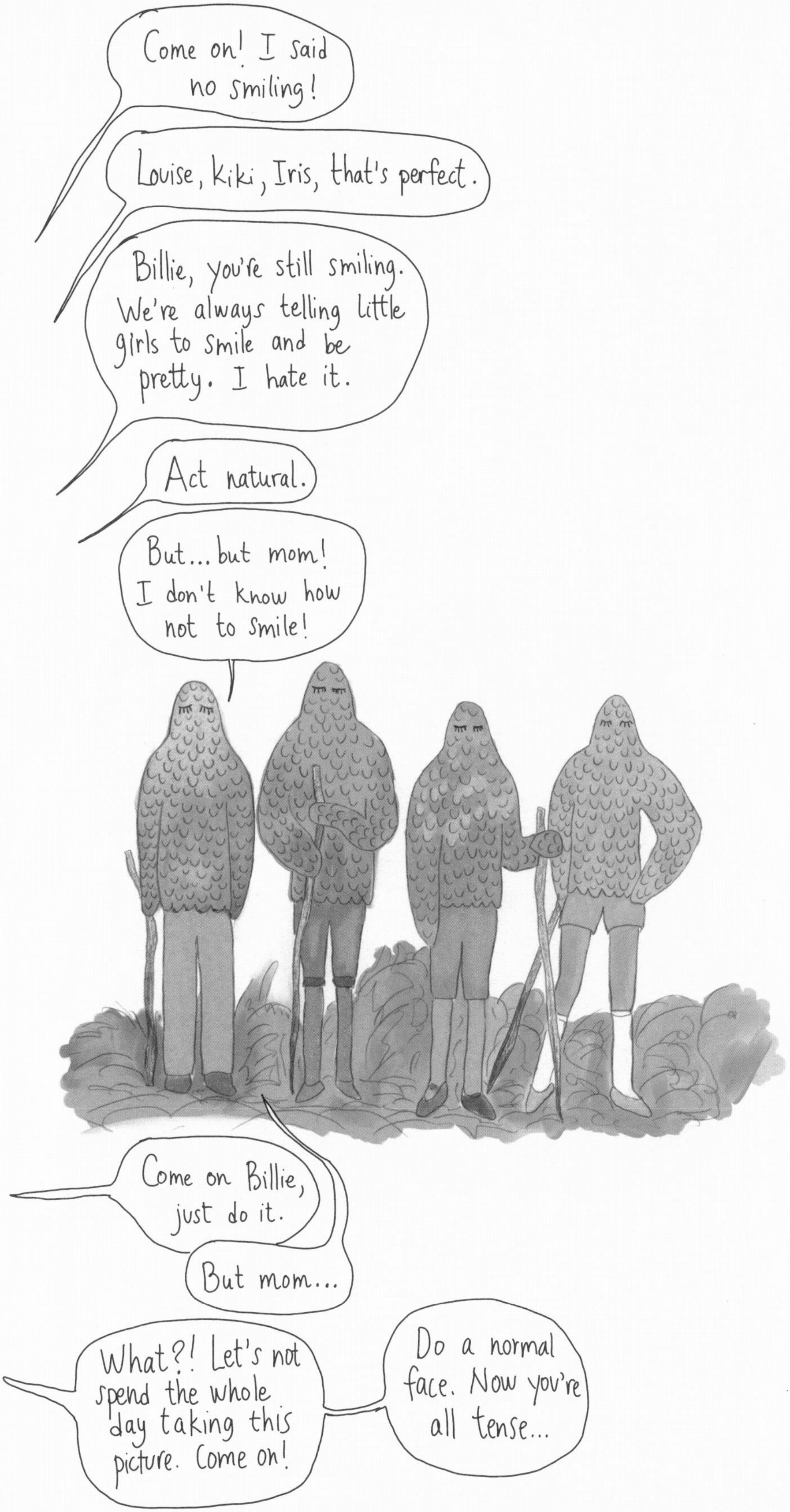
Come on! I said no smiling!
Louise, kiki, Iris, that's perfect.
Billie, you're still smiling. We're always telling little girls to smile and be pretty. I hate it.
Act natural.
But... but mom! I don't know how not to smile!
Come on Billie, just do it.
But mom...
What?! Let's not spend the whole day taking this picture. Come on!
Do a normal face. Now you're all tense...

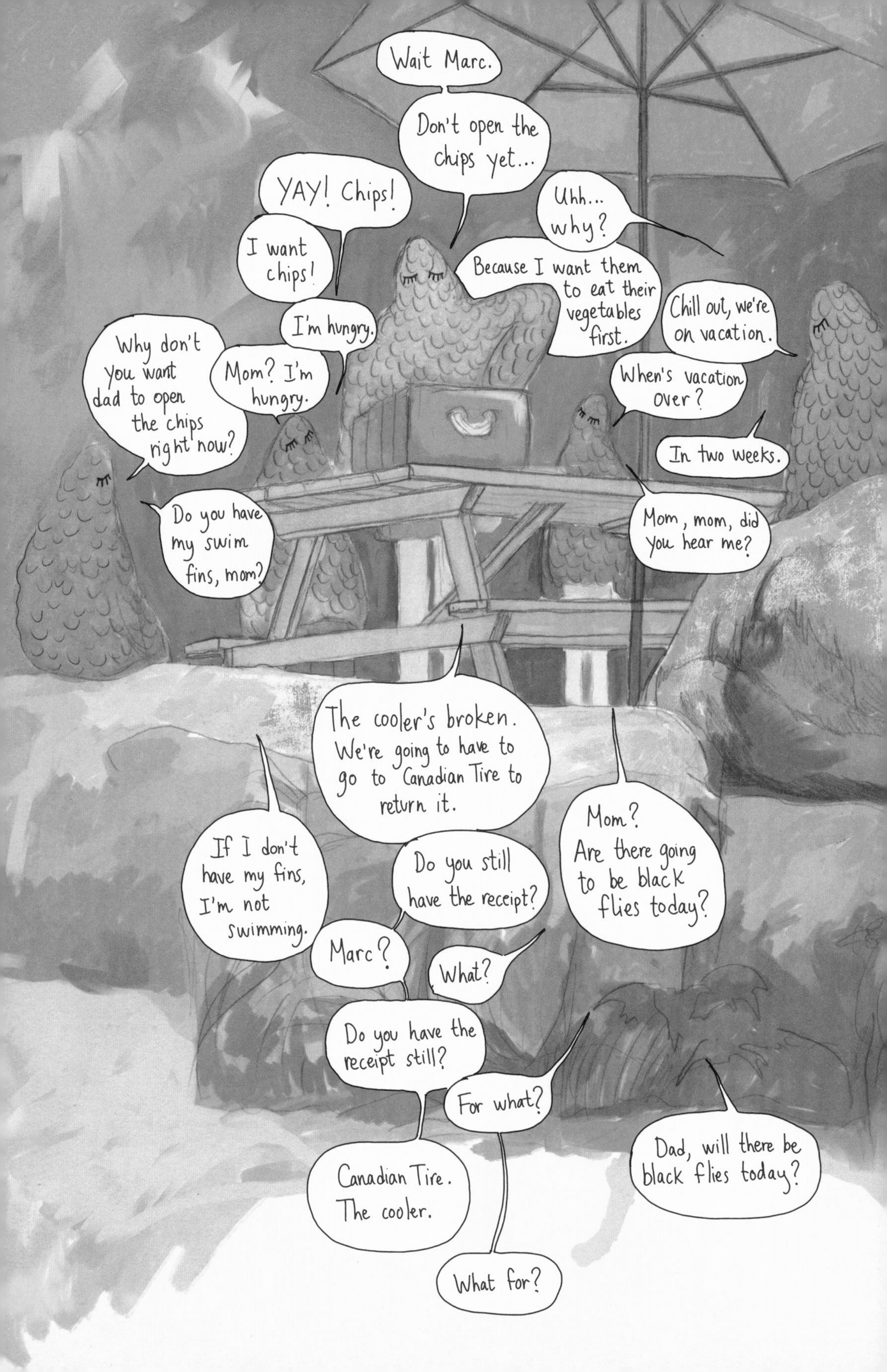
Wait Marc.
Don't open the chips yet...
YAY! Chips!
Uhh... why?
I want chips!
Because I want them to eat their vegetables first.
I'm hungry.
Chill out, we're on vacation.
Why don't you want dad to open the chips right now?
Mom? I'm hungry.
When's vacation over?
In two weeks.
Do you have my swim fins, mom?
Mom, mom, did you hear me?
The cooler's broken. We're going to have to go to Canadian Tire to return it.
If I don't have my fins, I'm not swimming.
Do you still have the receipt?
Mom? Are there going to be black flies today?
Marc?
What?
Do you have the receipt still?
For what?
Canadian Tire. The cooler.
Dad, will there be black flies today?
What for?

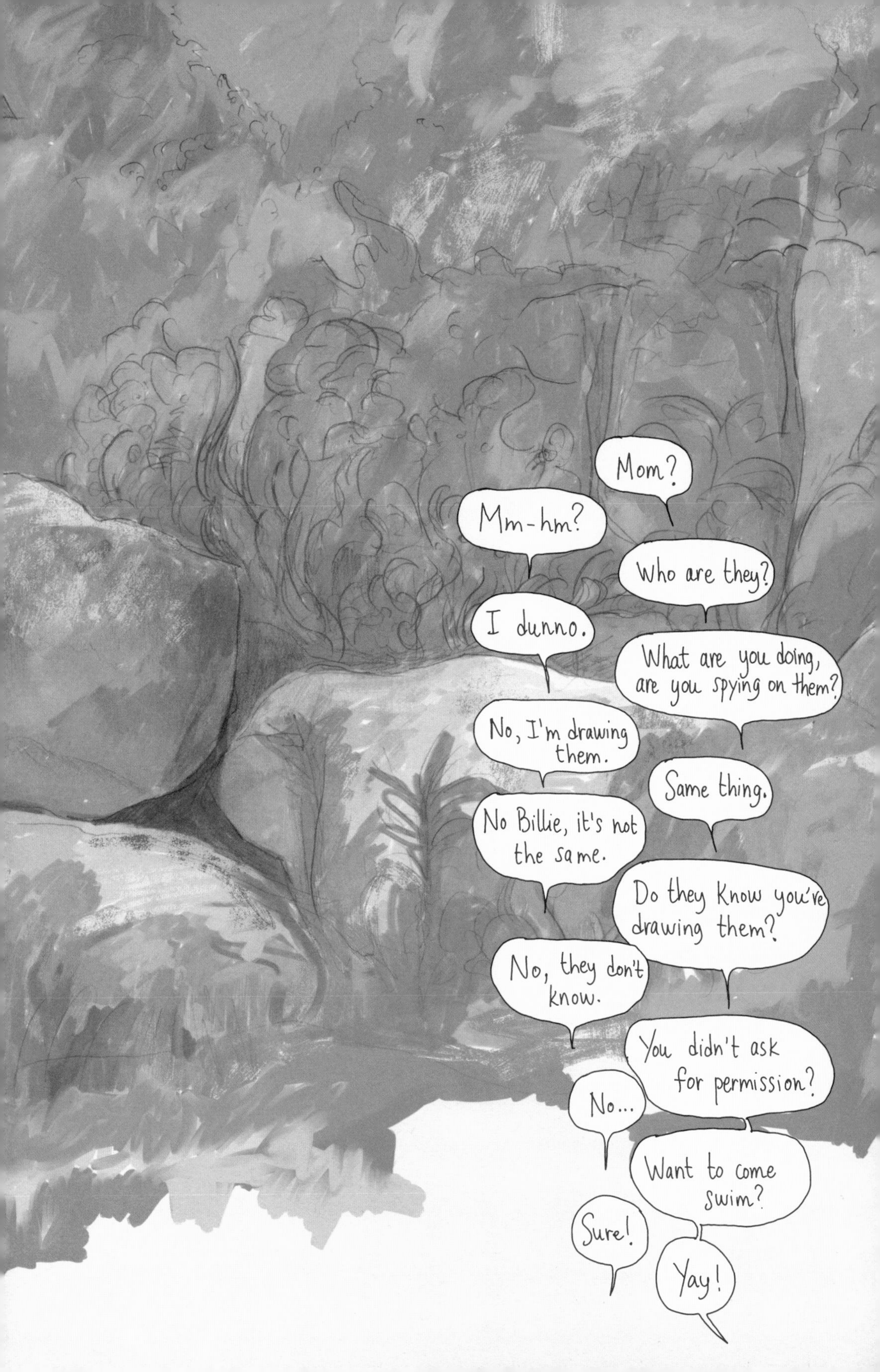
Mom?
Mm-hm?
Who are they?
I dunno.
What are you doing, are you spying on them?
No, I'm drawing them.
Same thing.
No Billie, it's not the same.
Do they know you're drawing them?
No, they don't know.
You didn't ask for permission?
No...
Want to come swim?
Sure!
Yay!

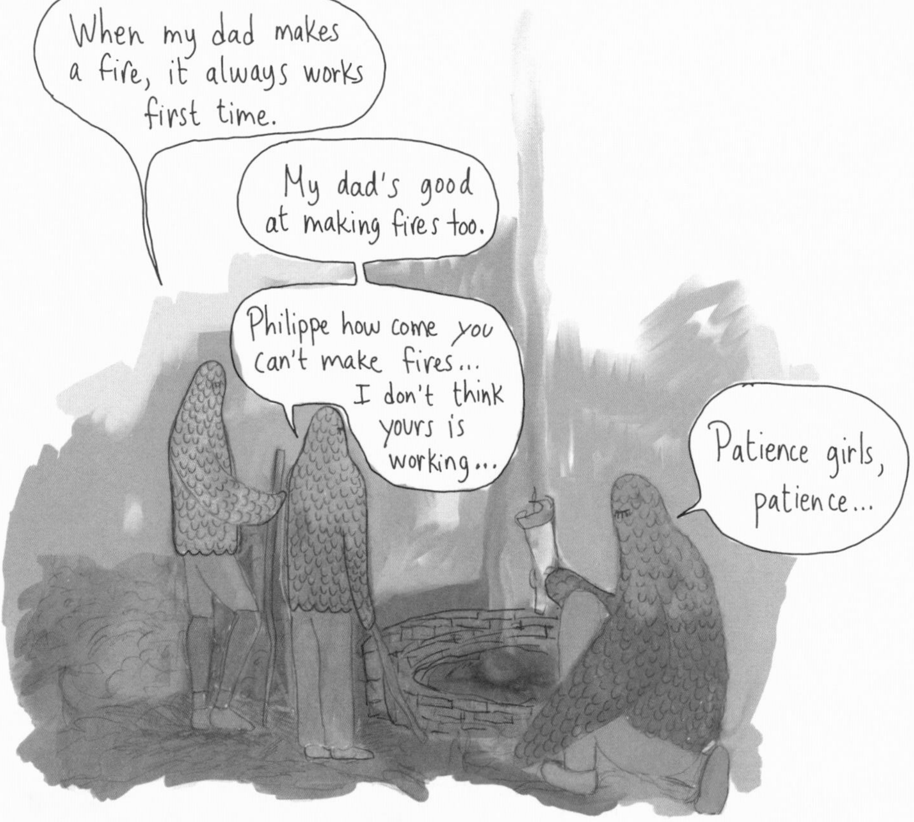
When my dad makes a fire, it always works first time.
My dad's good at making fires too.
Philippe how come you can't make fires... I don't think yours is working...
Patience girls, patience...

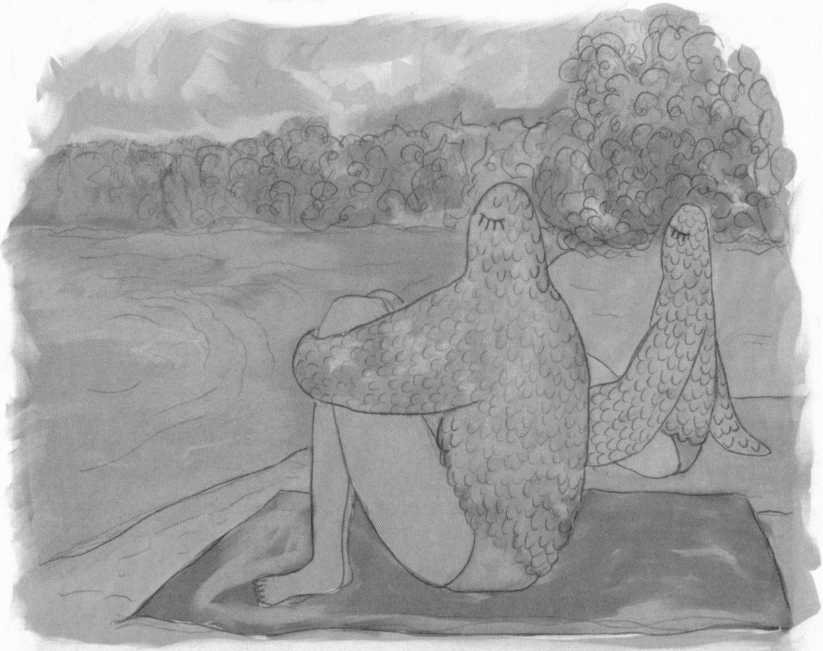

Mmmm. This apple's so good. Are you drawing, Catherine?
Yes Kiki, I'm drawing. I'm drawing you.
Do you like drawing, Catherine?
Yes, I do.
Are you an artist?
I don't know Kiki, I can't say.
My mom is an artist.
Yes, Natacha is an artist.
She's in New York right now.
Yes, I know.
New York is where Andy Worwall is from.
Catherine?
Yes Kiki?
Are you allergic to wasps?
I don't think so, but I've never been stung before.
My sister is allergic to wasps.
Yes, I know.
I'm not allergic to wasps, but I'm allergic to peanuts.
Mm-hm.
My apple's really good.
I'm glad, Kiki

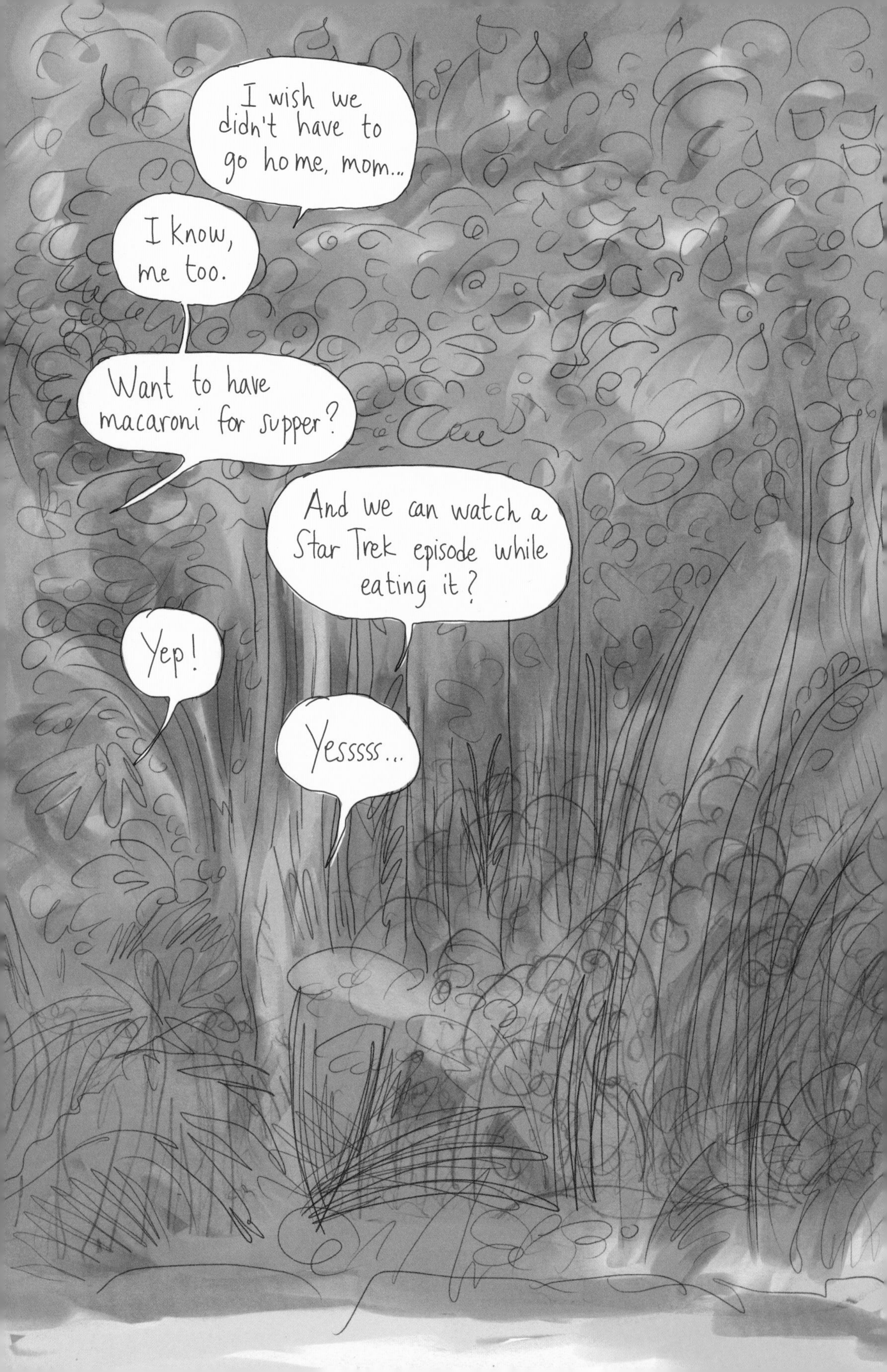
I wish we didn't have to go home, mom...
I know, me too.
Want to have macaroni for supper?
And we can watch a Star Trek episode while eating it?
Yep!
Yesssss...

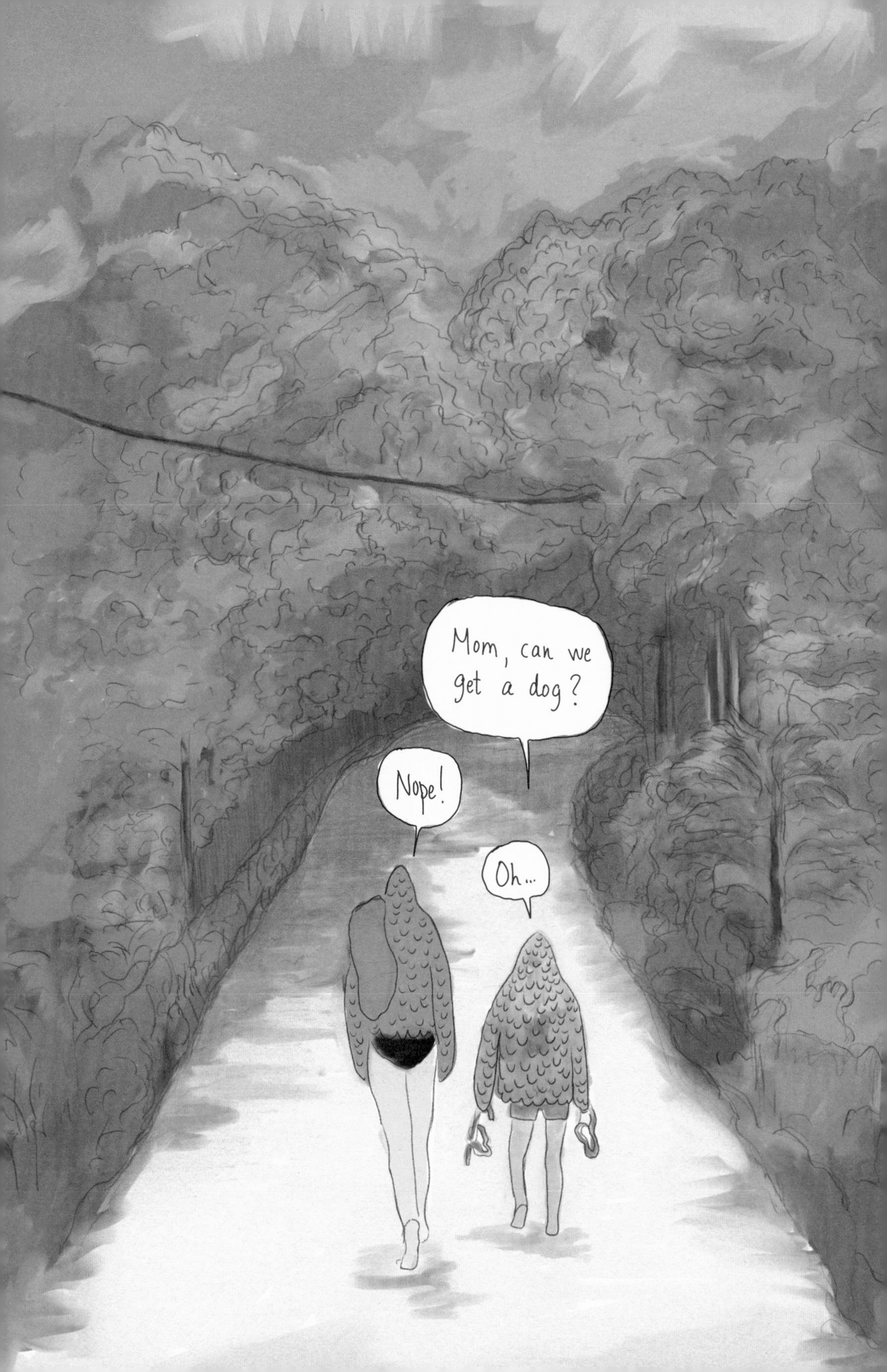
Mom, can we get a dog?
Nope!
Oh...

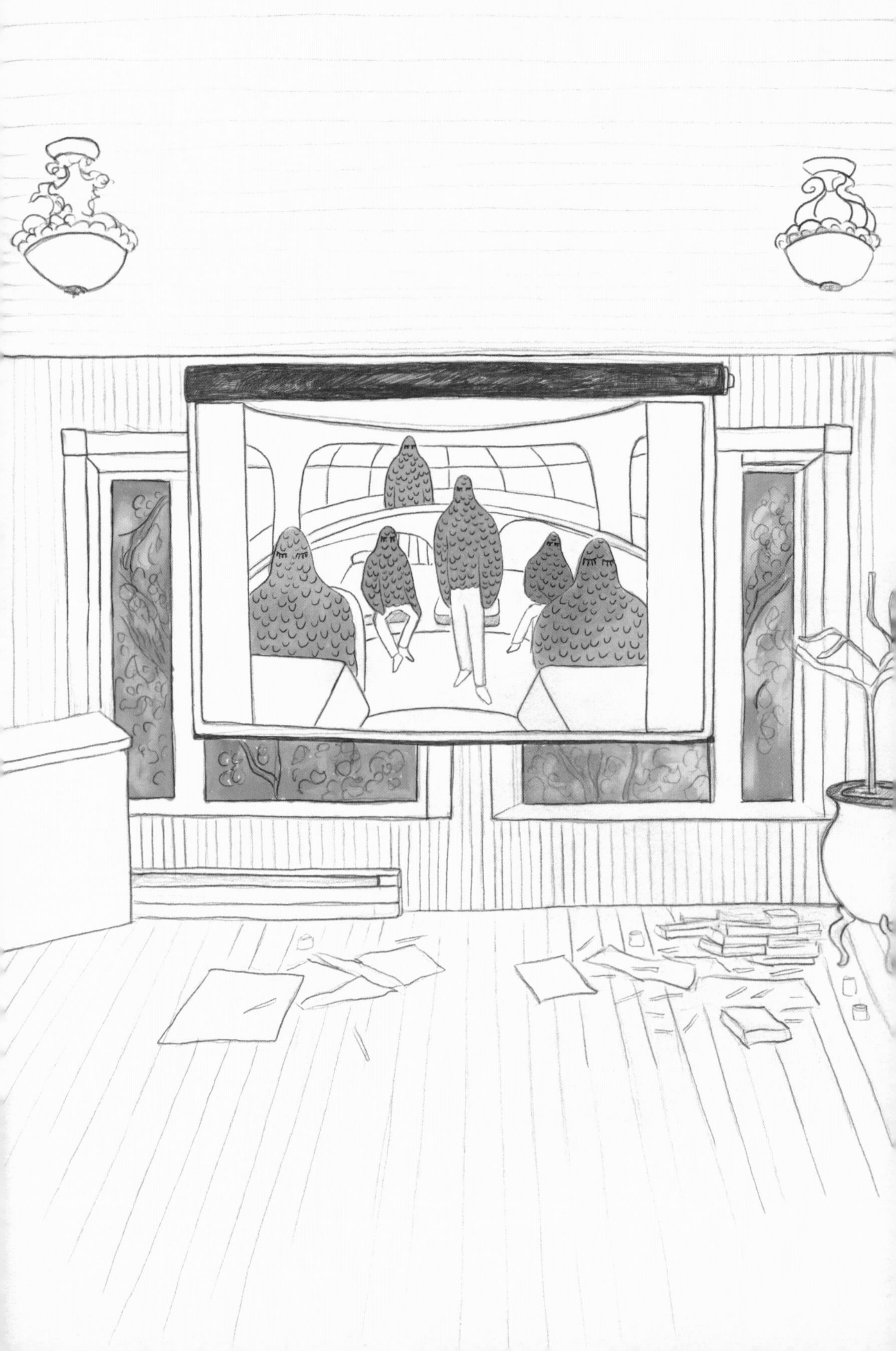

Emmanuelle

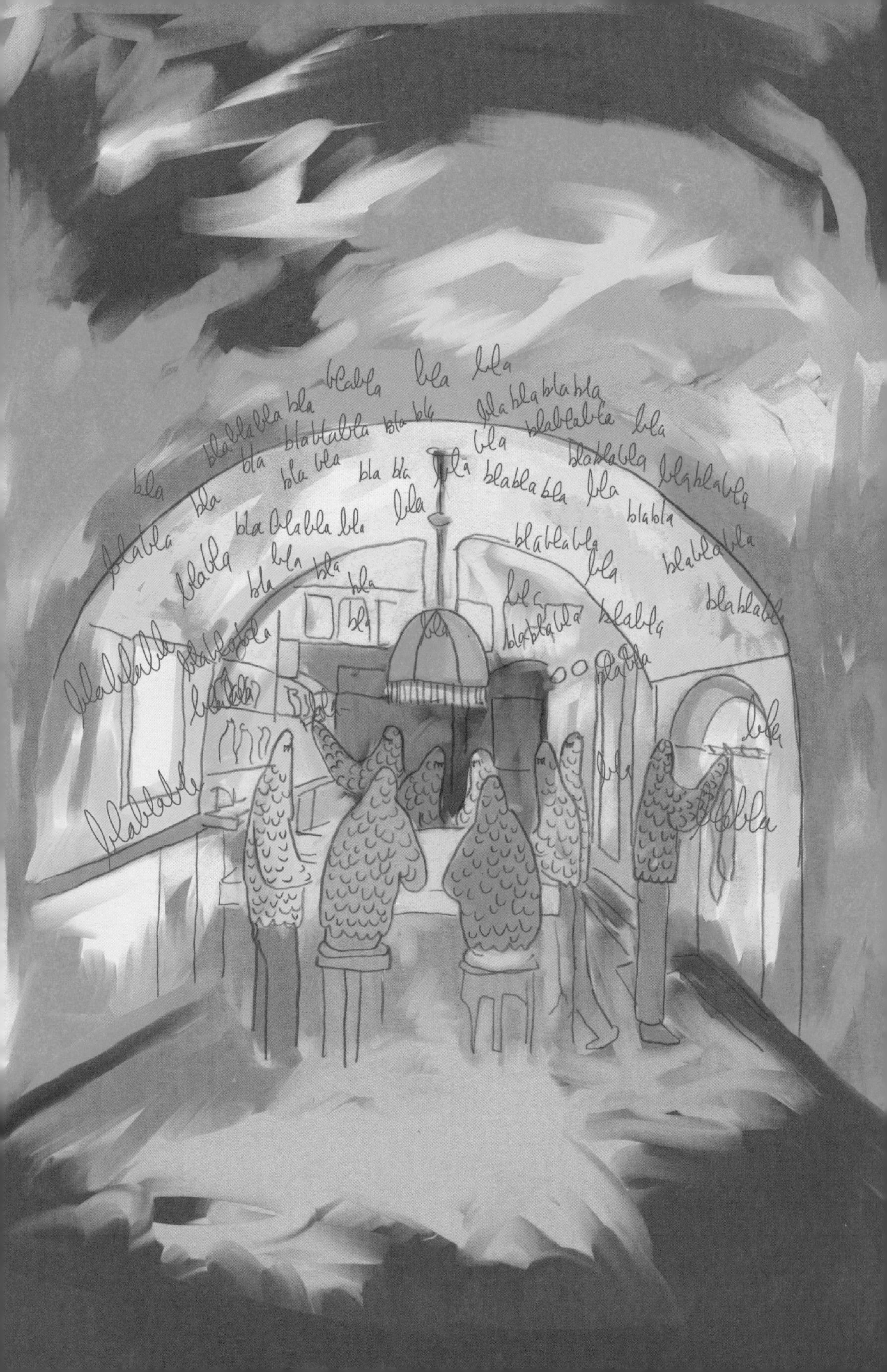
blabla bla bla
blablablabla bla
blablablabla bla bla
bla blablabla bla
bla bla bla bla bla bla
blablablabla bla
bla blablablabla bla
blabla bla blablabla bla bla
blabla blabla
blablabla
blabla bla bla bla
bla blablabla
blablabla
bla
blablabla
bla
blabla

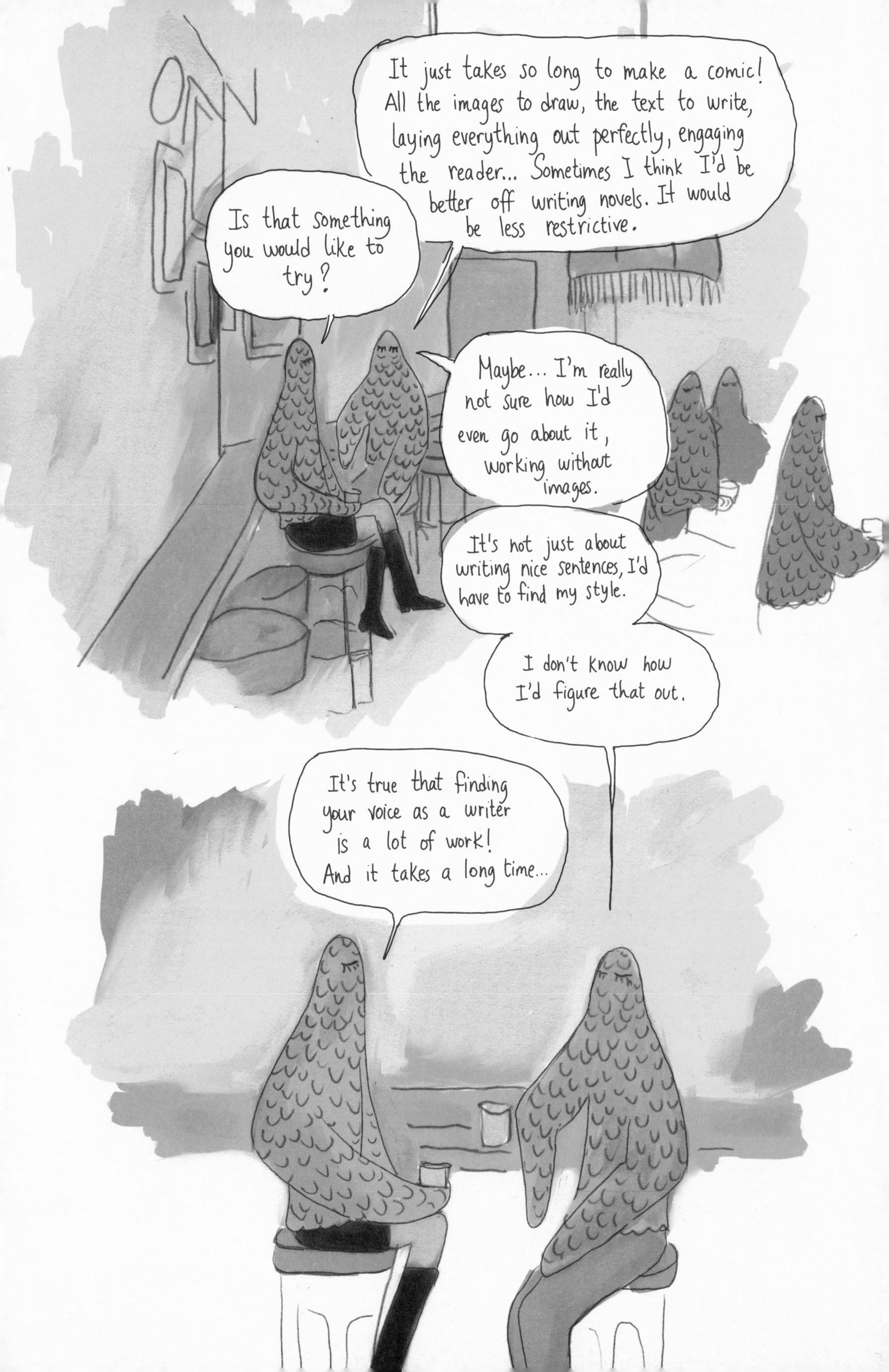
It just takes so long to make a comic! All the images to draw, the text to write, laying everything out perfectly, engaging the reader... Sometimes I think I'd be better off writing novels. It would be less restrictive.
Is that something you would like to try?
Maybe... I'm really not sure how I'd even go about it, working without images.
It's not just about writing nice sentences, I'd have to find my style.
I don't know how I'd figure that out.
It's true that finding your voice as a writer is a lot of work! And it takes a long time...

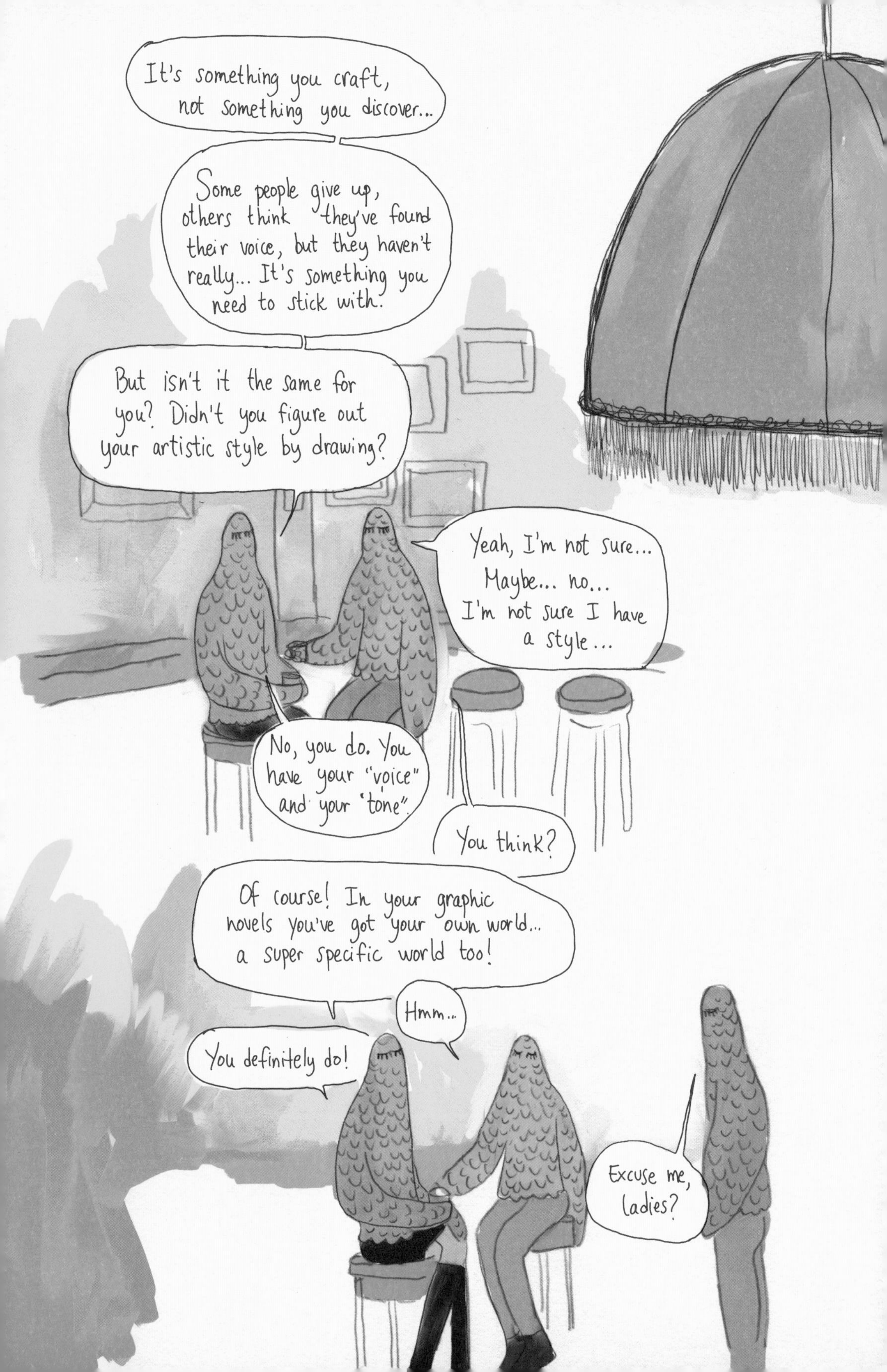
It's something you craft, not something you discover...
Some people give up, others think they've found their voice, but they haven't really... It's something you need to stick with.
But isn't it the same for you? Didn't you figure out your artistic style by drawing?
Yeah, I'm not sure... Maybe... no... I'm not sure I have a style...
No, you do. You have your "voice" and your "tone".
You think?
Of course! In your graphic novels you've got your own world... a super specific world too!
Hmm...
You definitely do!
Excuse me, ladies?

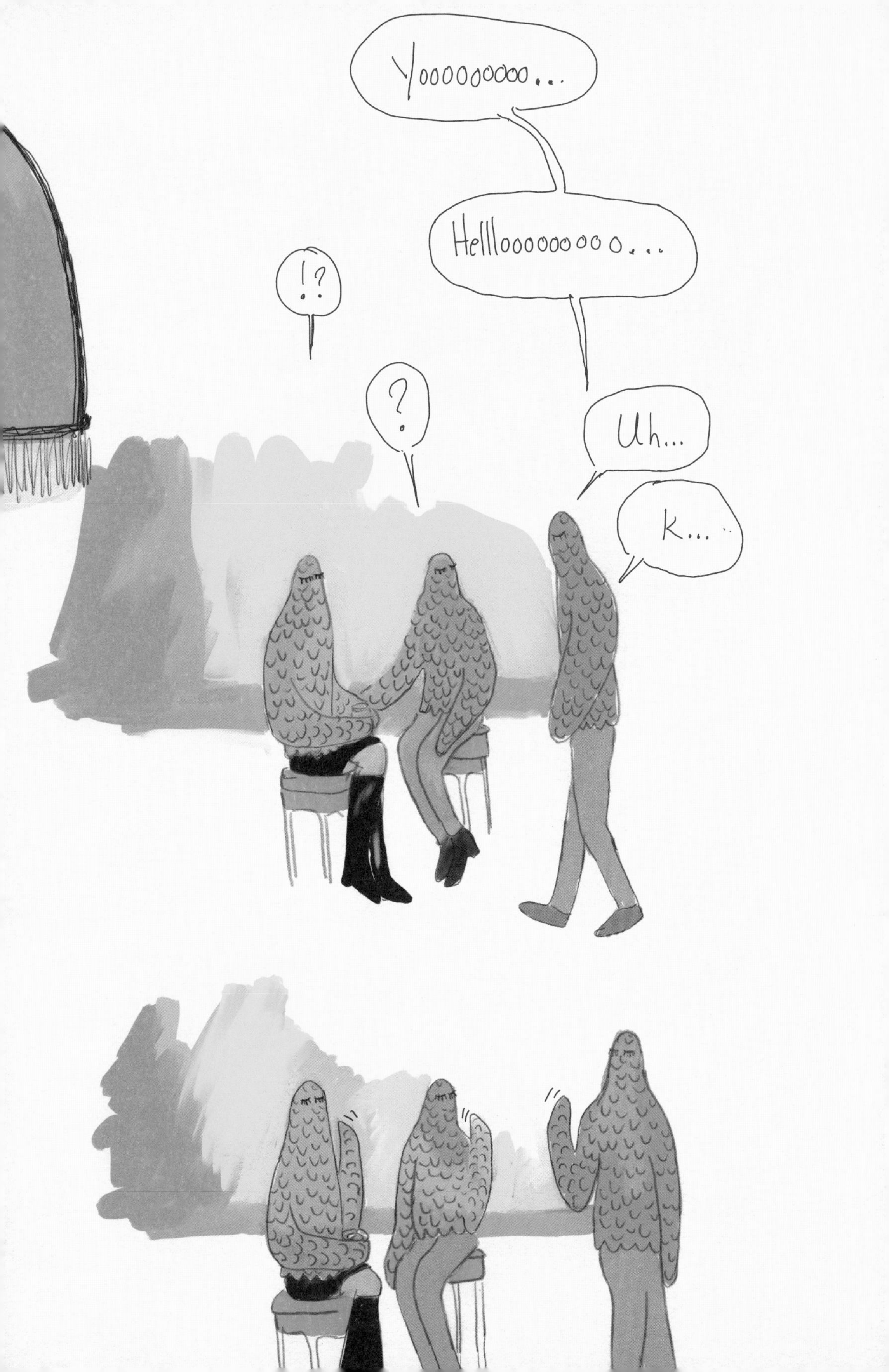
Yoooooooo...
Hellllooooooooo...
!?
?
Uh...
k...

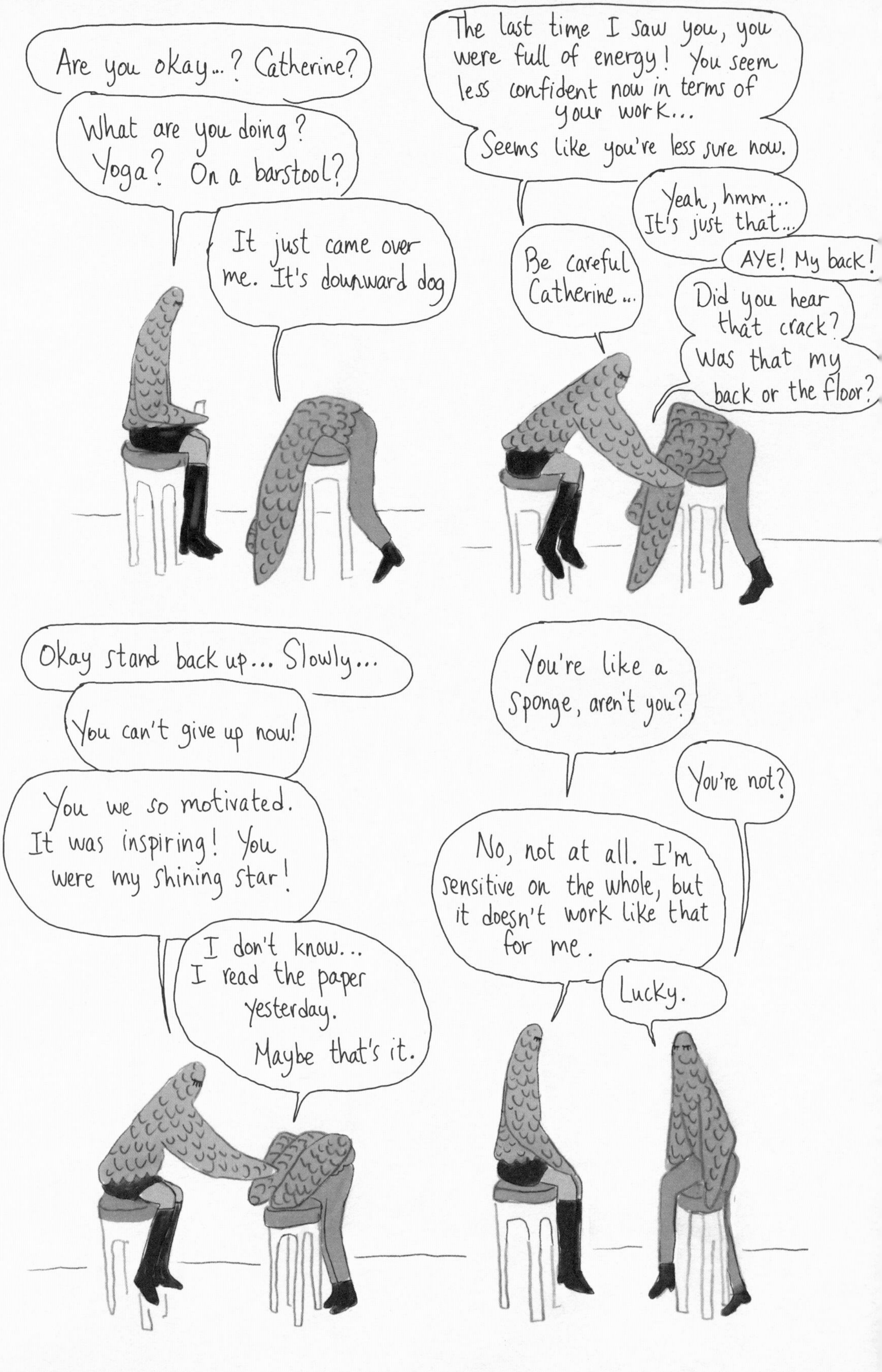
Are you okay...? Catherine?
What are you doing? Yoga? On a barstool?
It just came over me. It's downward dog
The last time I saw you, you were full of energy! You seem less confident now in terms of your work... Seems like you're less sure now.
Yeah, hmm... It's just that...
Be careful Catherine...
AYE! My back!
Did you hear that crack? Was that my back or the floor?
Okay stand back up... Slowly...
You can't give up now!
You we so motivated. It was inspiring! You were my shining star!
I don't know... I read the paper yesterday. Maybe that's it.
You're like a sponge, aren't you?
You're not?
No, not at all. I'm sensitive on the whole, but it doesn't work like that for me.
Lucky.

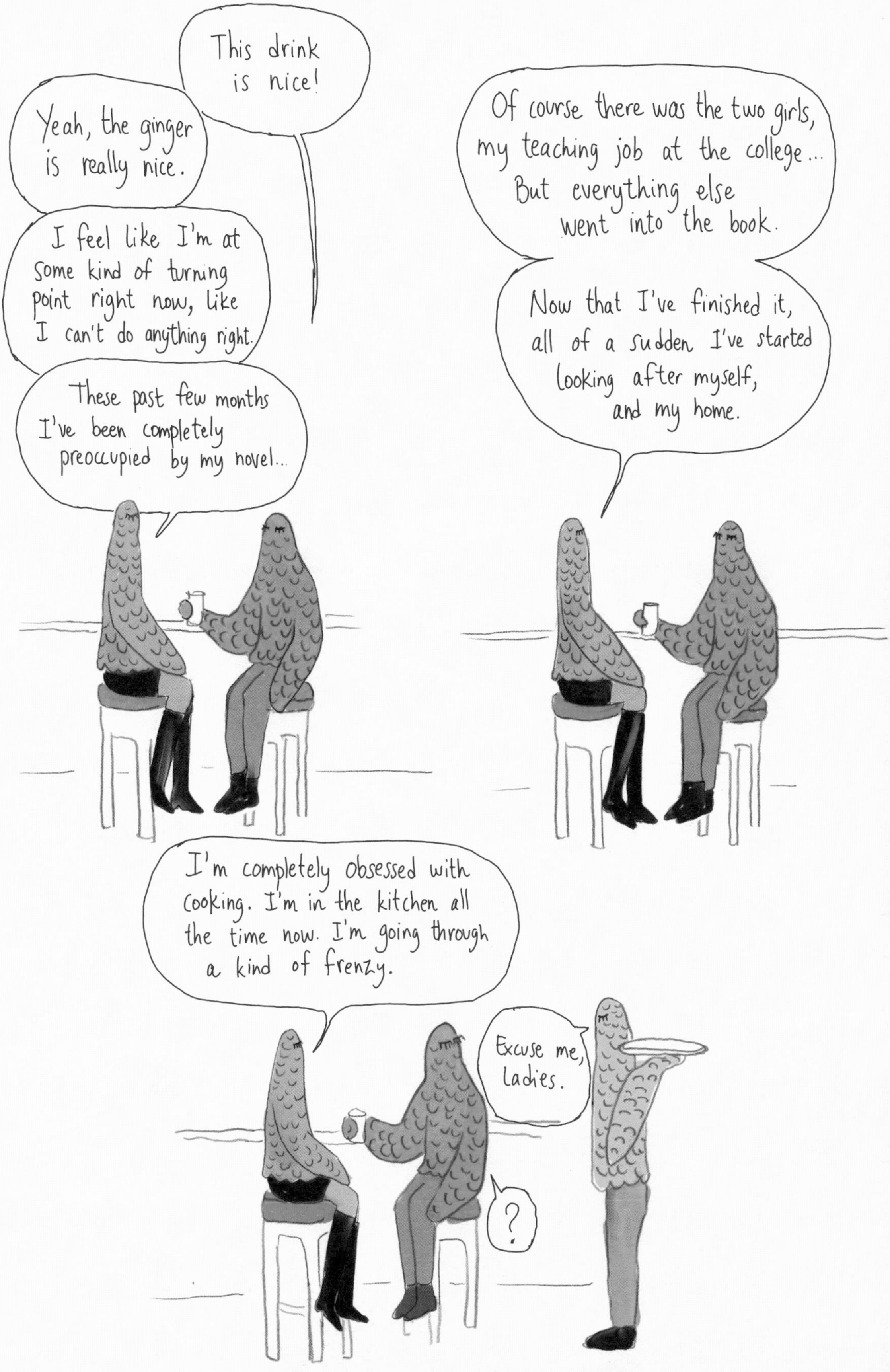
This drink is nice!
Yeah, the ginger is really nice.
I feel like I'm at some kind of turning point right now, like I can't do anything right.
These past few months I've been completely preoccupied by my novel...
Of course there was the two girls, my teaching job at the college... But everything else went into the book.
Now that I've finished it, all of a sudden I've started looking after myself, and my home.
I'm completely obsessed with cooking. I'm in the kitchen all the time now. I'm going through a kind of frenzy.
Excuse me, ladies.
?

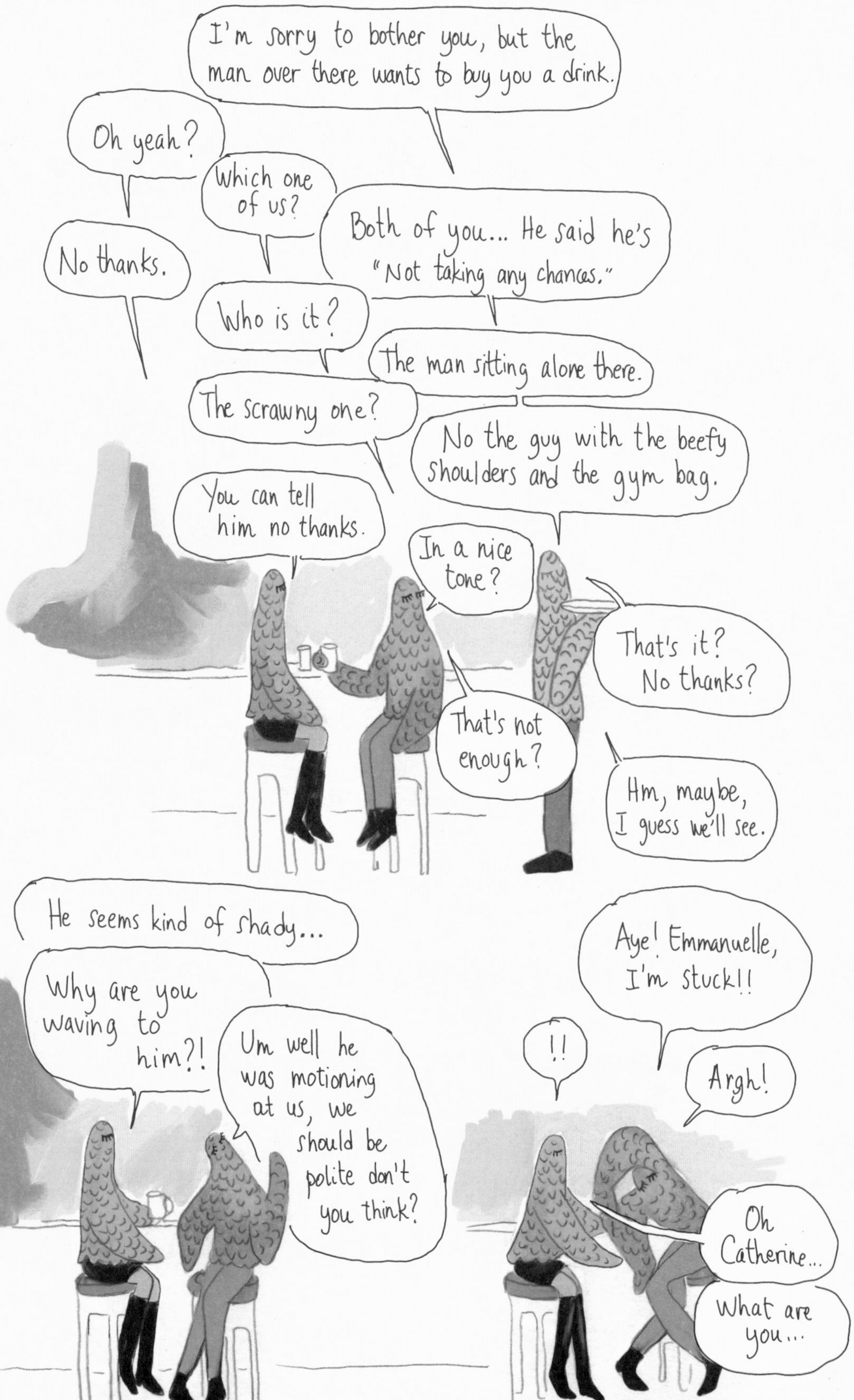

I'm sorry to bother you, but the man over there wants to buy you a drink.
Oh yeah?
Which one of us?
No thanks.
Both of you... He said he's "Not taking any chances."
Who is it?
The man sitting alone there.
The scrawny one?
No the guy with the beefy shoulders and the gym bag.
You can tell him no thanks.
In a nice tone?
That's it? No thanks?
That's not enough?
Hm, maybe, I guess we'll see.
He seems kind of shady...
Why are you waving to him?!
Um well he was motioning at us, we should be polite don't you think?
Aye! Emmanuelle, I'm stuck!!
!!
Argh!
Oh Catherine...
What are you...

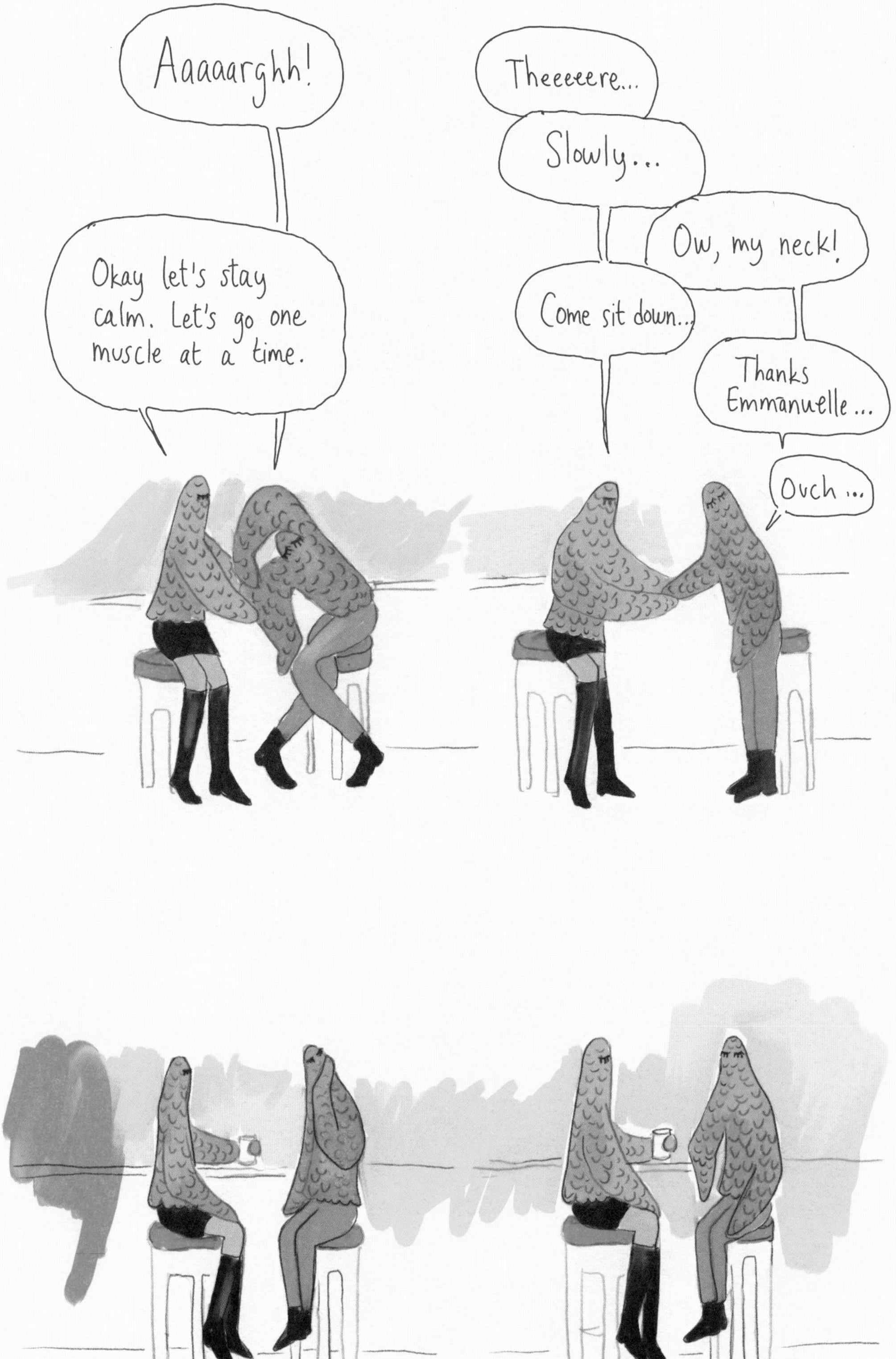
Aaaaarghh!
Okay let's stay calm. Let's go one muscle at a time.
Theeeeere...
Slowly...
Ow, my neck!
Come sit down...
Thanks Emmanuelle...
Ouch...

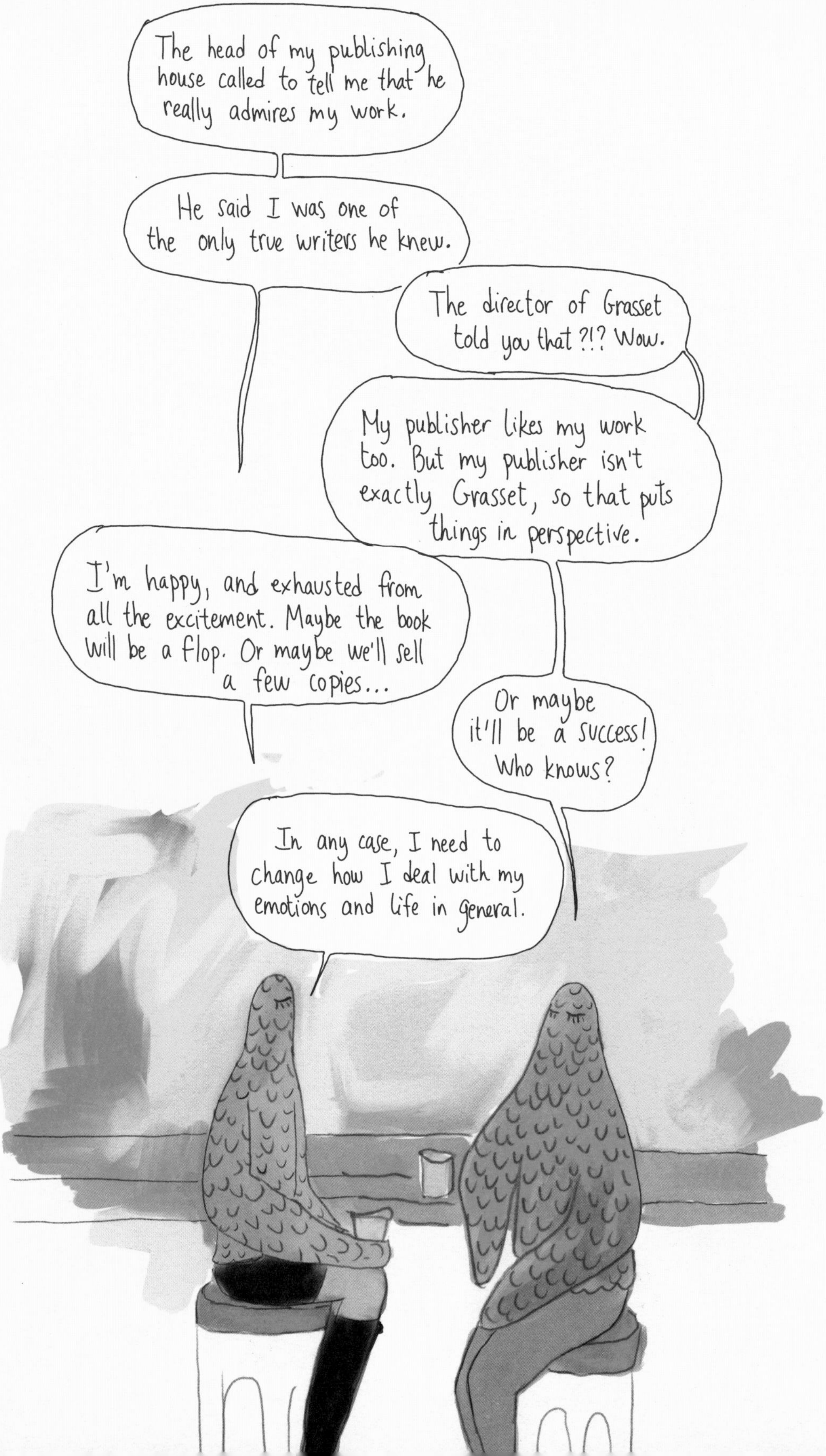

The head of my publishing house called to tell me that he really admires my work.
He said I was one of the only true writers he knew.
The director of Grasset told you that ?!? Wow.
My publisher likes my work too. But my publisher isn't exactly Grasset, so that puts things in perspective.
I'm happy, and exhausted from all the excitement. Maybe the book will be a flop. Or maybe we'll sell a few copies...
Or maybe it'll be a success! Who knows?
In any case, I need to change how I deal with my emotions and life in general.

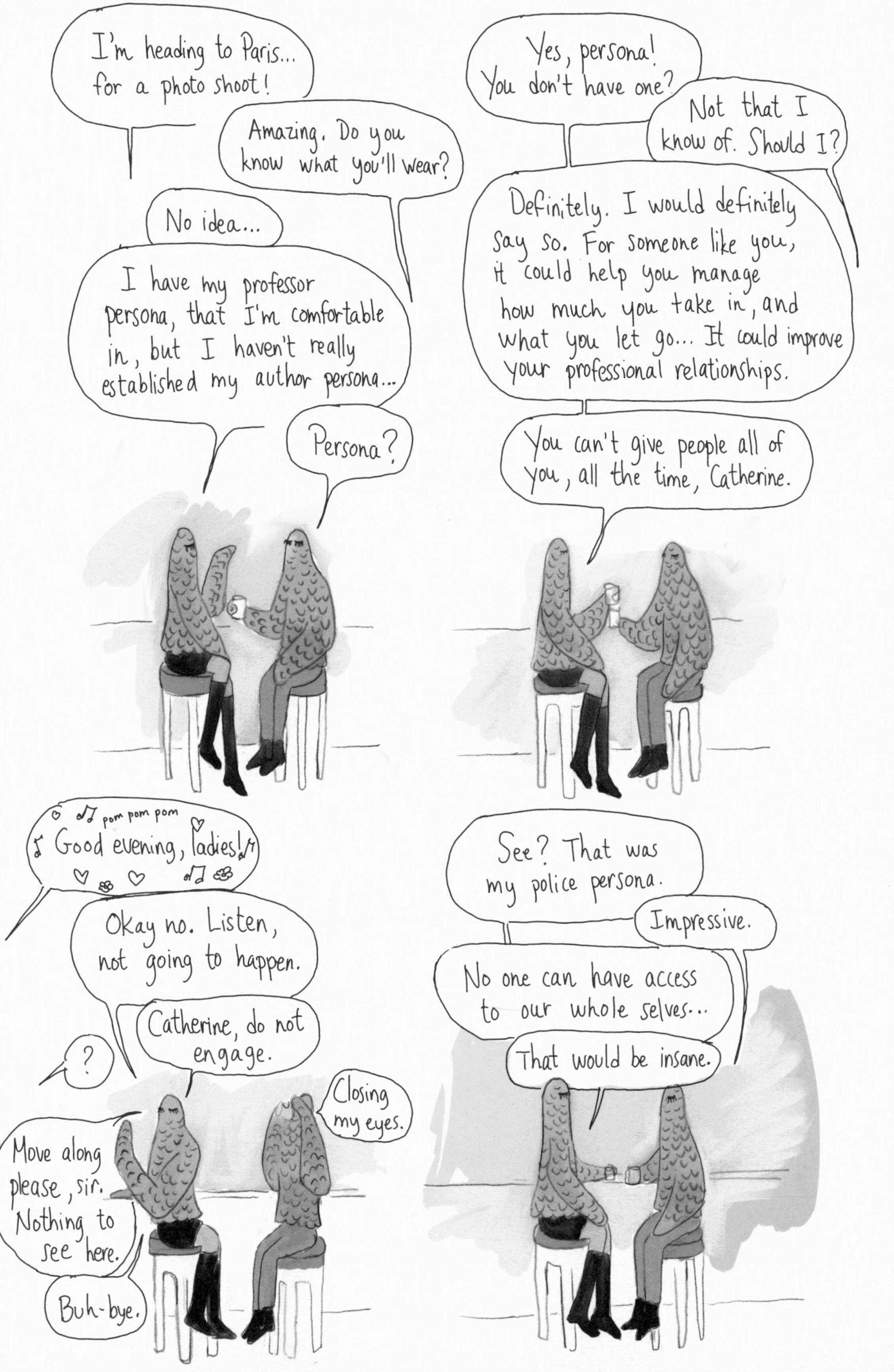
I'm heading to Paris... for a photo shoot!
Amazing. Do you know what you'll wear?
No idea...
I have my professor persona, that I'm comfortable in, but I haven't really established my author persona...
Persona?
Yes, persona! You don't have one?
Not that I know of. Should I?
Definitely. I would definitely say so. For someone like you, it could help you manage how much you take in, and what you let go... It could improve your professional relationships.
You can't give people all of you, all the time, Catherine.
pom pom pom
Good evening, ladies!
Okay no. Listen, not going to happen.
Catherine, do not engage.
?
Closing my eyes.
Move along please, sir. Nothing to see here.
Buh-bye.
See? That was my police persona.
Impressive.
No one can have access to our whole selves...
That would be insane.

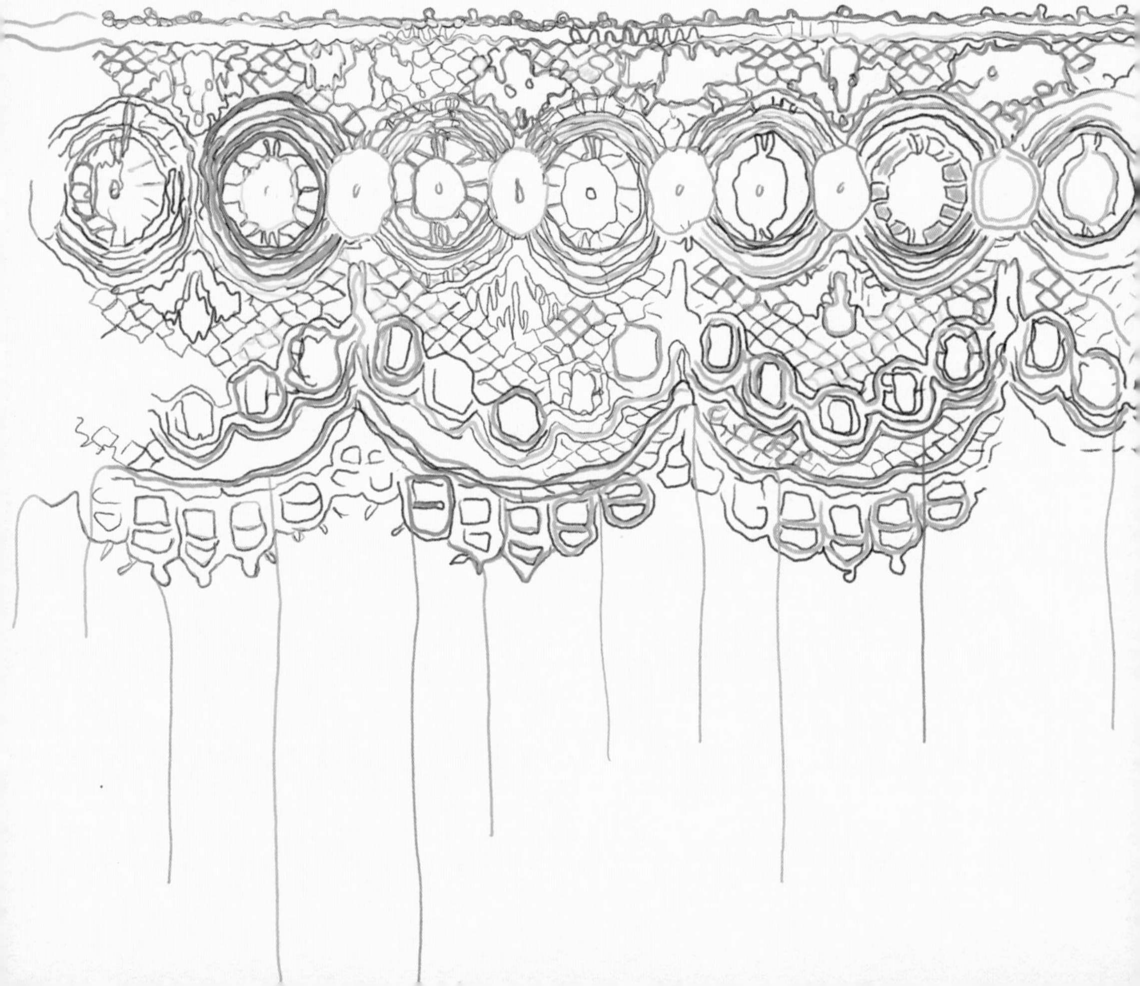

Sam

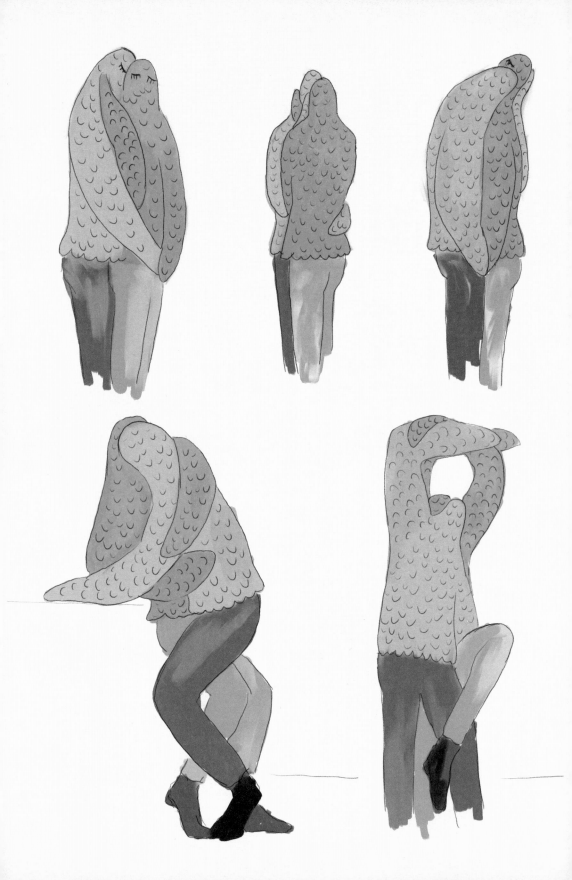

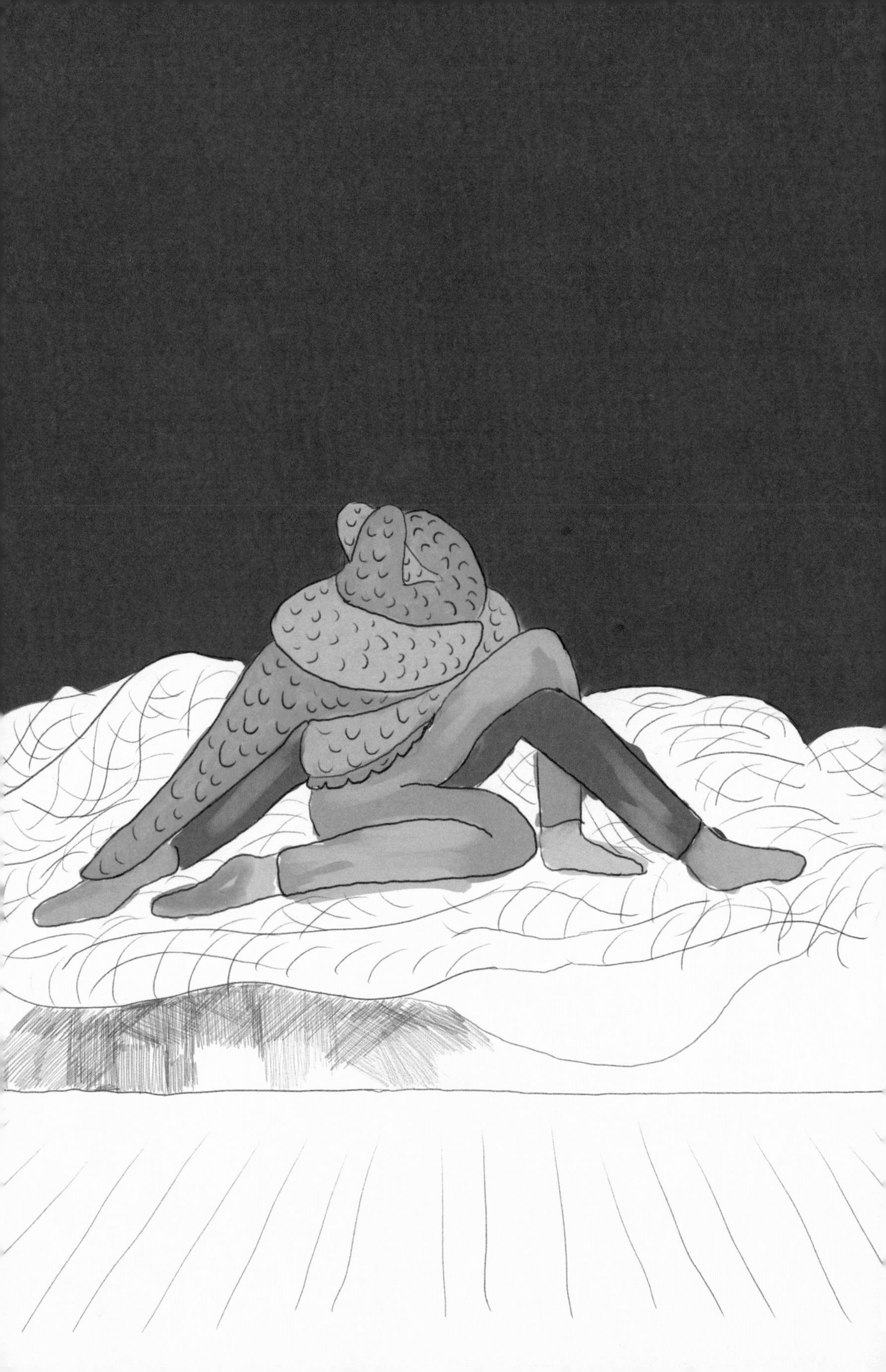

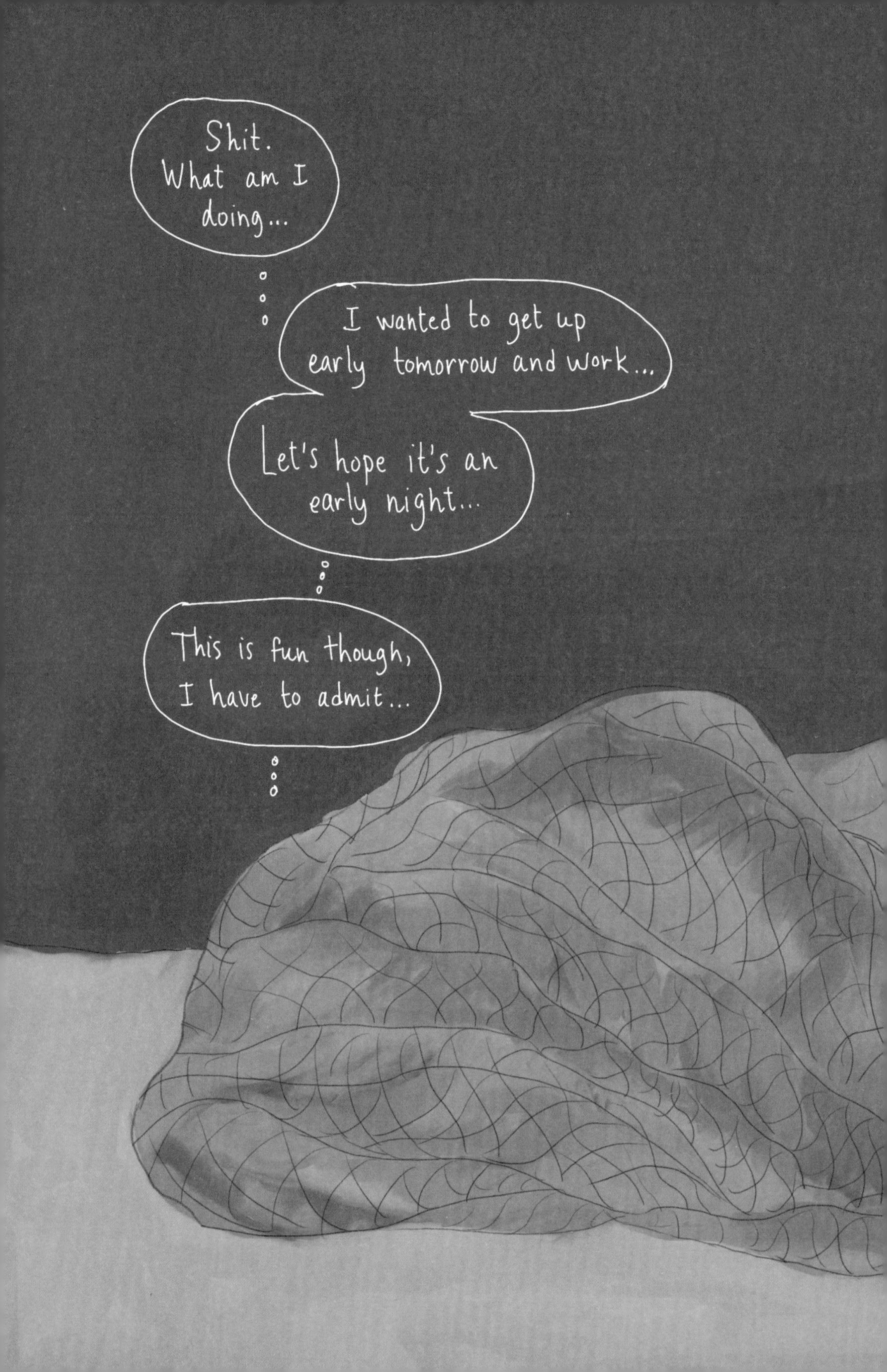
Shit. What am I doing...
I wanted to get up early tomorrow and work...
Let's hope it's an early night...
This is fun though, I have to admit...

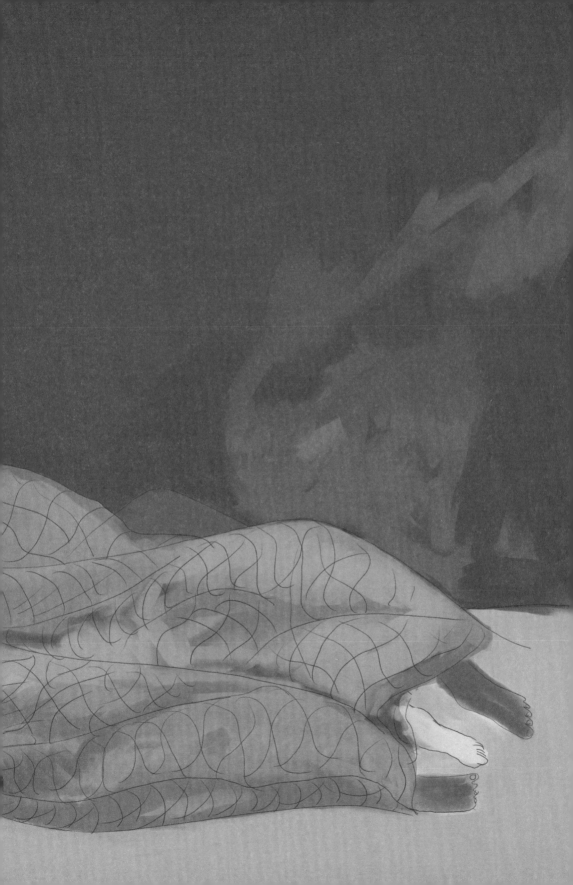

The next morning...

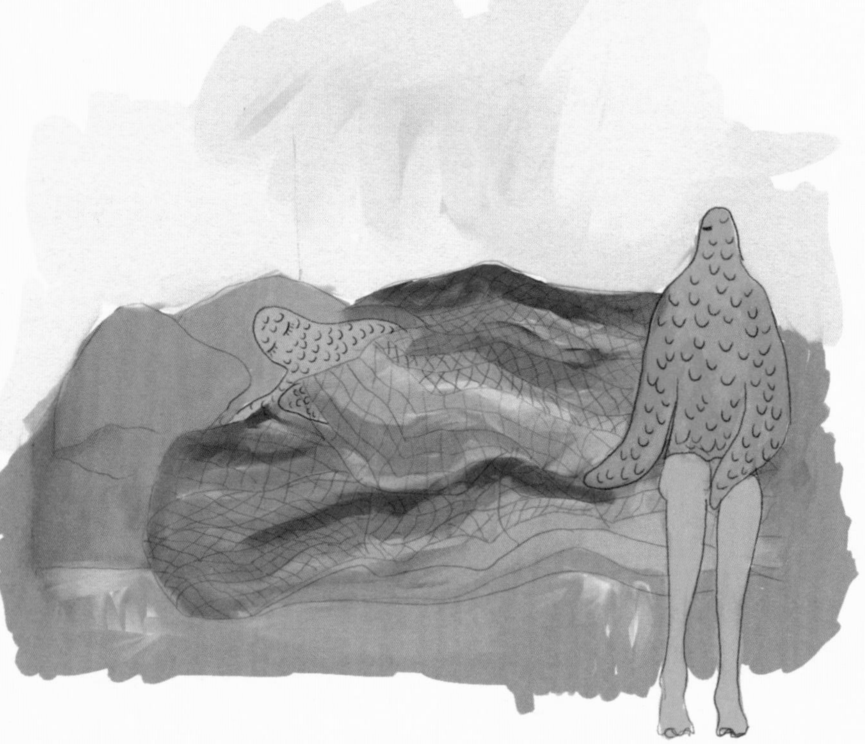

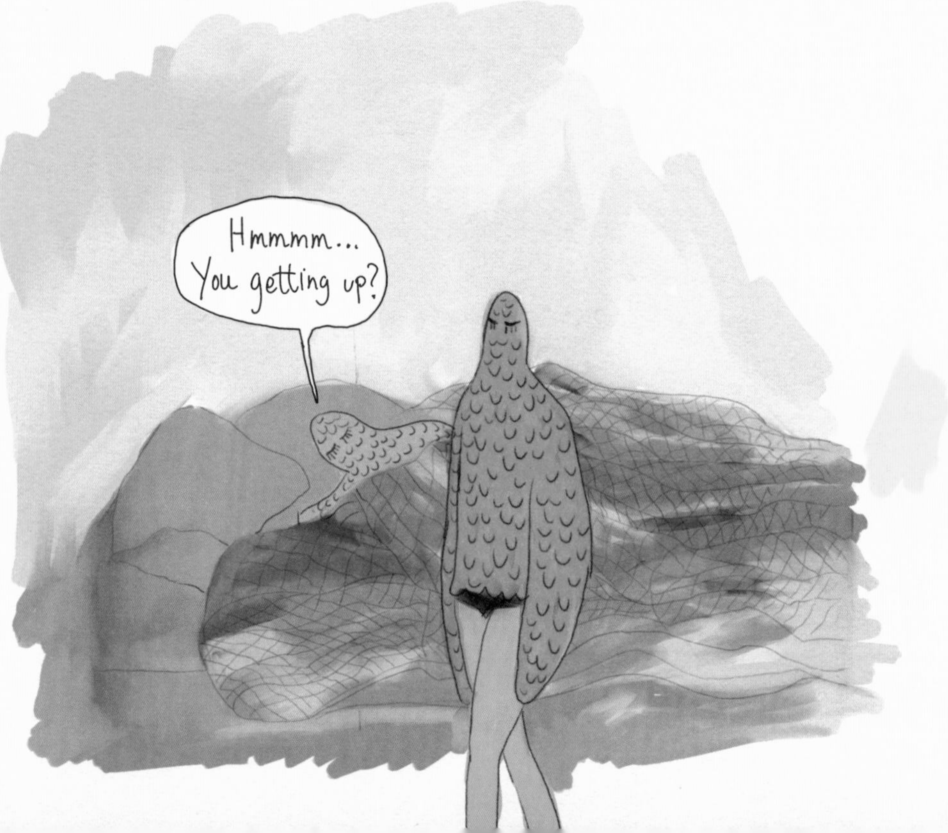
Hmmmm...
You getting up?

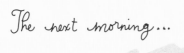

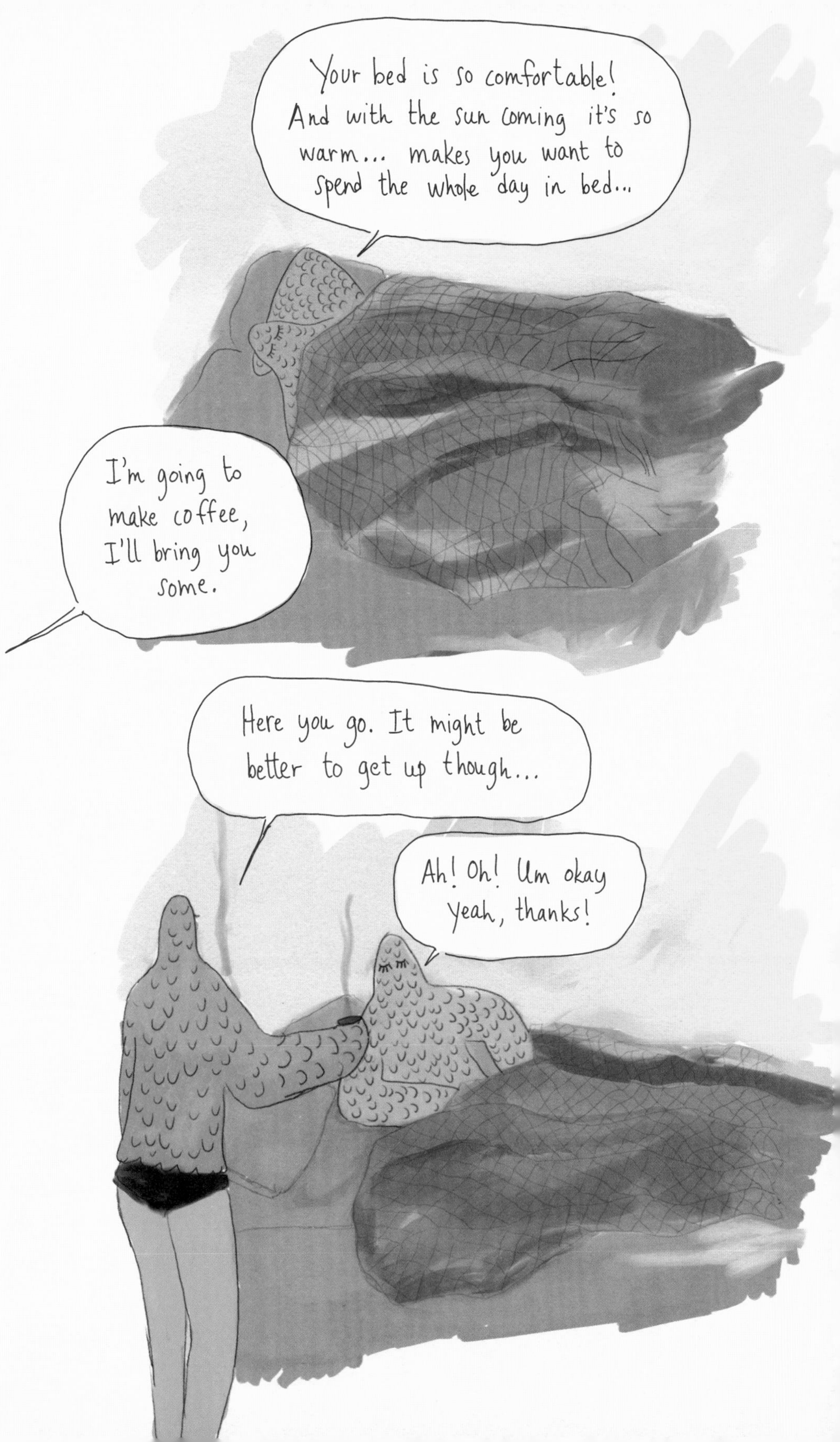
Your bed is so comfortable! And with the sun coming it's so warm... makes you want to spend the whole day in bed...
I'm going to make coffee, I'll bring you some.
Here you go. It might be better to get up though...
Ah! Oh! Um okay yeah, thanks!

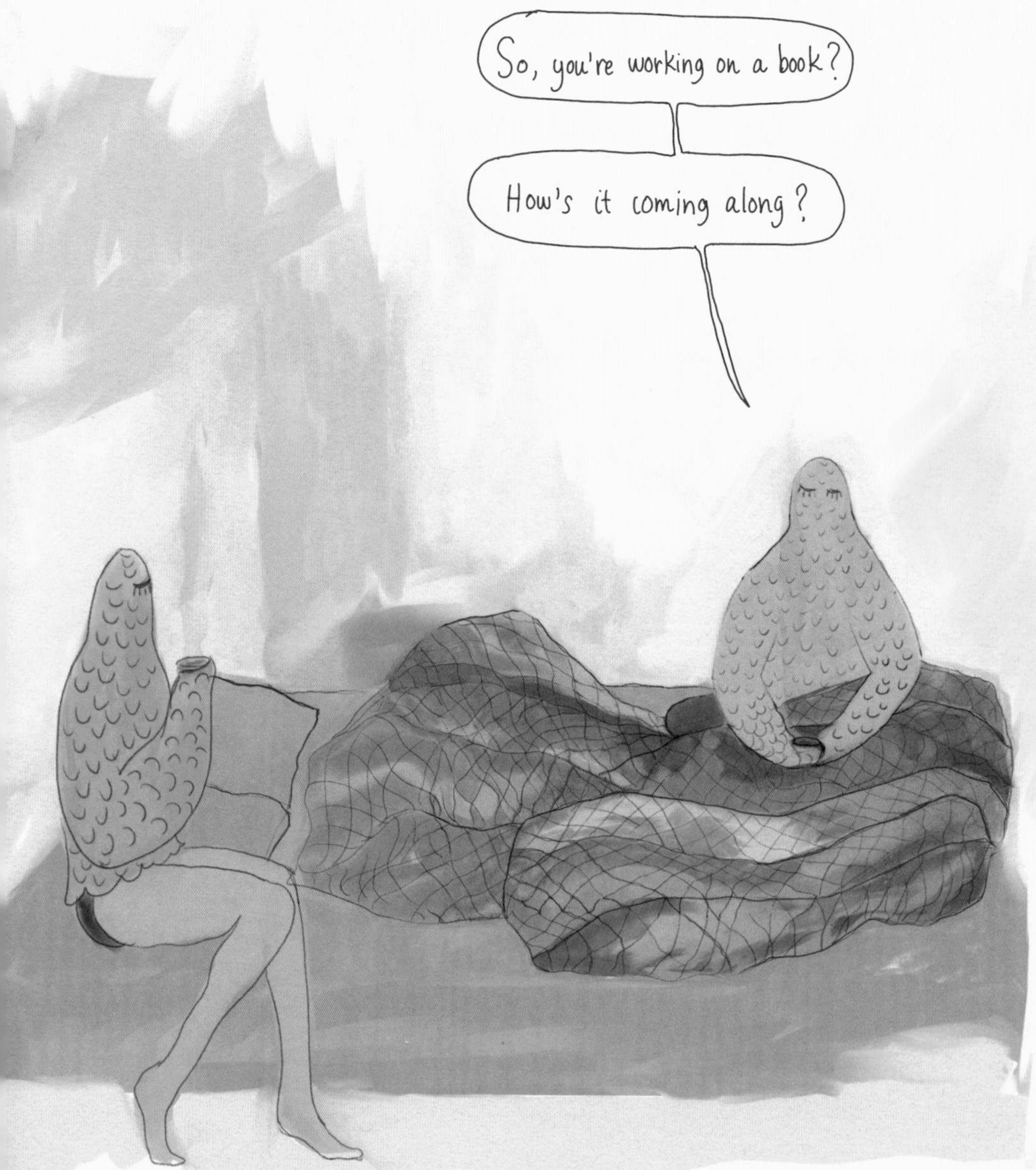
So, you're working on a book?
How's it coming along?

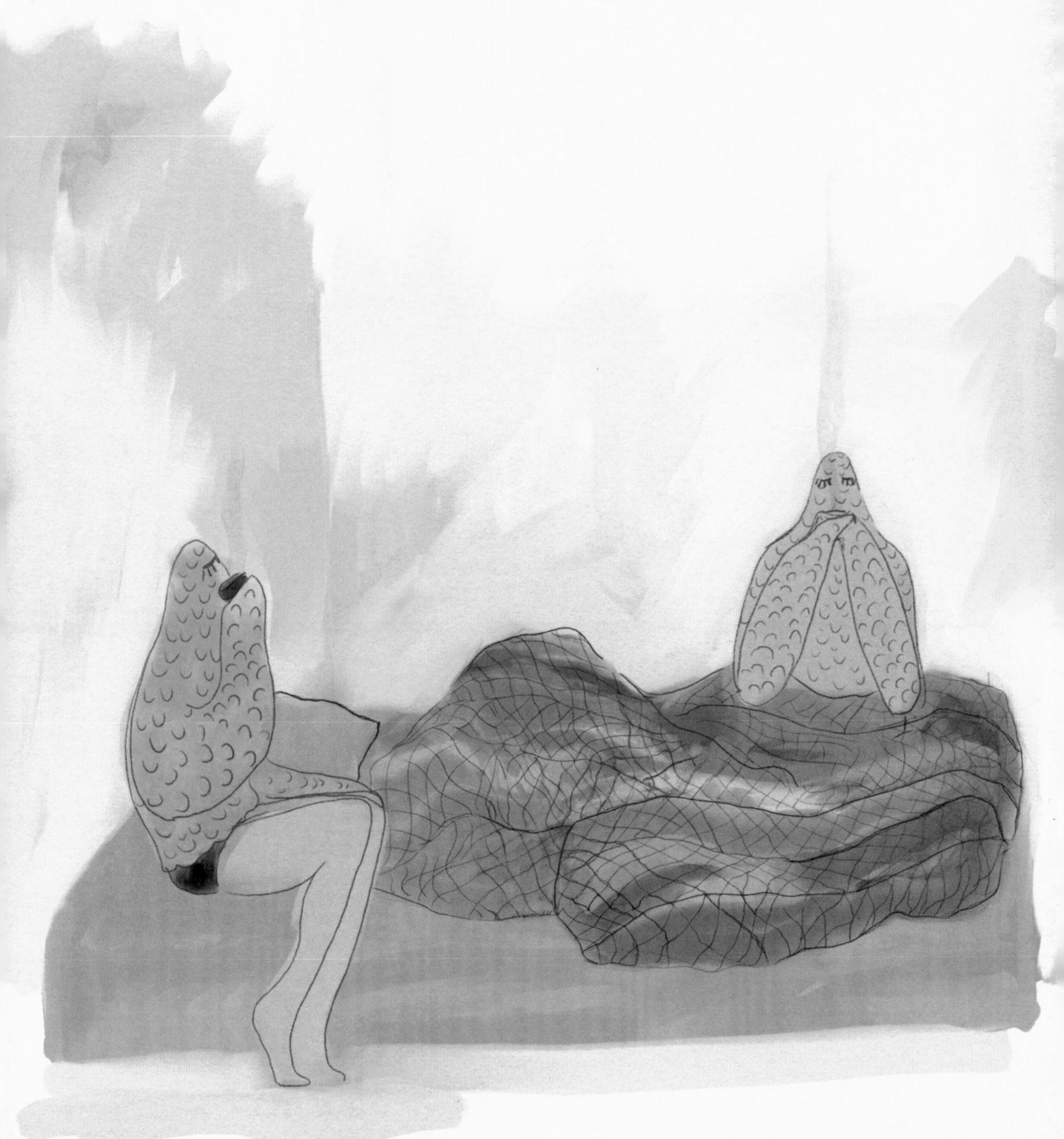

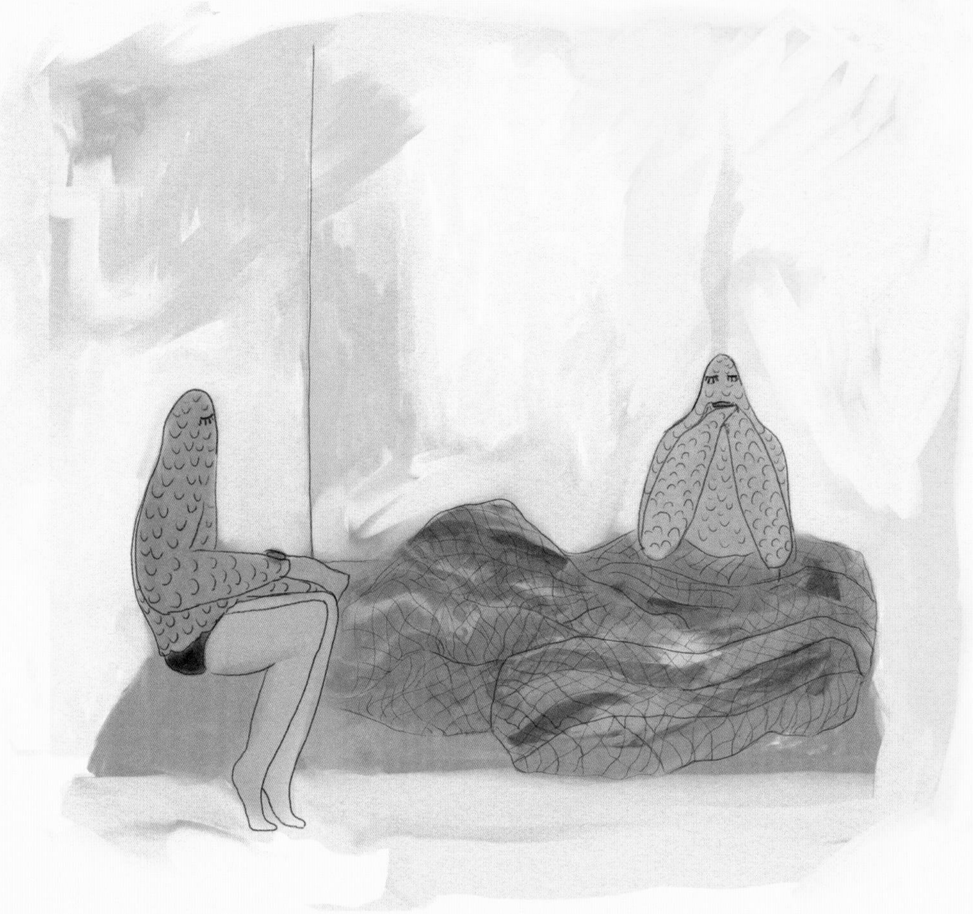

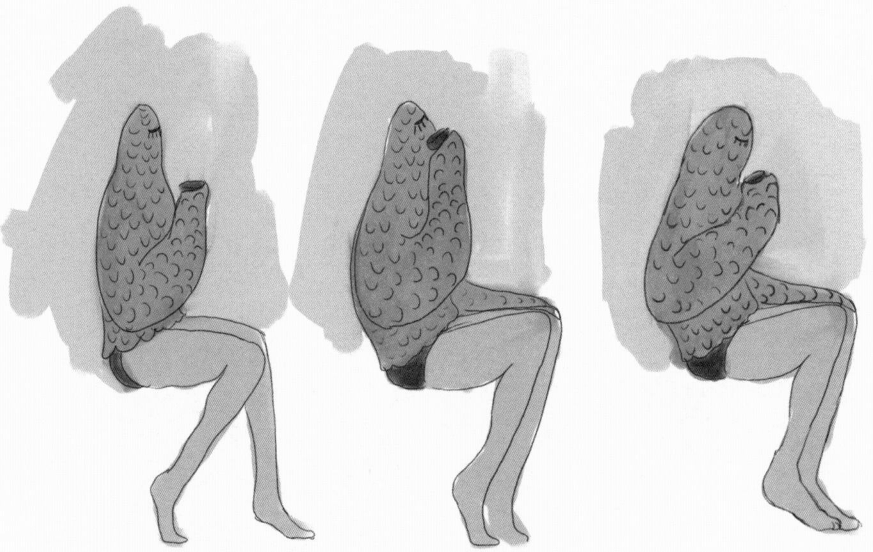

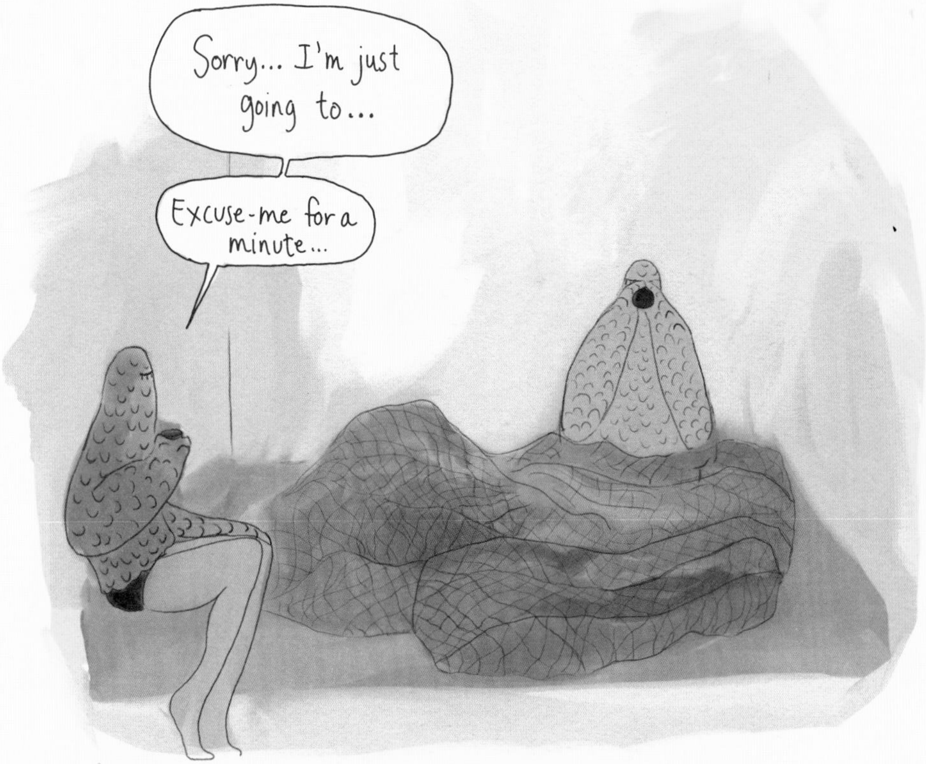
Sorry... I'm just going to...
Excuse-me for a minute...

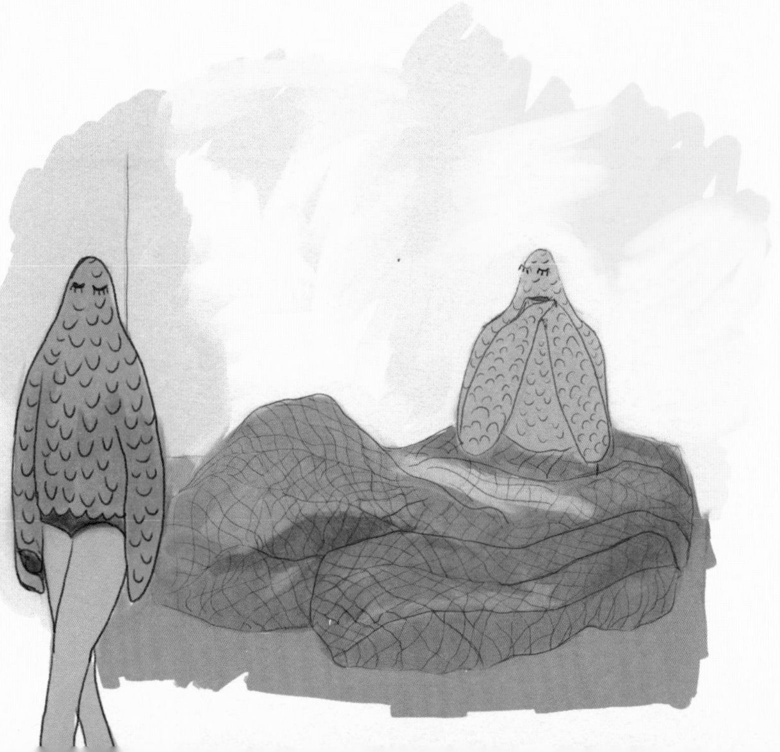

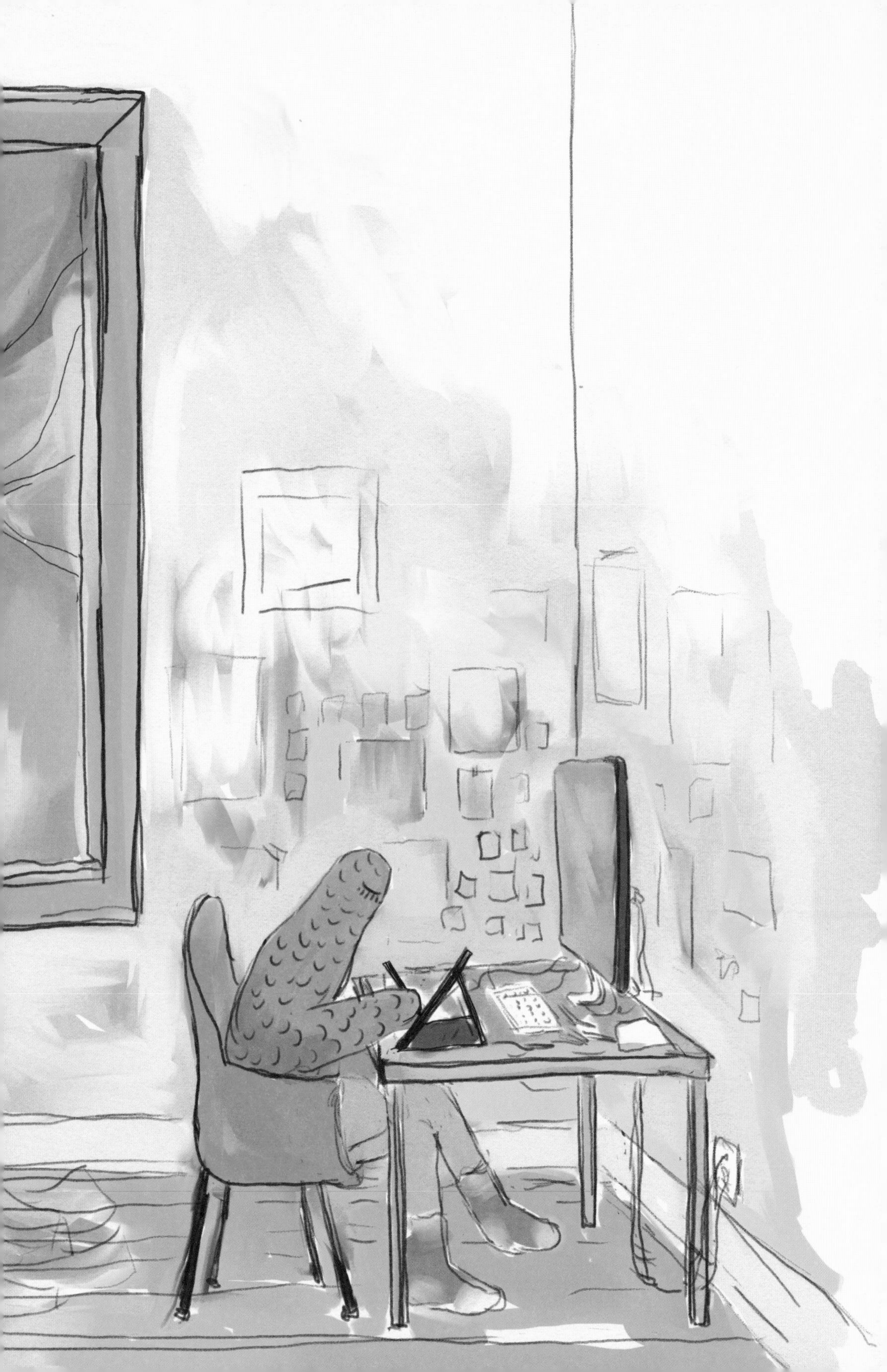

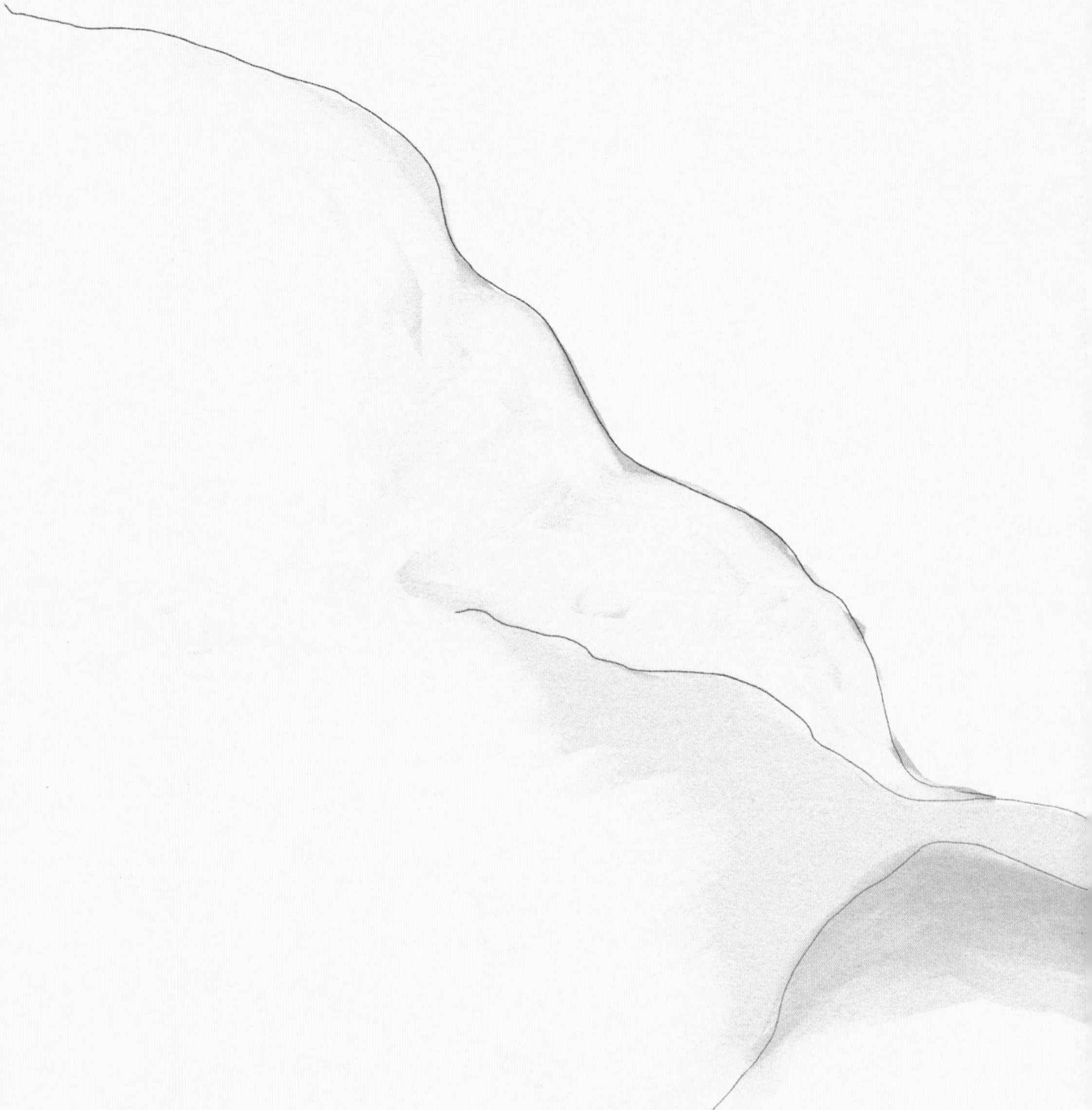

Billie

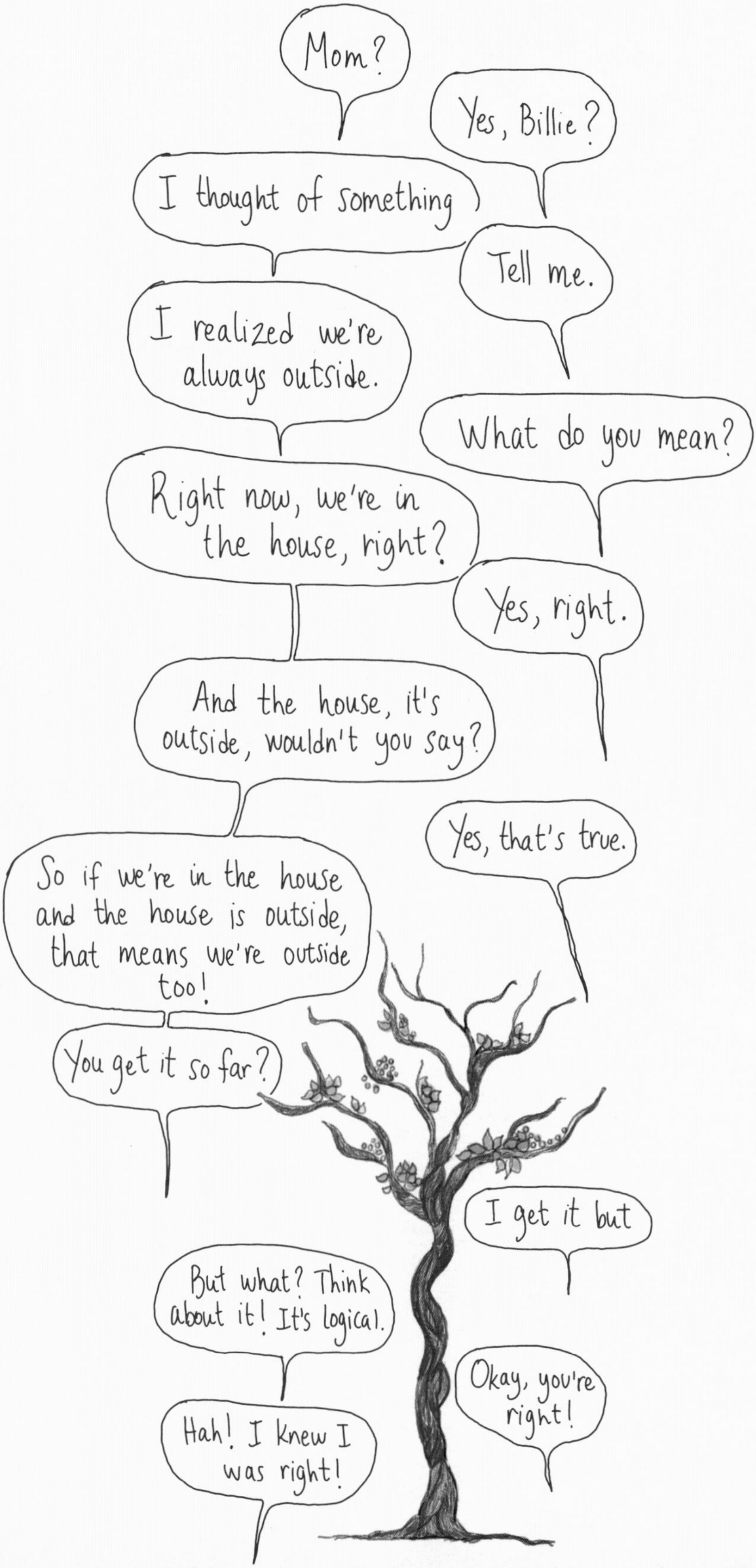
Mom?
Yes, Billie?
I thought of something
Tell me.
I realized we're always outside.
What do you mean?
Right now, we're in the house, right?
Yes, right.
And the house, it's outside, wouldn't you say?
Yes, that's true.
So if we're in the house and the house is outside, that means we're outside too!
You get it so far?
I get it but
But what? Think about it! It's logical.
Okay, you're right!
Hah! I knew I was right!

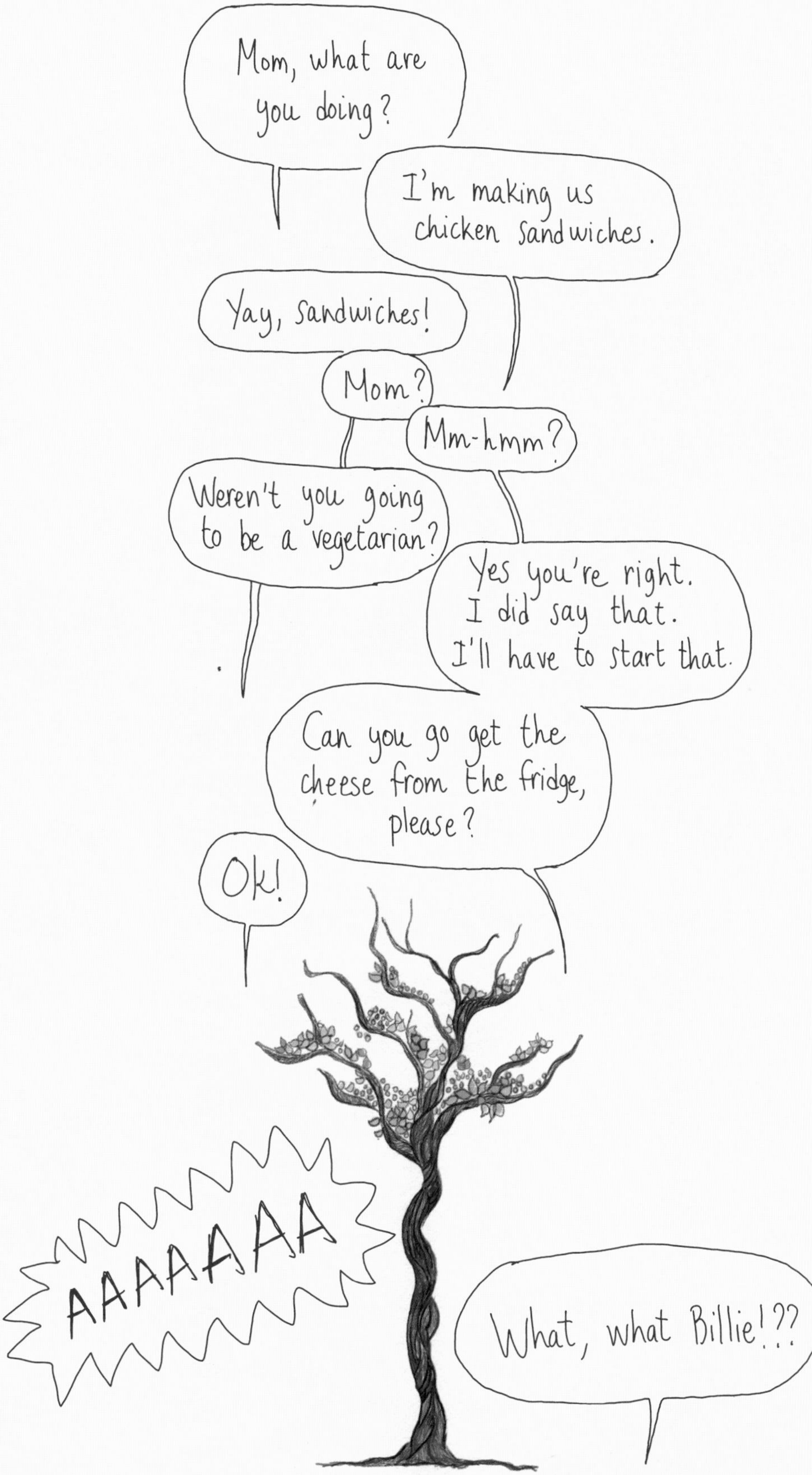
Mom, what are you doing?
I'm making us chicken sandwiches.
Yay, sandwiches!
Mom?
Mm-hmm?
Weren't you going to be a vegetarian?
Yes you're right. I did say that. I'll have to start that.
Can you go get the cheese from the fridge, please?
Ok!
AAAAAAA
What, what Billie!??

MOM there's a GIANT ant in the fridge! It looks like it even has HAIR!!!!
Aaaaaaaaaaaaaaa
It's crawling on the chocolate!!!
Oh wow. You're right, it's massive!
Let me see.
Hang on... there we go!
squiiiiish
There, all fixed.
...
Sniff...
Billie are you crying?
But... why are you crying sweetheart?
Why... why'd you kill it, mom...
Huh?

Why... why'd you kill it, mom...
But... you thought it was gross...
... you could've... sniff!
I don't know...
You could've brought it outside...
sniff...
It wasn't its fault that it's not pretty...
boohoohoo...
Oh Billie... I'm so sorry...

Rafaël

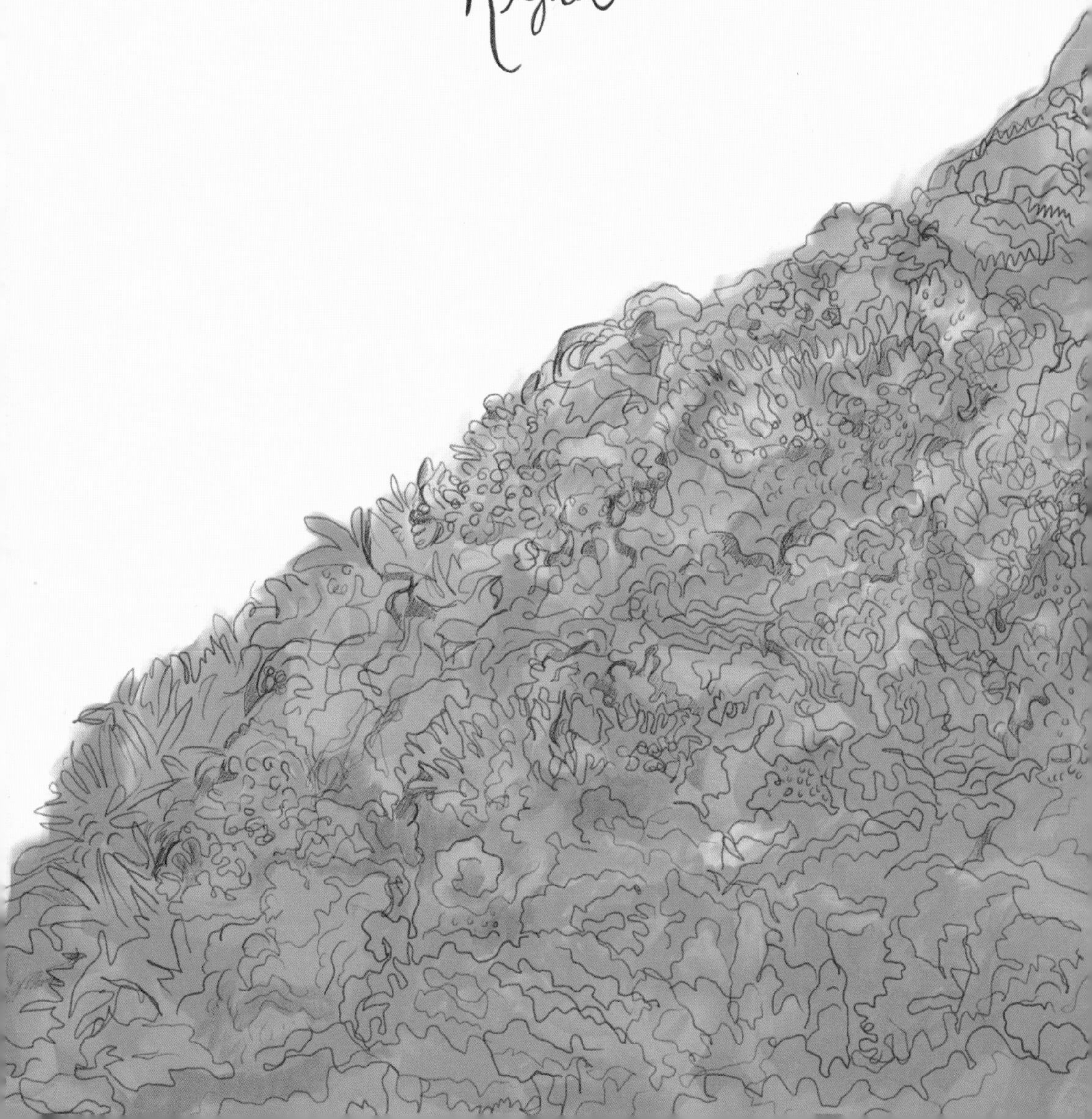

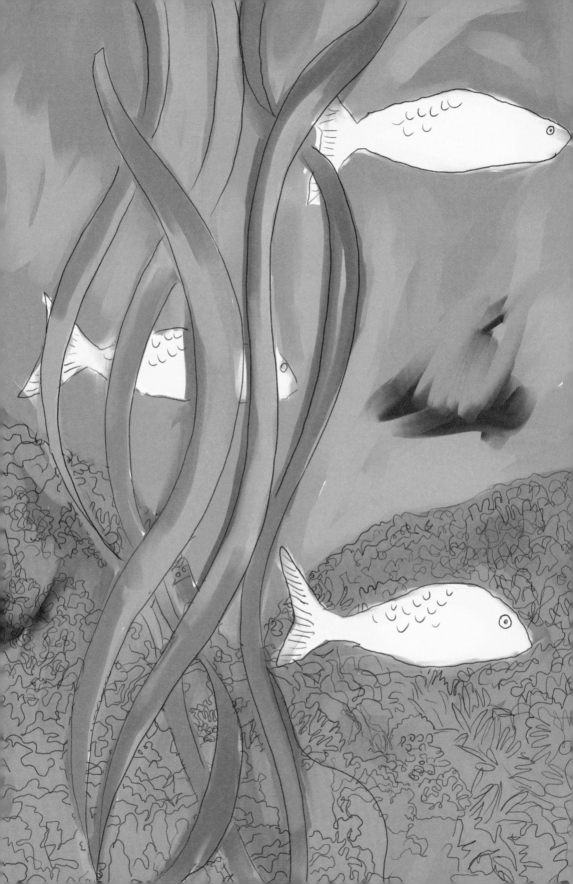

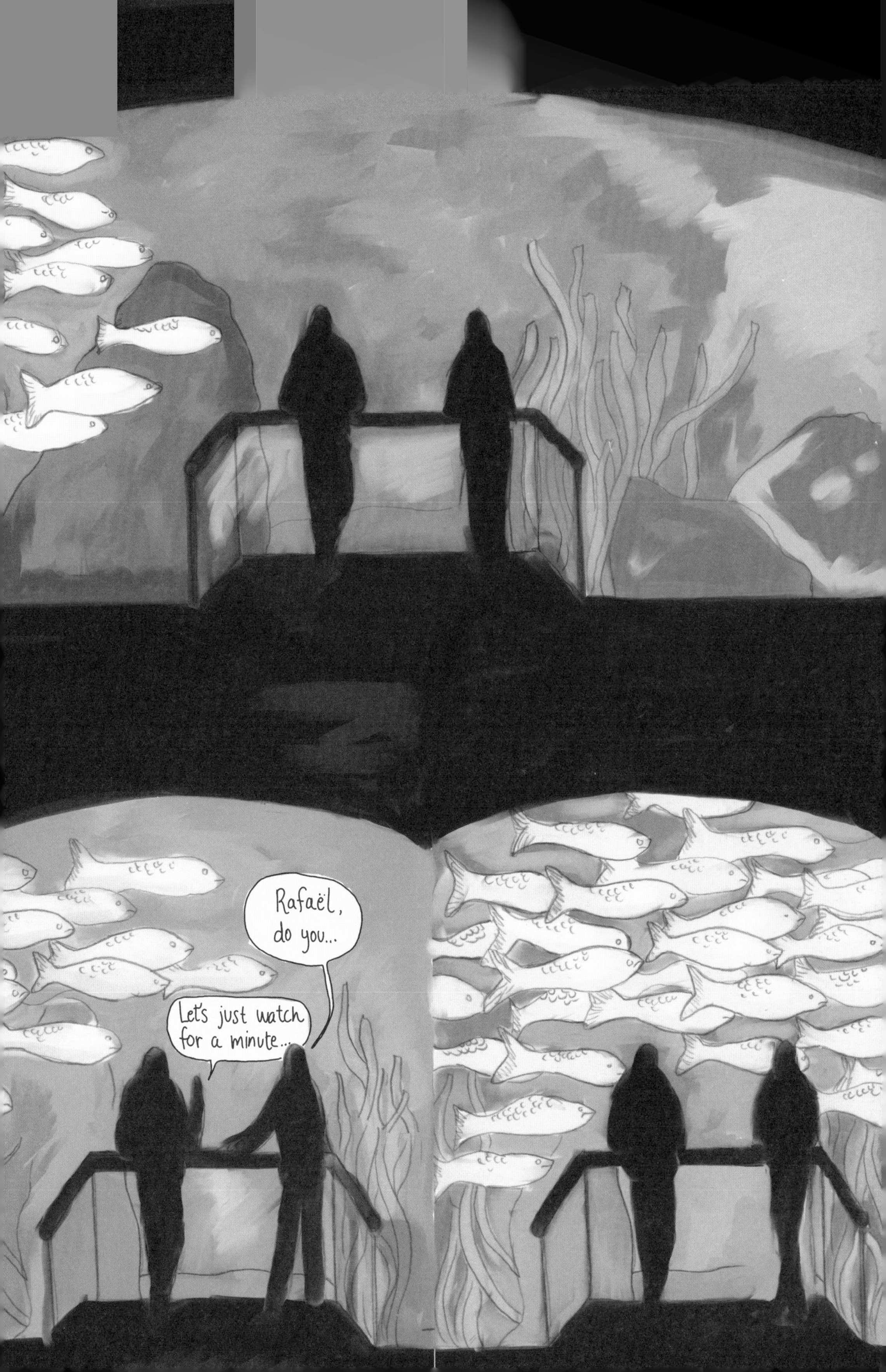
Rafaël, do you...
Let's just watch for a minute...

When I was growing up in Dégelis, I was a big fish in a tiny pond...
In Montreal, it's different...
Here, I'm a small fish in a big pond.

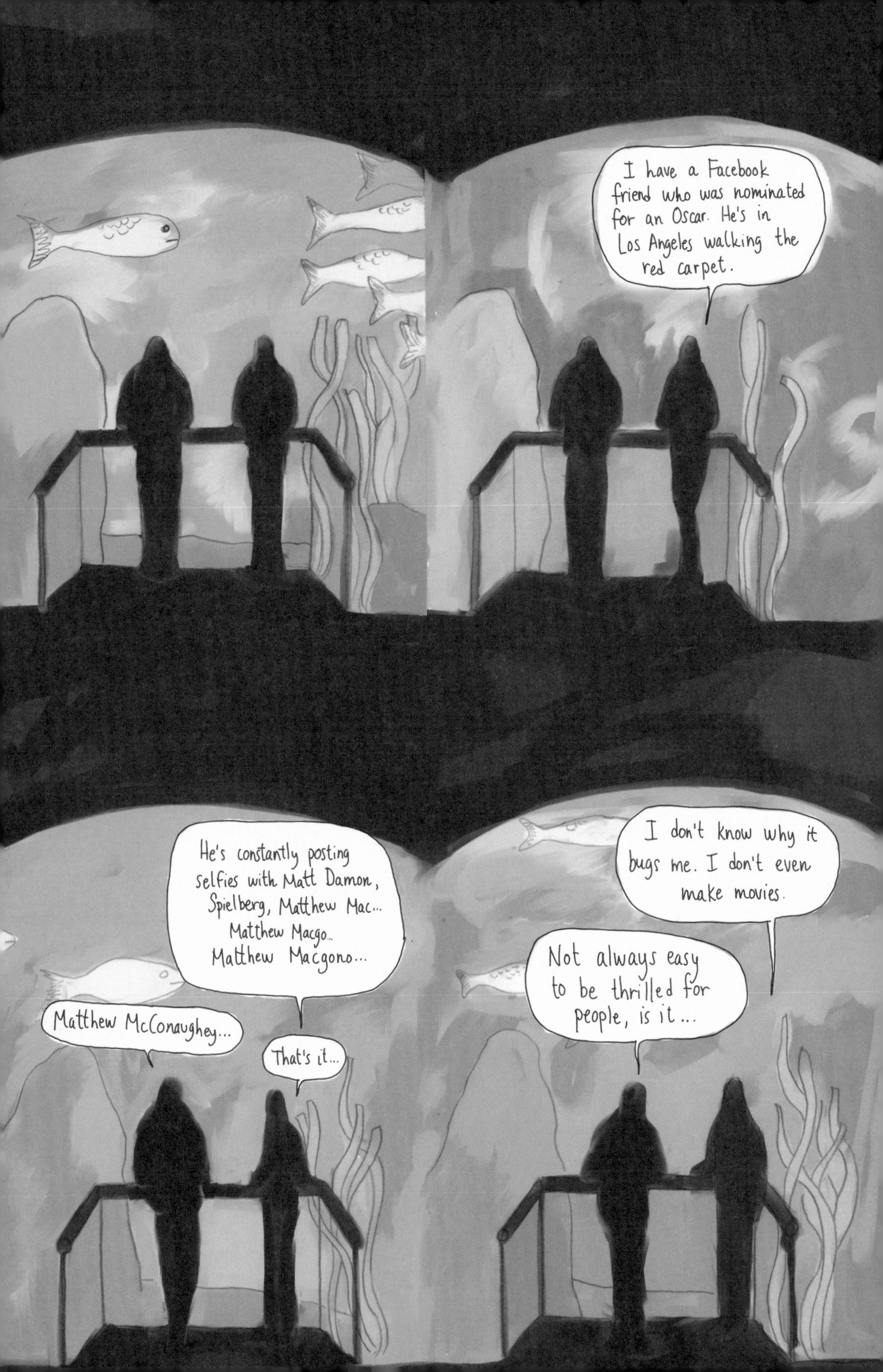
I have a Facebook friend who was nominated for an Oscar. He's in Los Angeles walking the red carpet.
He's constantly posting selfies with Matt Damon, Spielberg, Matthew Mac... Matthew Macgo... Matthew Macgono...
Matthew McConaughey...
That's it...
I don't know why it bugs me. I don't even make movies.
Not always easy to be thrilled for people, is it...

At one point I had two very good friends making movies at the same time I was. One of them did really well, big numbers at the box office, a ton of commercial success.
The other was at all the festivals, rave reviews, Cannes, Venice, etc.
And I was between the two. A little car between two big trucks. I felt stuck.
It was motivating, but difficult to deal with.
Being around successful people, who are making it - it can be stimulating but also demoralizing...
Maybe but...
I'm not sure surrounding yourself with losers would make you feel better...
I know.

I have this writer friend who puts out a book a year. He has a full-time job and a seven-year-old. He jots down all his ideas on the bus to work every day. And he writes every night after his son goes to bed...
I wish I was that disciplined.
For me it's not a question of discipline. I've just been in this kind of paralyzed state for a while now.
Didn't you just finish a big TV series? I feel like I always read about you. Aren't you on the radio every week?
Yeah... but I don't mean that.

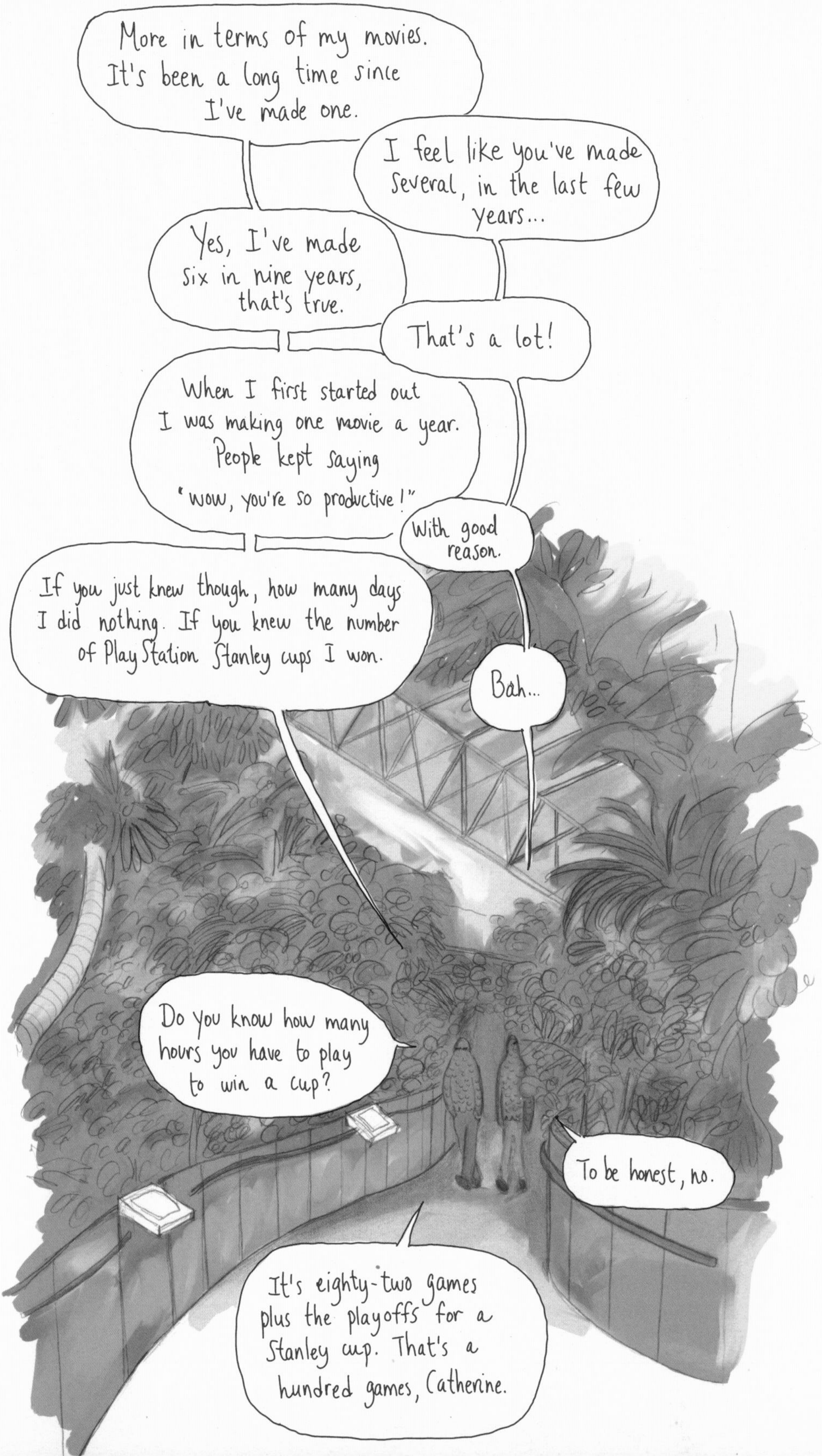
More in terms of my movies. It's been a long time since I've made one.
I feel like you've made several, in the last few years...
Yes, I've made six in nine years, that's true.
That's a lot!
When I first started out I was making one movie a year. People kept saying "wow, you're so productive!"
With good reason.
If you just knew though, how many days I did nothing. If you knew the number of PlayStation Stanley cups I won.
Bah...
Do you know how many hours you have to play to win a cup?
To be honest, no.
It's eighty-two games plus the playoffs for a Stanley cup. That's a hundred games, Catherine.

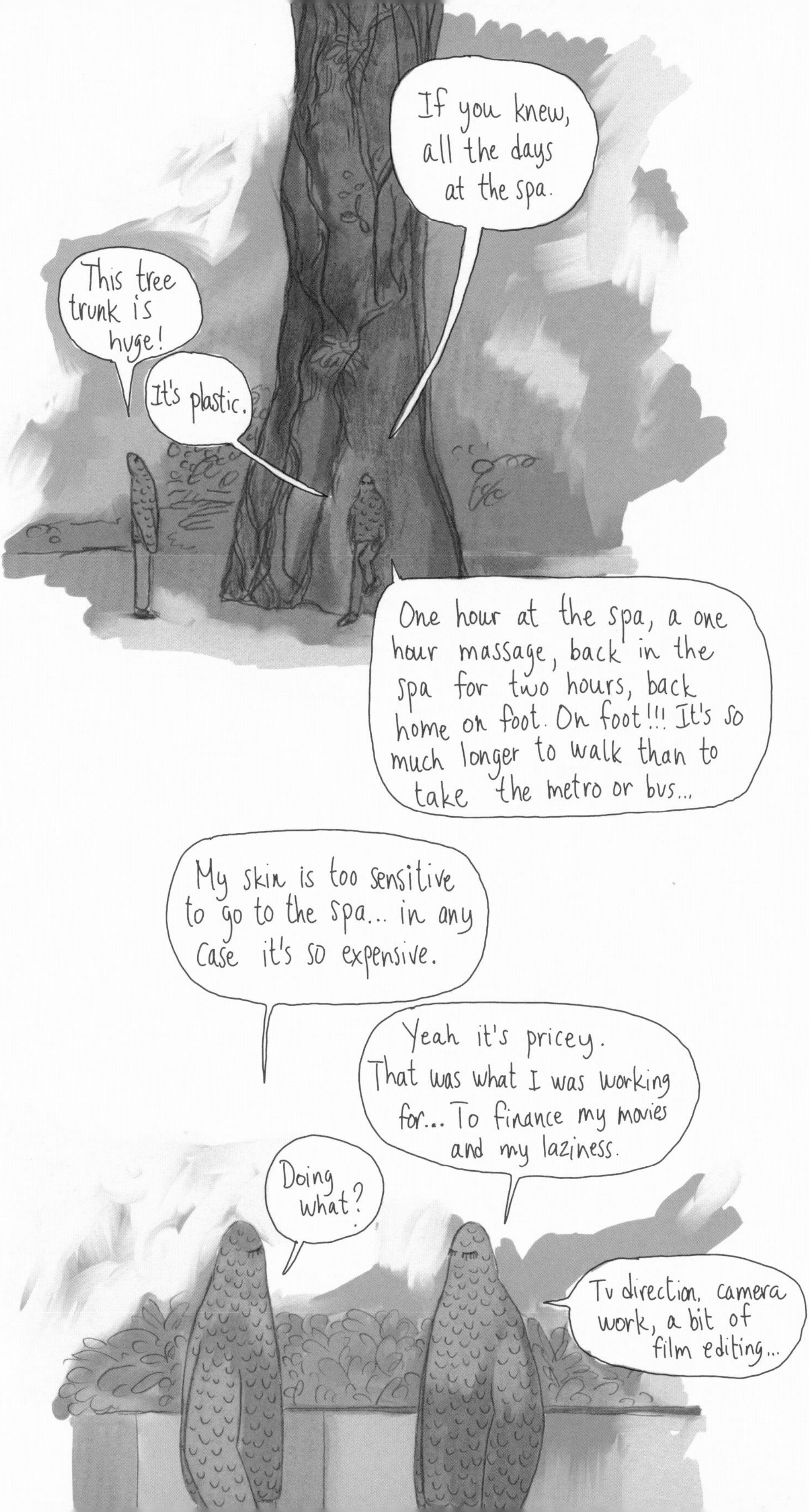
If you knew, all the days at the spa.
This tree trunk is huge!
It's plastic.
One hour at the spa, a one hour massage, back in the spa for two hours, back home on foot. On foot!!! It's so much longer to walk than to take the metro or bus...
My skin is too sensitive to go to the spa... in any case it's so expensive.
Yeah it's pricey. That was what I was working for... To finance my movies and my laziness.
Doing what?
Tv direction, camera work, a bit of film editing...

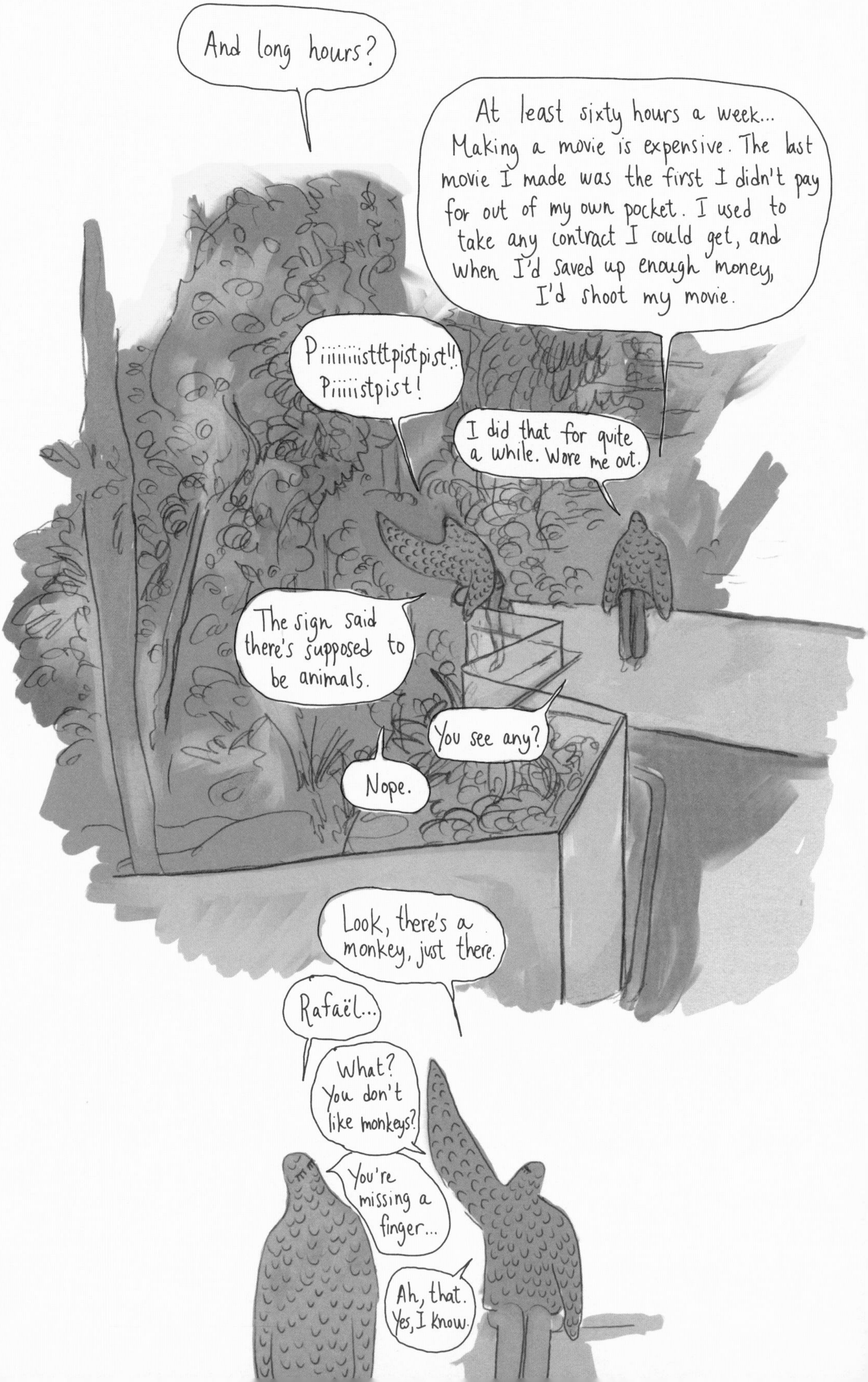
And long hours?
At least sixty hours a week... Making a movie is expensive. The last movie I made was the first I didn't pay for out of my own pocket. I used to take any contract I could get, and when I'd saved up enough money, I'd shoot my movie.
Piiiiiiistttpistpist!! Piiiiistpist!
I did that for quite a while. Wore me out.
The sign said there's supposed to be animals.
You see any?
Nope.
Look, there's a monkey, just there.
Rafaël...
What? You don't like monkeys?
You're missing a finger...
Ah, that. Yes, I know.

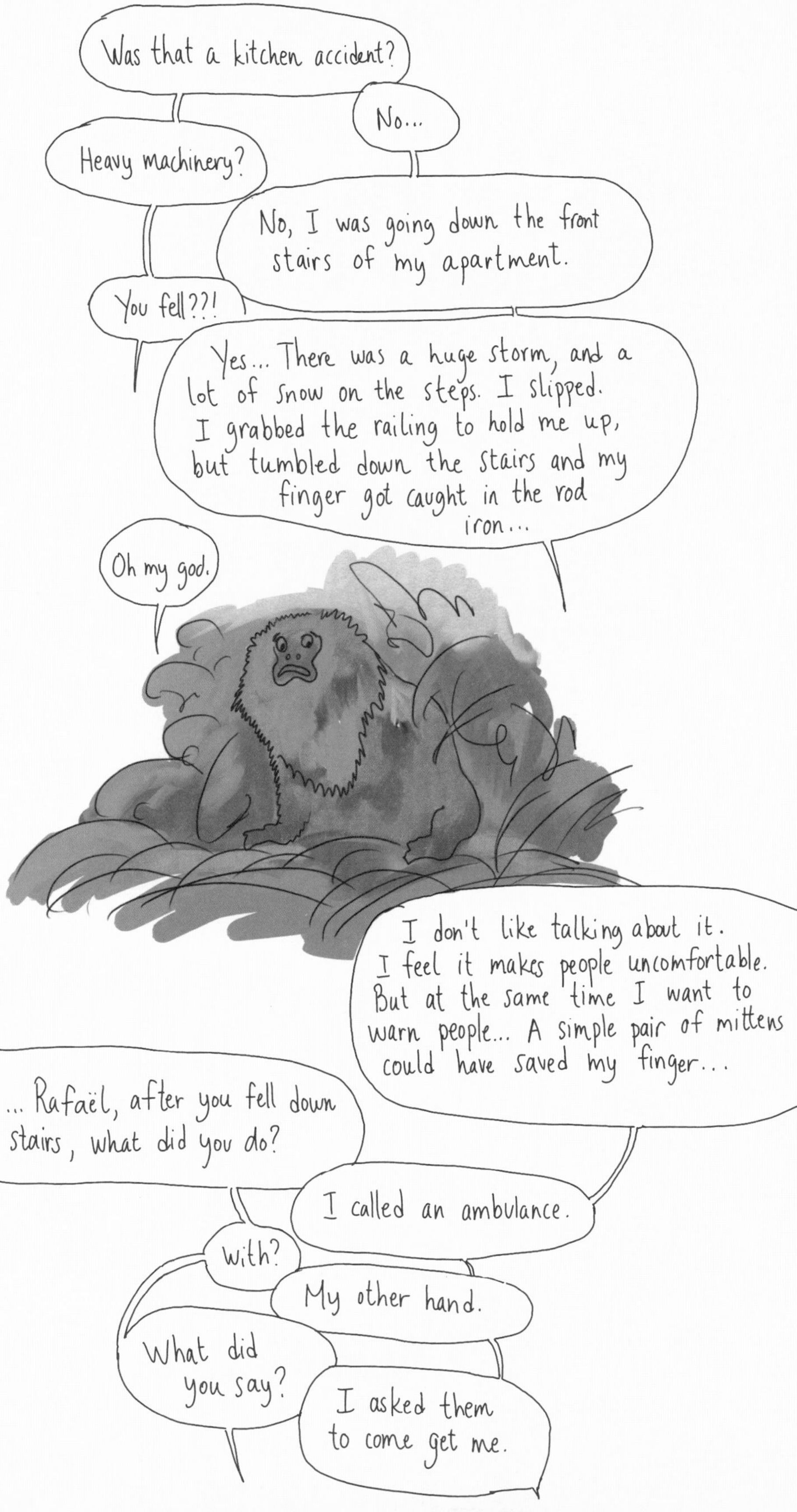
Was that a kitchen accident?
No...
Heavy machinery?
No, I was going down the front stairs of my apartment.
You fell??!
Yes... There was a huge storm, and a lot of snow on the steps. I slipped. I grabbed the railing to hold me up, but tumbled down the stairs and my finger got caught in the rod iron...
Oh my god.
I don't like talking about it. I feel it makes people uncomfortable. But at the same time I want to warn people... A simple pair of mittens could have saved my finger...
But... Rafaël, after you fell down the stairs, what did you do?
I called an ambulance.
With?
My other hand.
What did you say?
I asked them to come get me.

I had to wait a long time because of the storm, so I stayed on the phone with the woman. I told her "I've got my hand in a snow bank". She said, "That's not a good idea."
She was criticizing you?!?
No, not really. She told me how to make a bandage out of my coat to preserve the tissue in my hand. And what to do with the finger.
Which was?
I put it in a flyer bag.
...
Yeah...
But in the end they couldn't reattach it, as you can see.
...
WTF
Where are we going now...?
To the North Pole, I think.

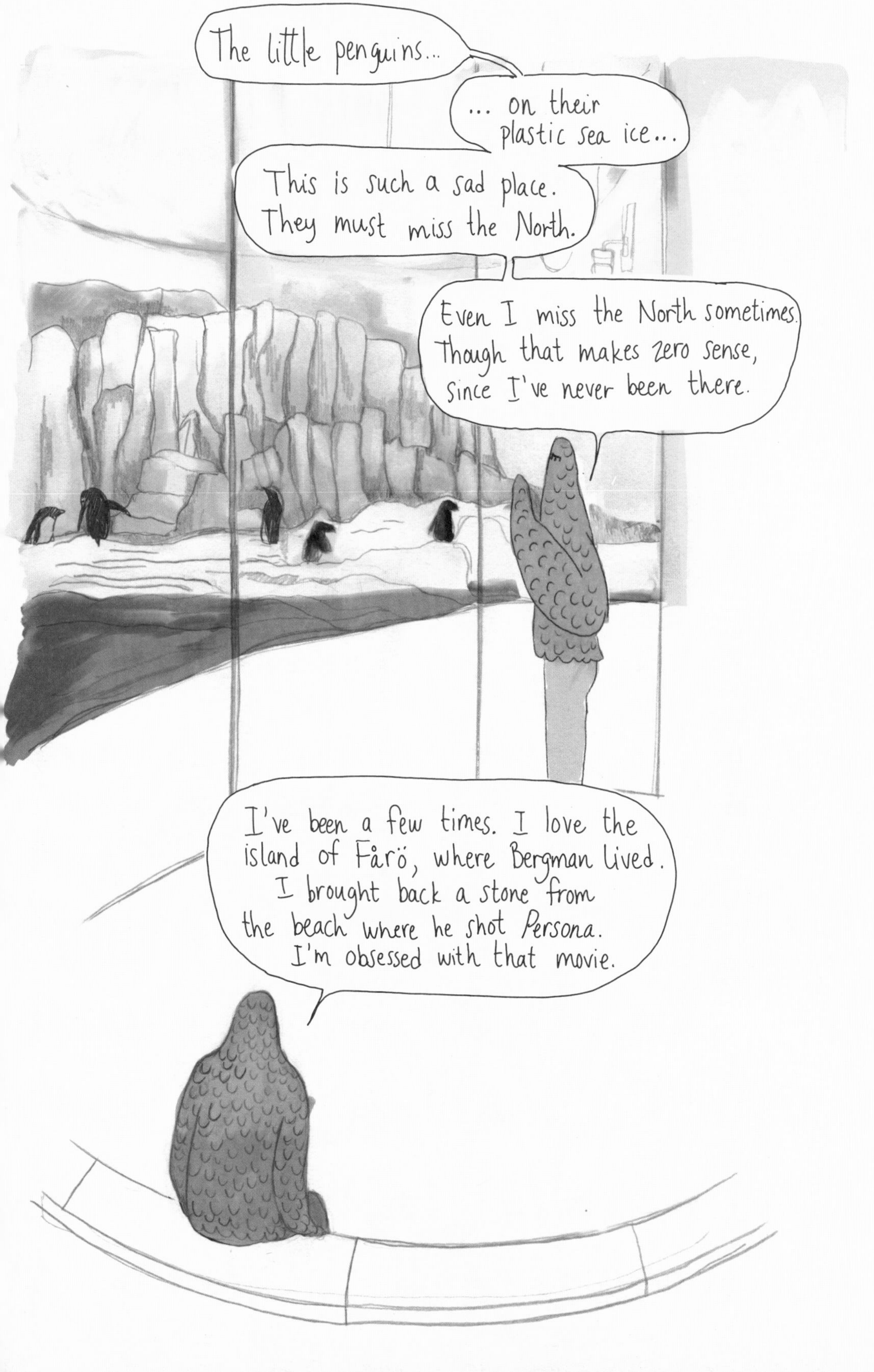
The little penguins...
... on their plastic sea ice...
This is such a sad place. They must miss the North.
Even I miss the North sometimes. Though that makes zero sense, since I've never been there.
I've been a few times. I love the island of Fårö, where Bergman lived. I brought back a stone from the beach where he shot *Persona*. I'm obsessed with that movie.

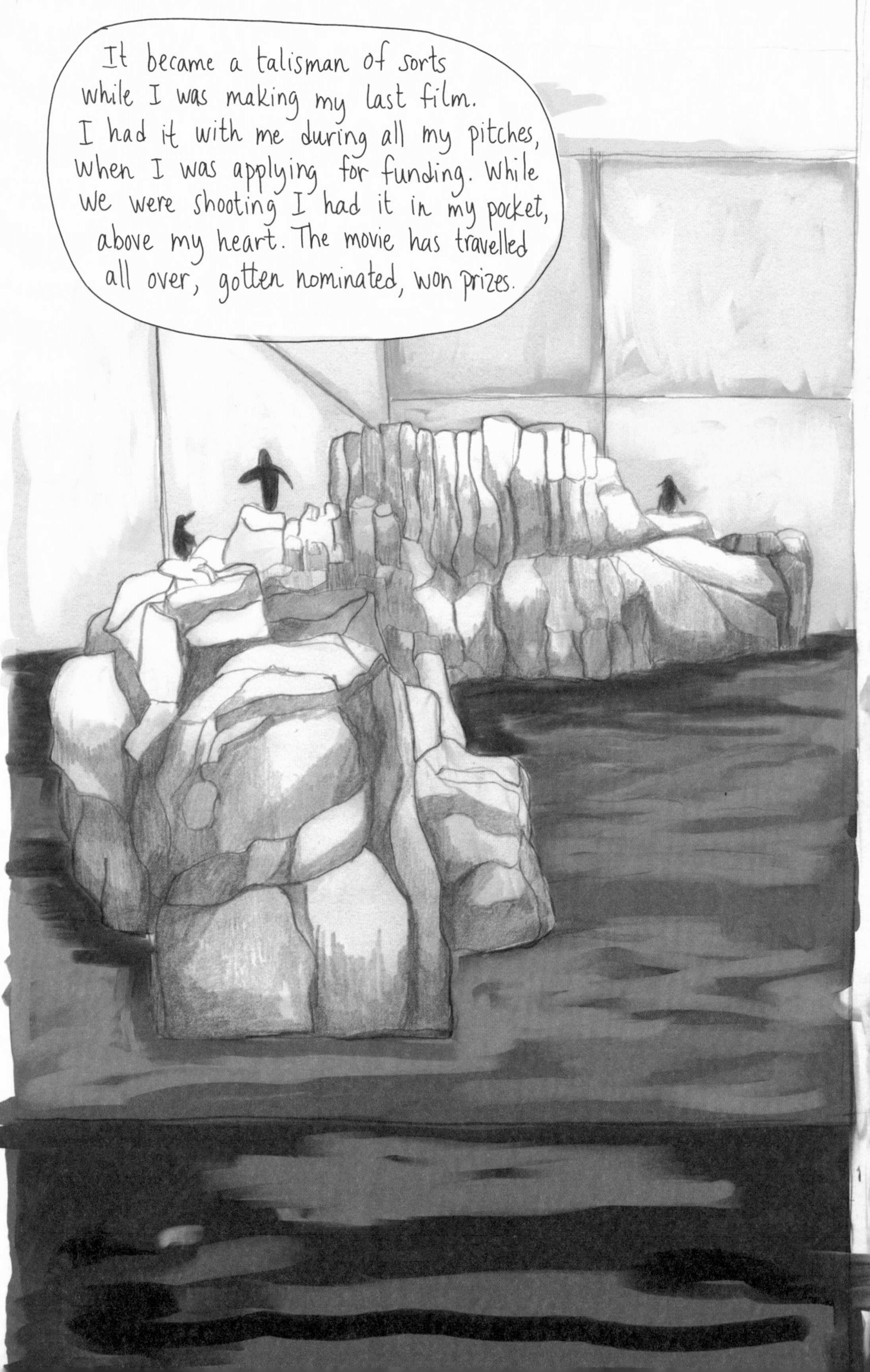
It became a talisman of sorts while I was making my last film. I had it with me during all my pitches, when I was applying for funding. While we were shooting I had it in my pocket, above my heart. The movie has travelled all over, gotten nominated, won prizes.

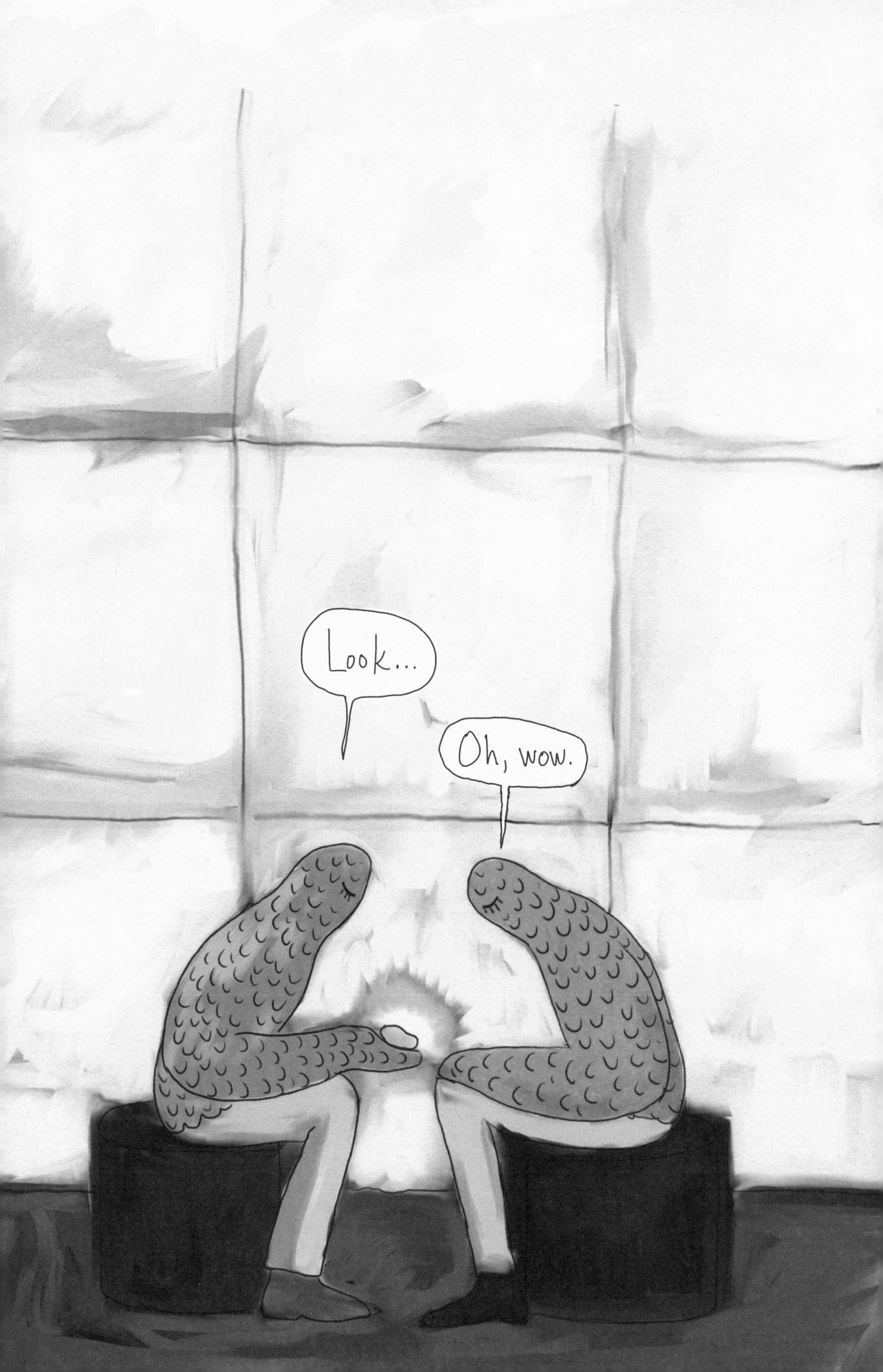
Look...
Oh, wow.

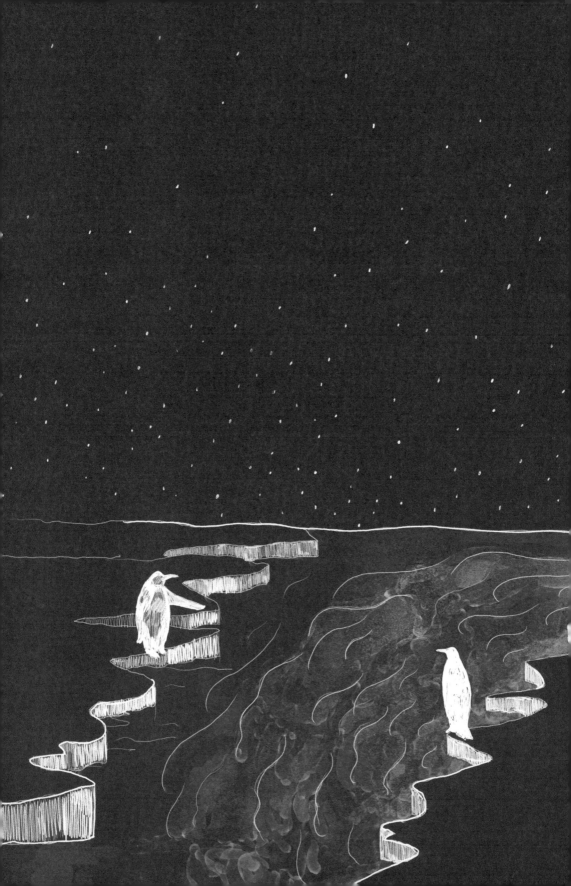

Mom

The planet is much closer to gargantua than we thought.

Landing there takes us dangerously close ...

Gravity on our planet will slow our clock compared to Earth's. Drastically.

How bad?

Every hour we spend on that planet will be 7 years back on Earth.

That's relativity folks.

(Scene from Christopher Nolan's movie Interstellar)

Well, we can't just drop down there!
HEY we have a MISSION!
Oooofffff... Feels good to relax.
Billie wants a dog... Maybe we should get one.
You can't just think about your family You have to think bigger than that!
Should I stop watching TV and do some work?
Why are they arguing about the theory of relativity?
This movie is so complicated. Can't tune out for two seconds...

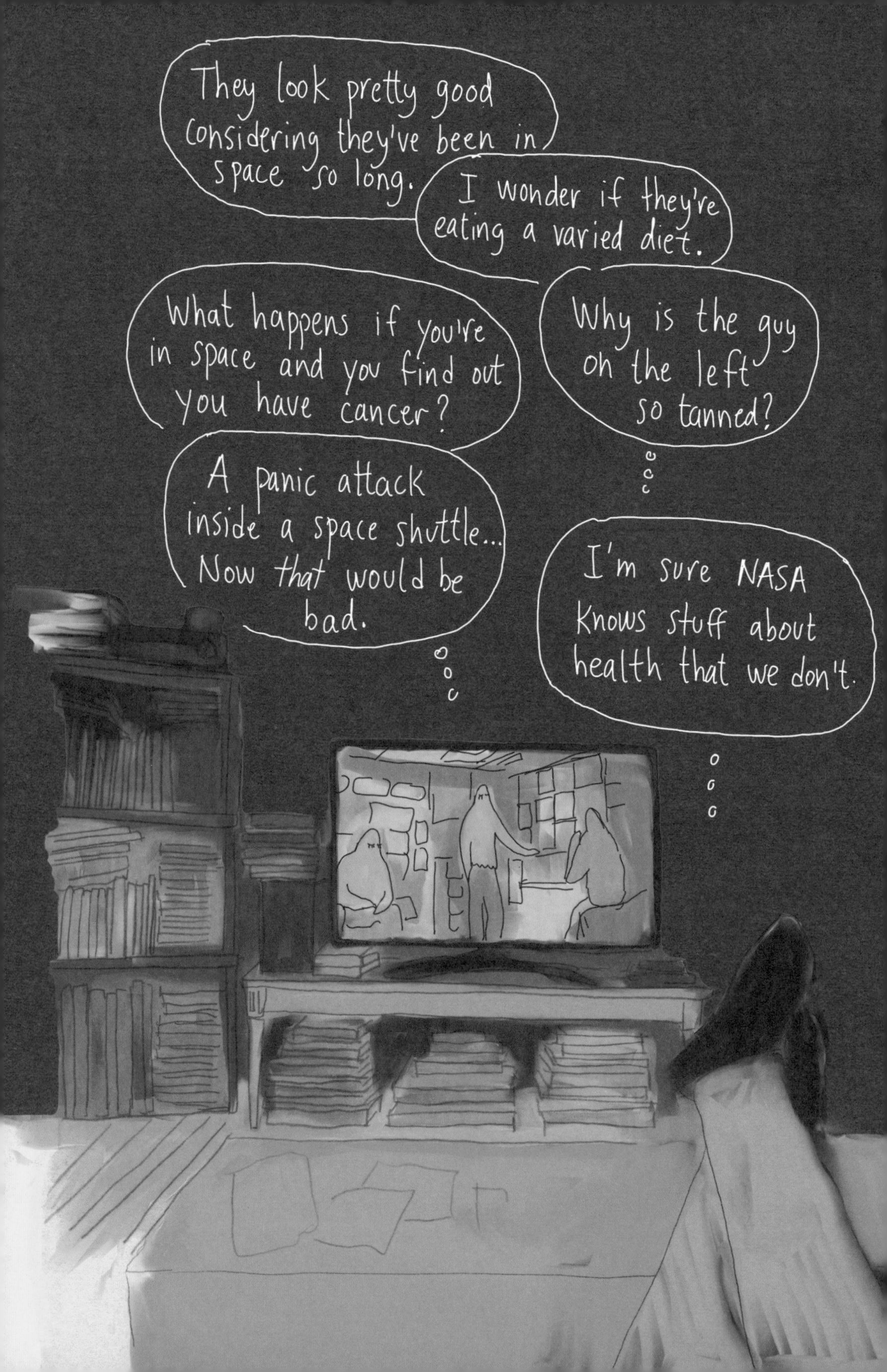
They look pretty good considering they've been in space so long.
I wonder if they're eating a varied diet.
What happens if you're in space and you find out you have cancer?
Why is the guy on the left so tanned?
A panic attack inside a space shuttle... Now *that* would be bad.
I'm sure NASA knows stuff about health that we don't.

We want to get there fast, don't we?
Actually, we want to get there in one piece.
Hang on.

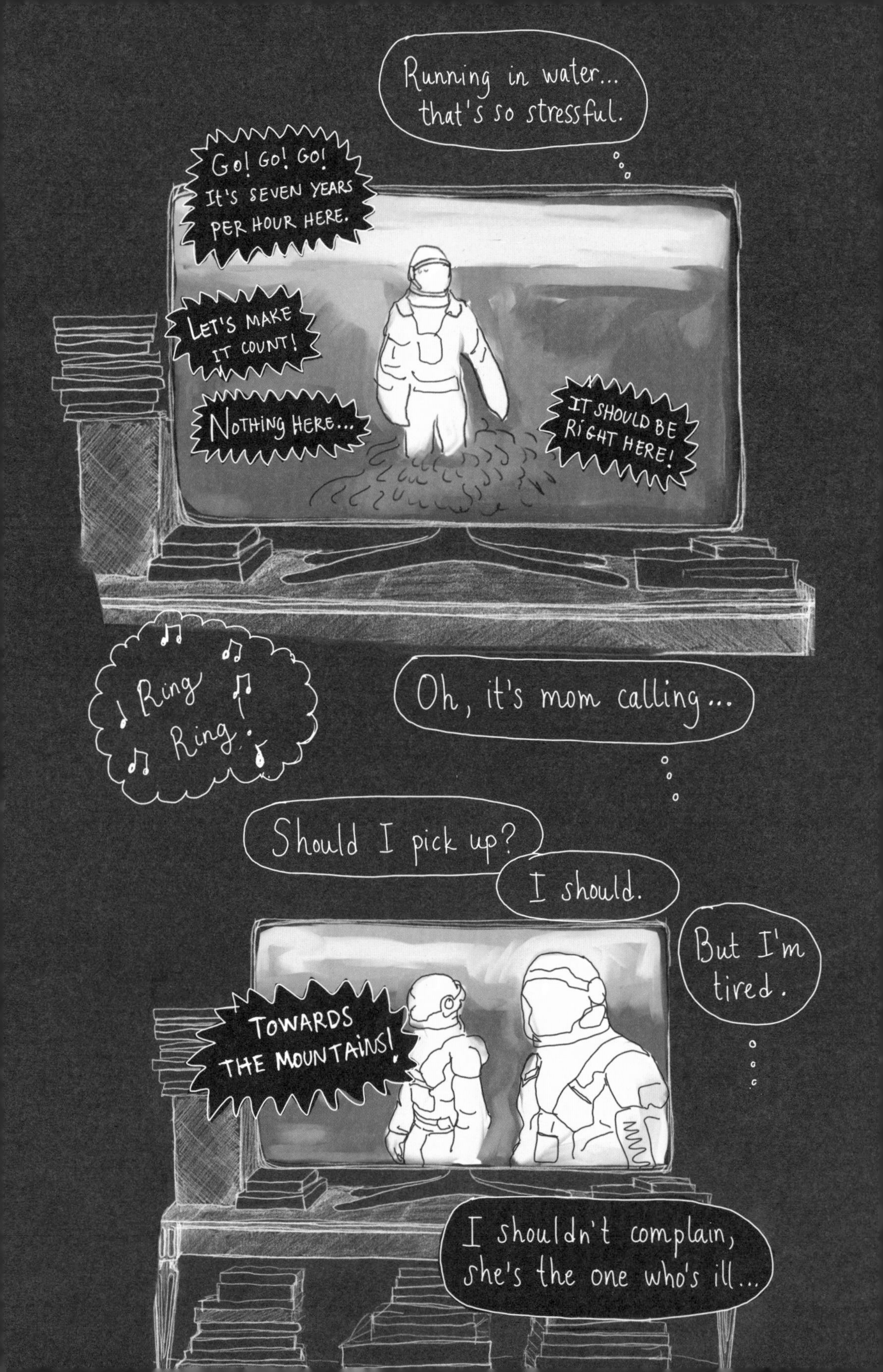
Running in water... that's so stressful.
Go! Go! Go! It's SEVEN YEARS PER HOUR HERE.
LET'S MAKE IT COUNT!
NOTHING HERE...
IT SHOULD BE RIGHT HERE!
Ring Ring!
Oh, it's mom calling...
Should I pick up?
I should.
But I'm tired.
TOWARDS THE MOUNTAINS!
I shouldn't complain, she's the one who's ill...

Hello?
Mom?
Everything ok?
Mom, is something covering the receiver?
ssssrrchs
I can't hear you...
Those aren't mountains... THEY'RE WAVES.
Mom! Hello?!!!
Did you drop the phone or something?
There you are!
Oh BEEP! Cath BEEP haven BEEP in a long BEEP! I just want BEEP! BEEP! to BEEP!
Mom, you're hitting the buttons while you talk.
Can you hold the phone some other way please?
Biiiiiiiiiiiip
Mom?

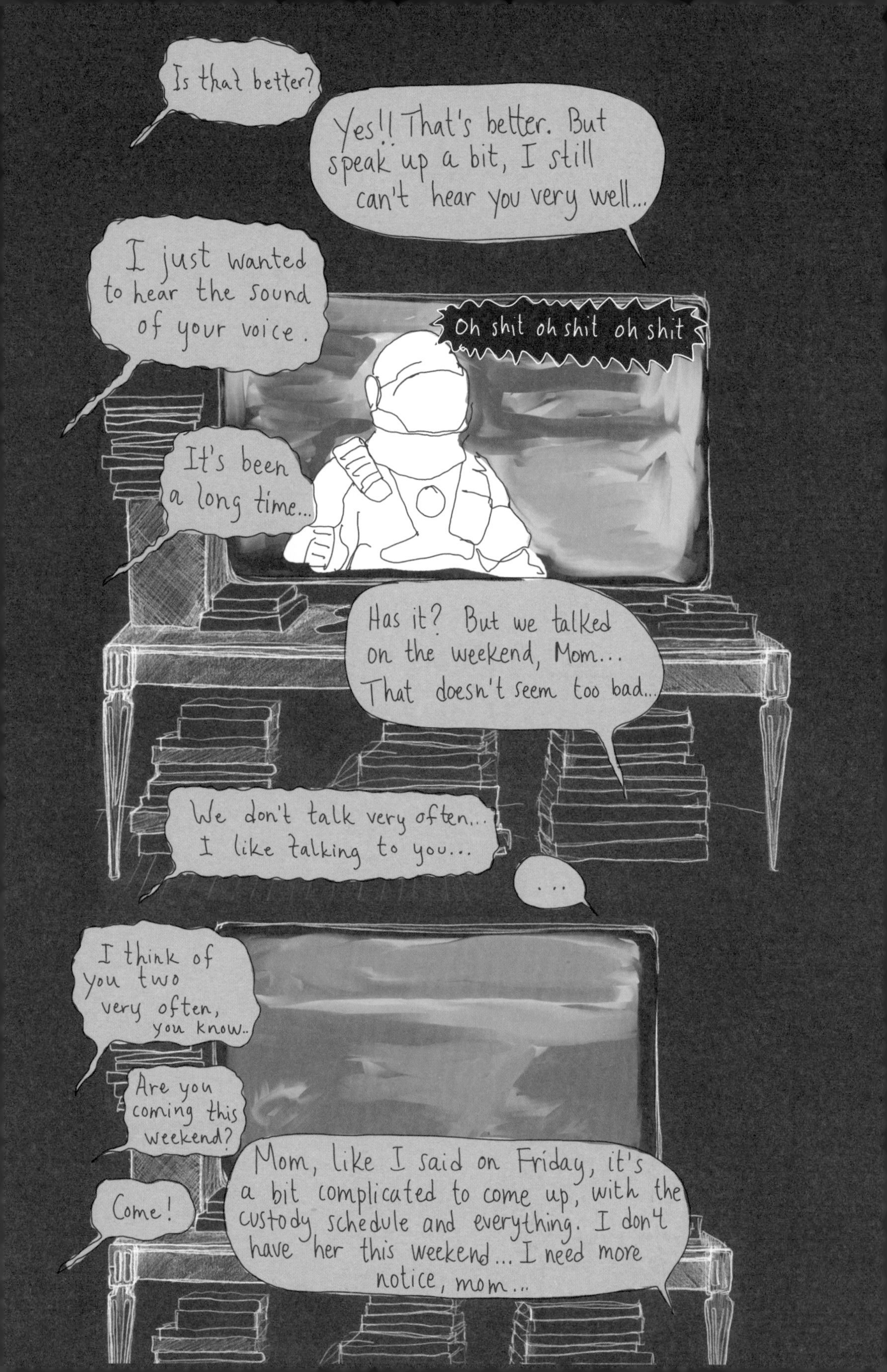

Is that better?
Yes!! That's better. But speak up a bit, I still can't hear you very well...
I just wanted to hear the sound of your voice.
Oh shit oh shit oh shit
It's been a long time...
Has it? But we talked on the weekend, Mom... That doesn't seem too bad...
We don't talk very often... I like talking to you...
...
I think of you two very often, you know..
Are you coming this weekend?
Come!
Mom, like I said on Friday, it's a bit complicated to come up, with the custody schedule and everything. I don't have her this weekend... I need more notice, mom...

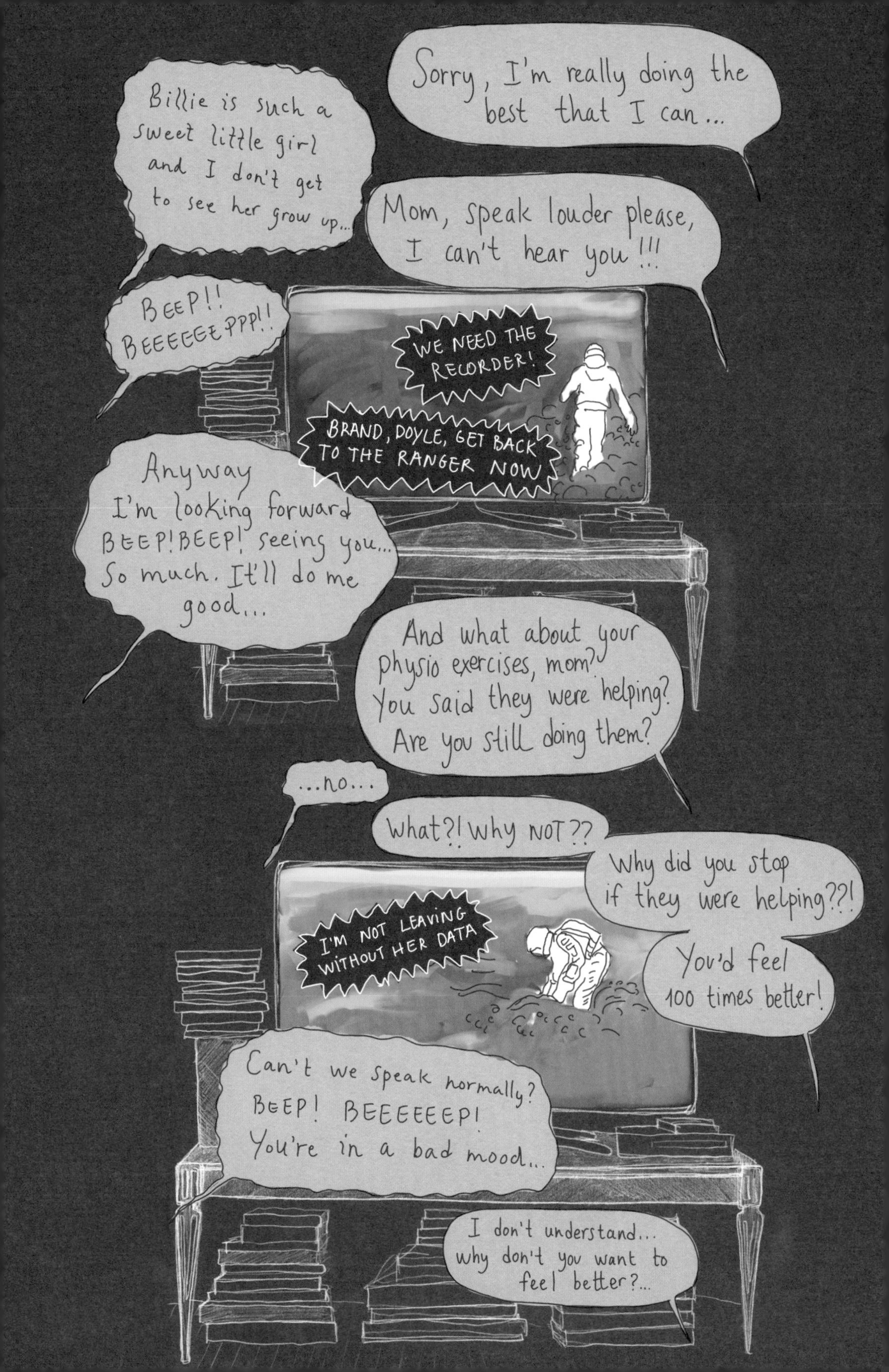

Sorry, I'm really doing the best that I can...
Billie is such a sweet little girl and I don't get to see her grow up...
Mom, speak louder please, I can't hear you!!!
BEEP!! BEEEEEEPPP!!
WE NEED THE RECORDER!
BRAND, DOYLE, GET BACK TO THE RANGER NOW
Anyway I'm looking forward BEEP!BEEP! seeing you... So much. It'll do me good...
And what about your physio exercises, mom? You said they were helping? Are you still doing them?
...no...
What?! Why NOT??
Why did you stop if they were helping??!
I'M NOT LEAVING WITHOUT HER DATA
You'd feel 100 times better!
Can't we speak normally? BEEP! BEEEEEEP! You're in a bad mood...
I don't understand... why don't you want to feel better?...

GET BACK HERE NOW WE DON'T HAVE TIME
Don't you have someBEEP! nice to tell me?
THE SECOND WAVE IS COMING
WE'RE IN THE MIDDLE OF THE SWIRL
BEEEEEP!! BEEP!
Hello?
Mom! Please mom please can you try to stop hitting the buttons? It's so loud... Please...
And so now
Crrrrshhhrrn
Mom... please... you know you shouldn't call when you're having a shaking episode...
It's impossible for us to talk when you're like this...
COOPER, go! GO! I CAN'T MAKE IT!!
BRAND, GET BACK HERE, NOW!
Mom?
You still there...?
I can't hear you at all... Are you there? Please, please take care of yourself...
I'm so sorry... I love you...
I'm going to hang up now...
Bye, mom...
CLICK!

GET UP! GET UP, BRAND!
I'M NOT GOING TO MAKE IT...
GO!
YES YOU ARE,
YES YOU ARE!
Mom?
Are you crying?
Billie!?!

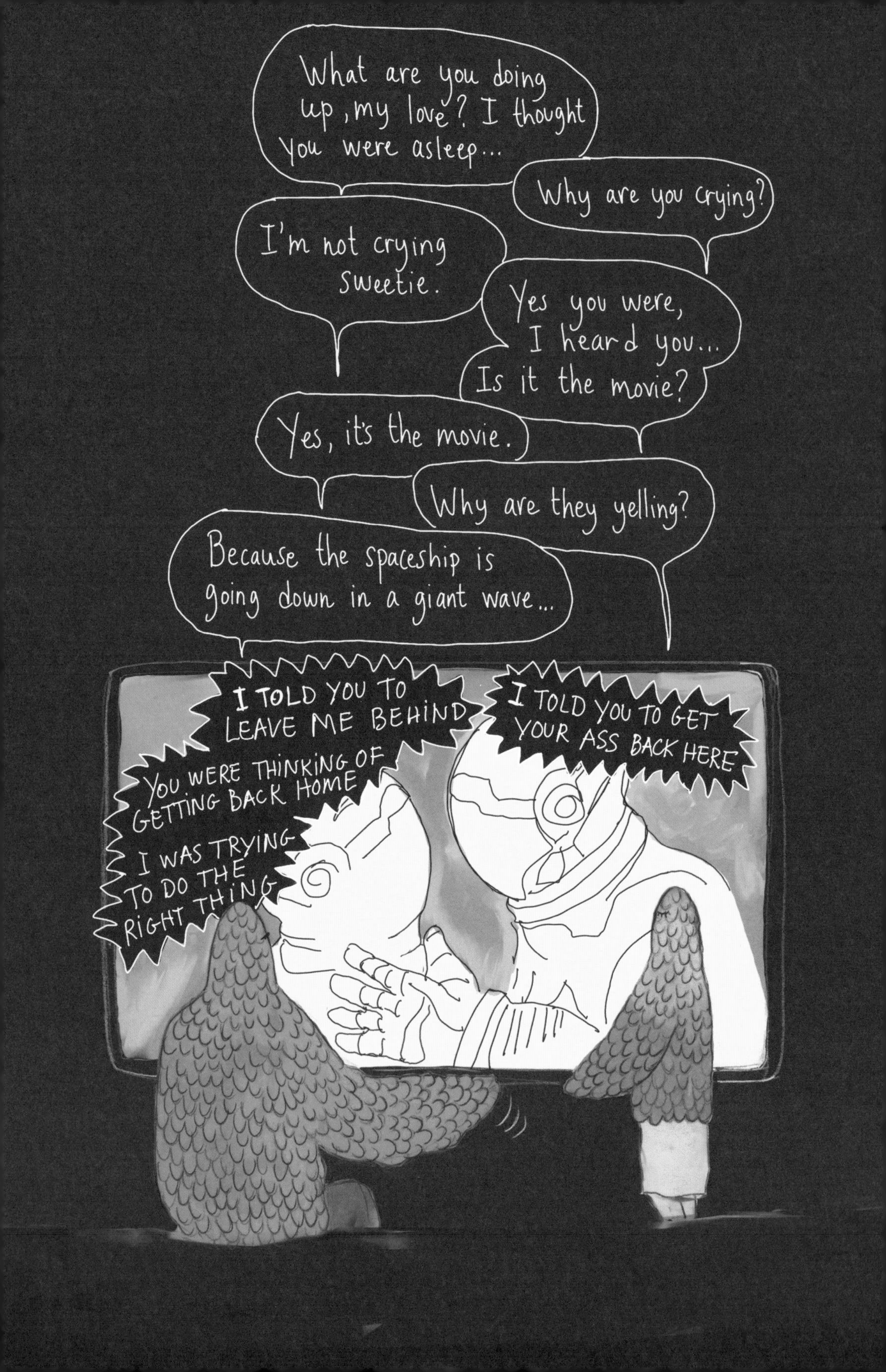
What are you doing up, my love? I thought you were asleep...
Why are you crying?
I'm not crying sweetie.
Yes you were, I heard you... Is it the movie?
Yes, it's the movie.
Why are they yelling?
Because the spaceship is going down in a giant wave...
I TOLD YOU TO LEAVE ME BEHIND
I TOLD YOU TO GET YOUR ASS BACK HERE
YOU WERE THINKING OF GETTING BACK HOME
I WAS TRYING TO DO THE RIGHT THING

That's what made you cry?
I think it's the soundtrack. Sometimes it's too much.
Ah.
If we had a dog, you wouldn't be sad when we watch movies.
Nice try, but no.
Okay. So can I watch the rest with you?
No, my love.
But mom, I don't have school tomorrow!
That's true. OK then.
Yesss!!
What is this going to cost us, Brand...
A lot...
Decades...
I love you, mom.
I love you too, Billie.

Saint André,
Saint Joseph,
Rachel / Rachelle

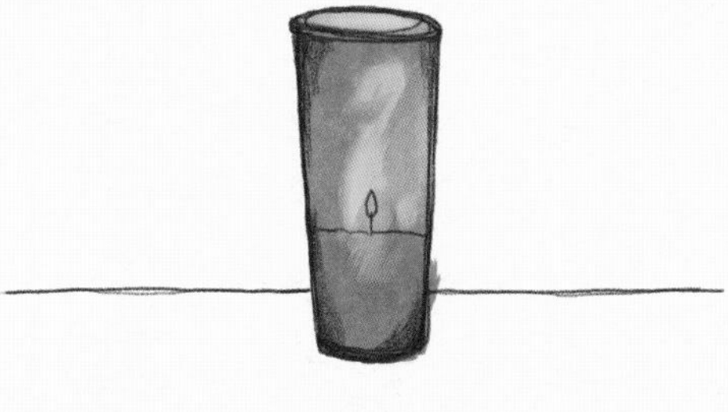

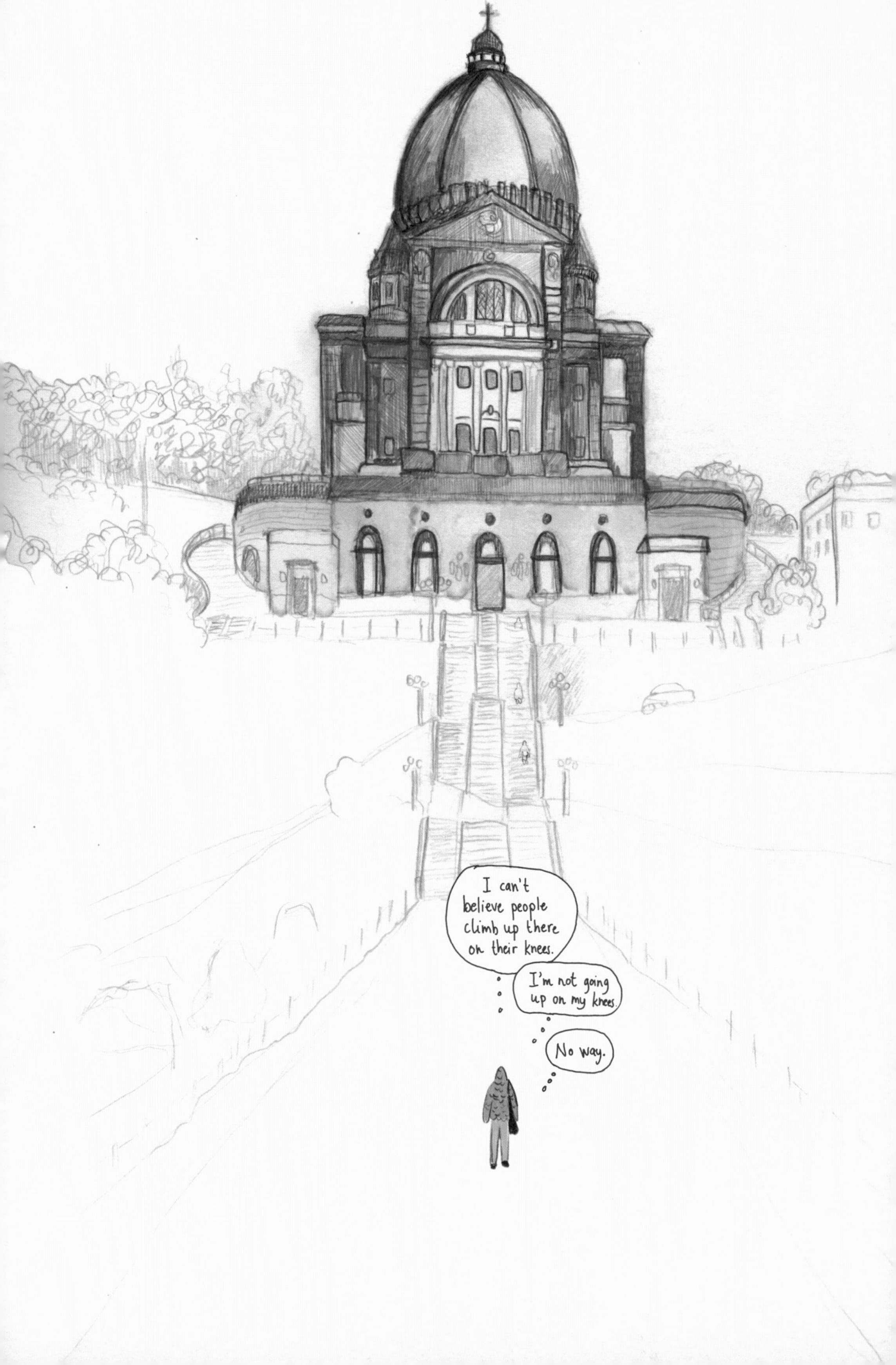
I can't believe people climb up there on their knees.
I'm not going up on my knees.
No way.

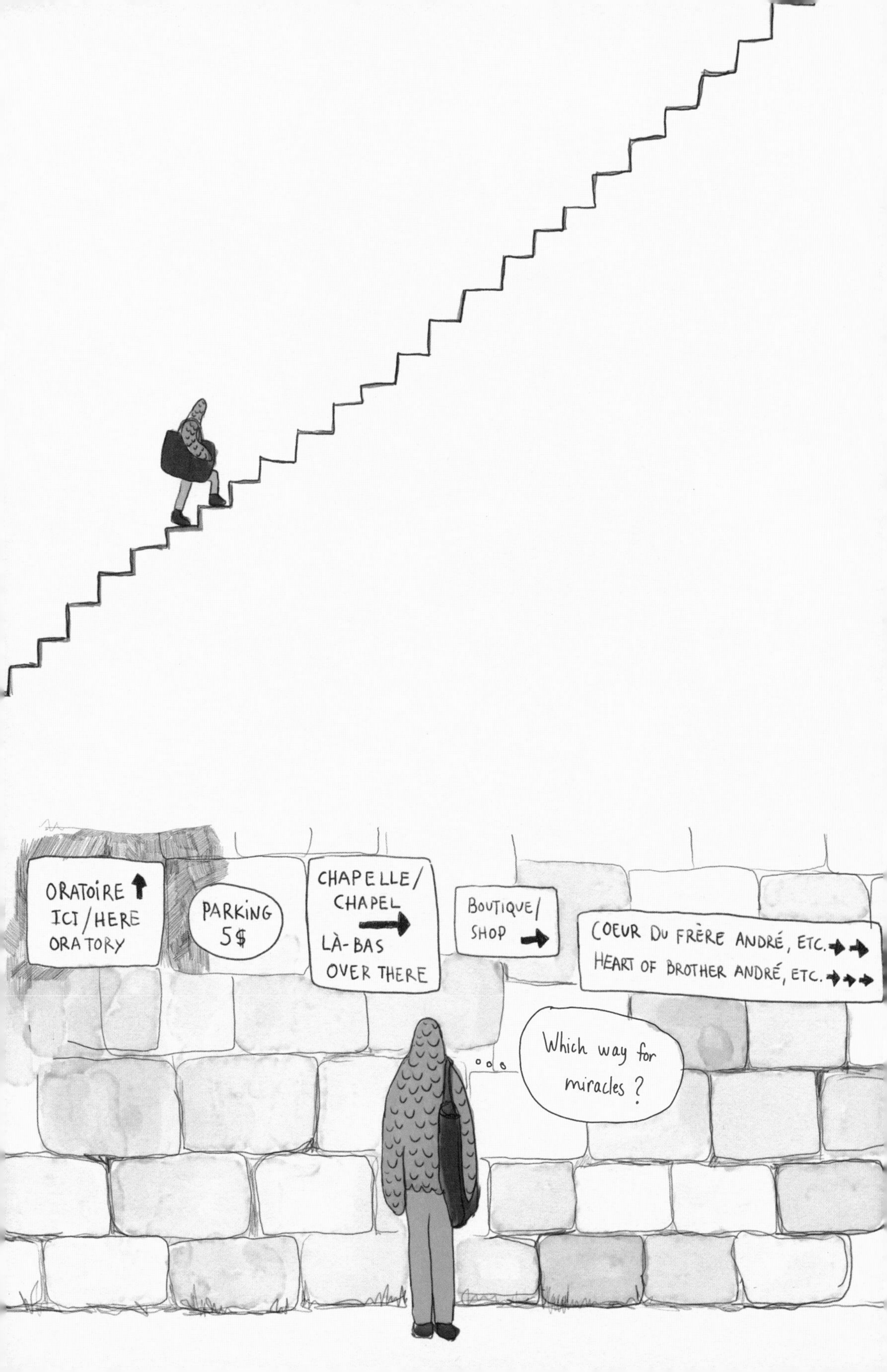
ORATOIRE ICI/HERE ORATORY
PARKING 5$
CHAPELLE/ CHAPEL LÀ-BAS OVER THERE
BOUTIQUE/ SHOP
COEUR DU FRÈRE ANDRÉ, ETC.
HEART OF BROTHER ANDRÉ, ETC.
Which way for miracles ?

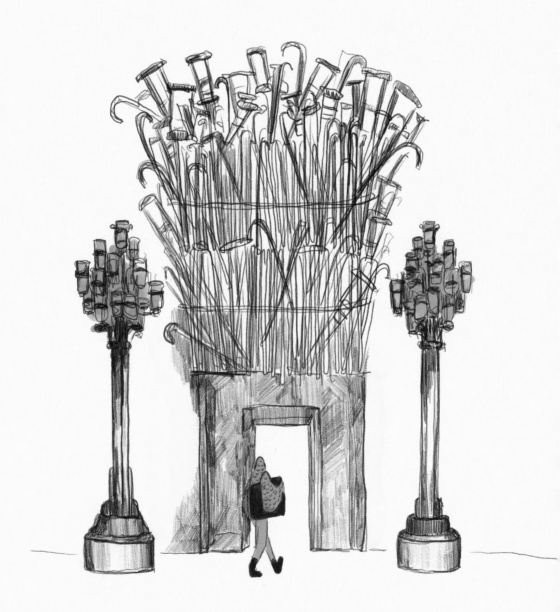

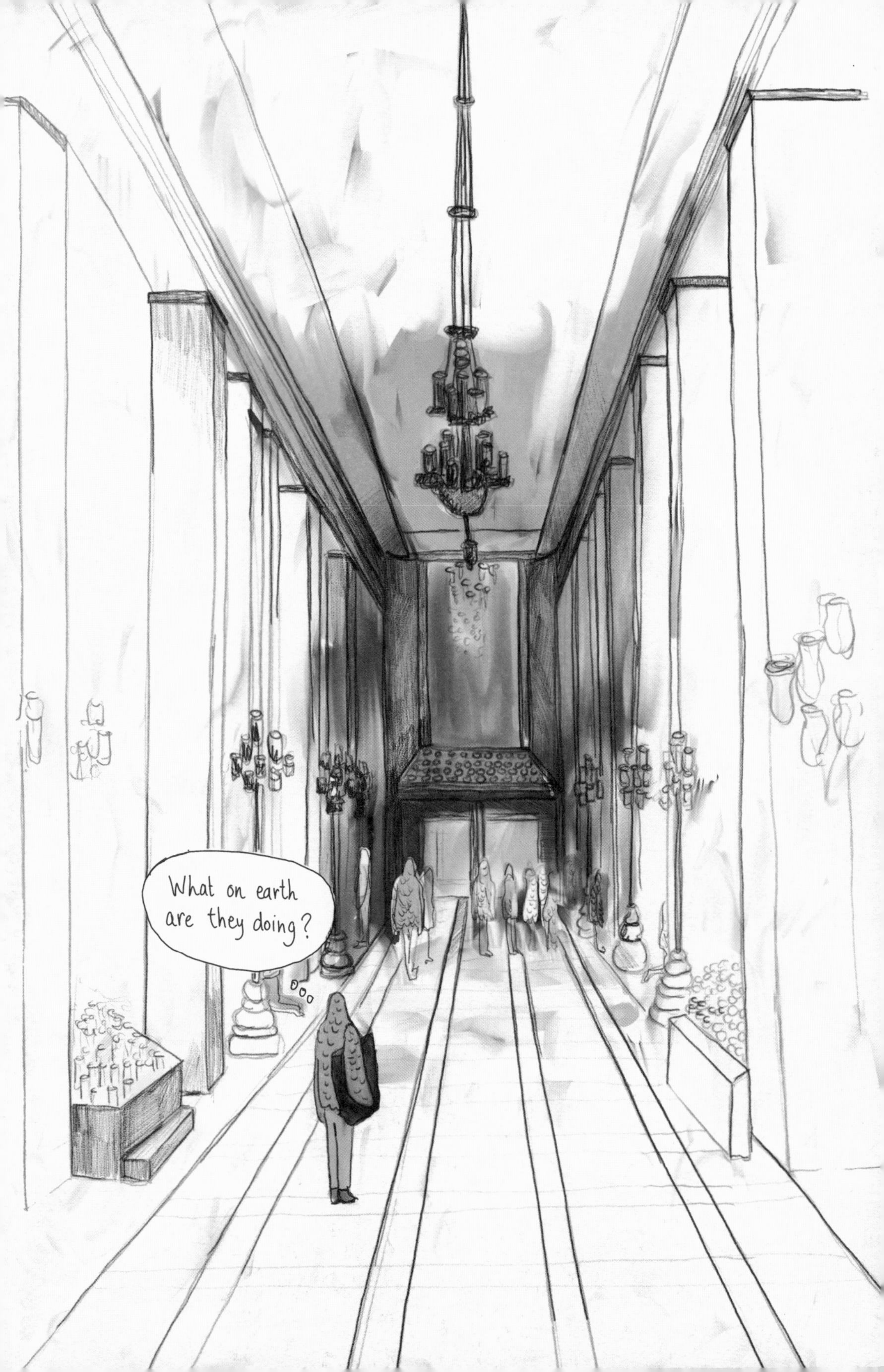
What on earth are they doing?

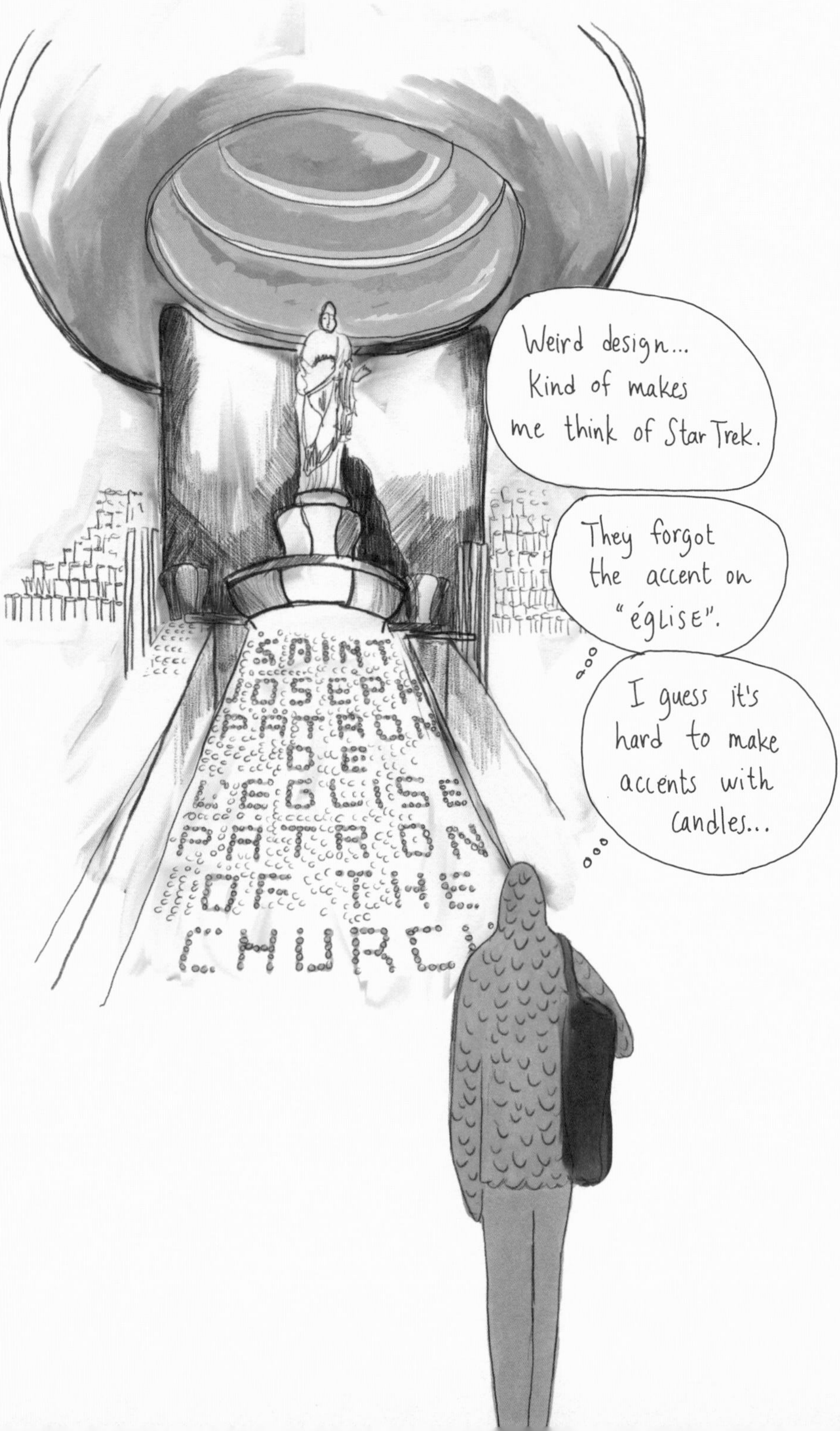
SAINT
JOSEPH
PATRON
DE
L'EGLISE
PATRON
OF THE
CHURC
Weird design... Kind of makes me think of Star Trek.
They forgot the accent on "église".
I guess it's hard to make accents with candles...

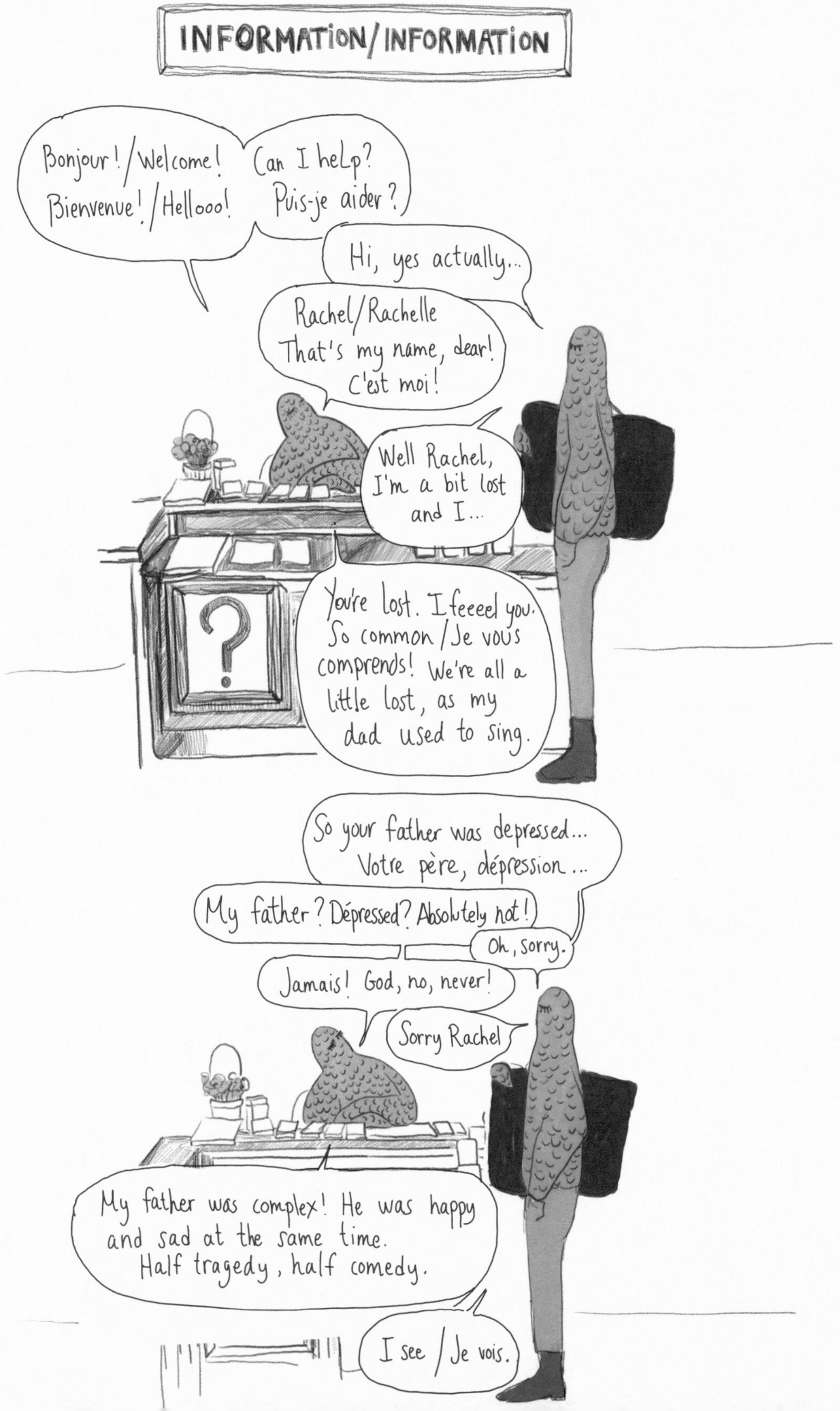
INFORMATION/INFORMATION
Bonjour!/Welcome! Bienvenue!/Hellooo!
Can I heLp? Puis-je aider?
Hi, yes actually...
Rachel/Rachelle That's my name, dear! C'est moi!
Well Rachel, I'm a bit lost and I...
You're lost. I feeeel you. So common/Je vous comprends! We're all a little lost, as my dad used to sing.
?
So your father was depressed... Votre père, dépression...
My father? Dépressed? Absolutely not!
Oh, sorry.
Jamais! God, no, never!
Sorry Rachel
My father was complex! He was happy and sad at the same time. Half tragedy, half comedy.
I see/Je vois.

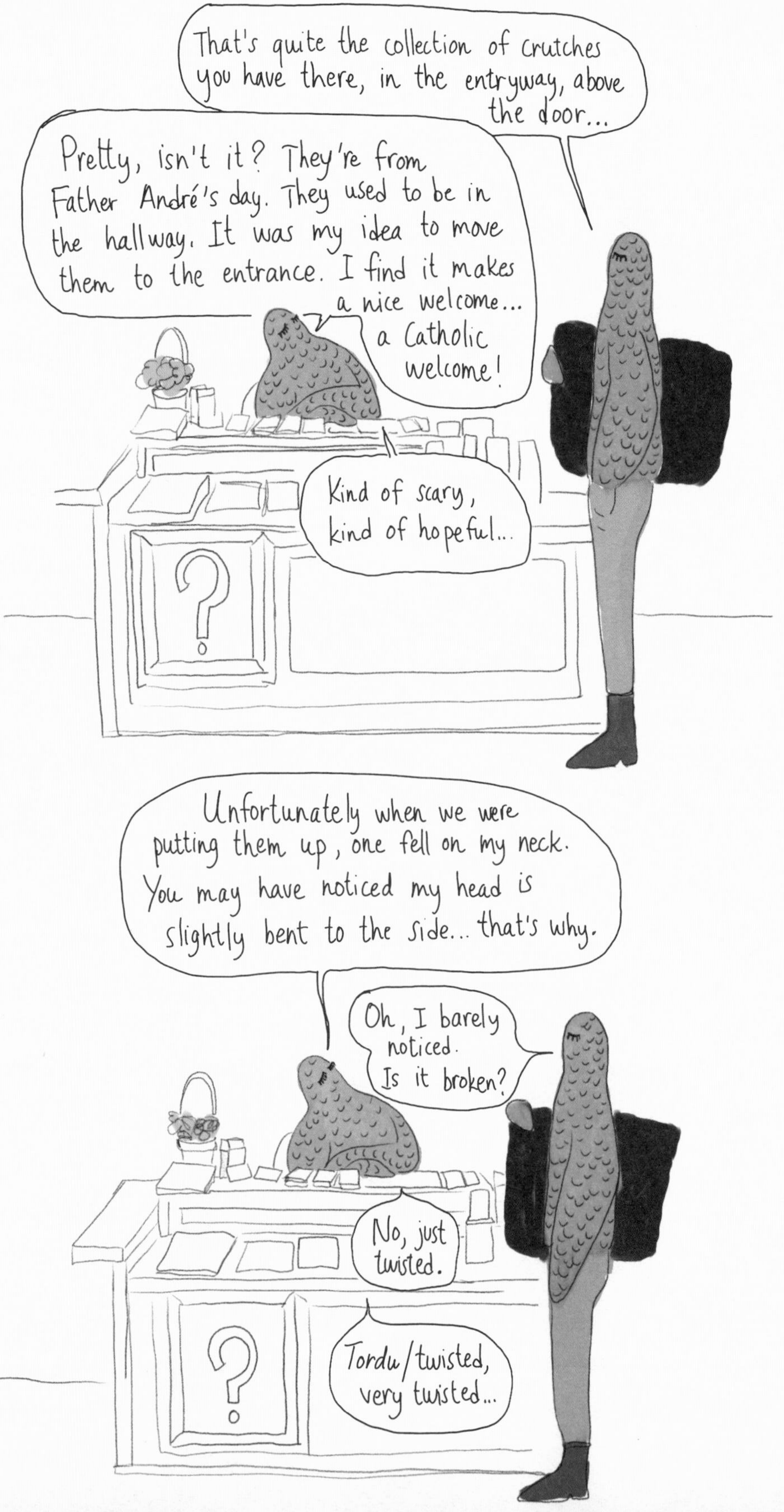
That's quite the collection of crutches you have there, in the entryway, above the door...
Pretty, isn't it? They're from Father André's day. They used to be in the hallway. It was my idea to move them to the entrance. I find it makes a nice welcome... a Catholic welcome!
Kind of scary, kind of hopeful...
Unfortunately when we were putting them up, one fell on my neck. You may have noticed my head is slightly bent to the side... that's why.
Oh, I barely noticed. Is it broken?
No, just twisted.
Tordu/twisted, very twisted...

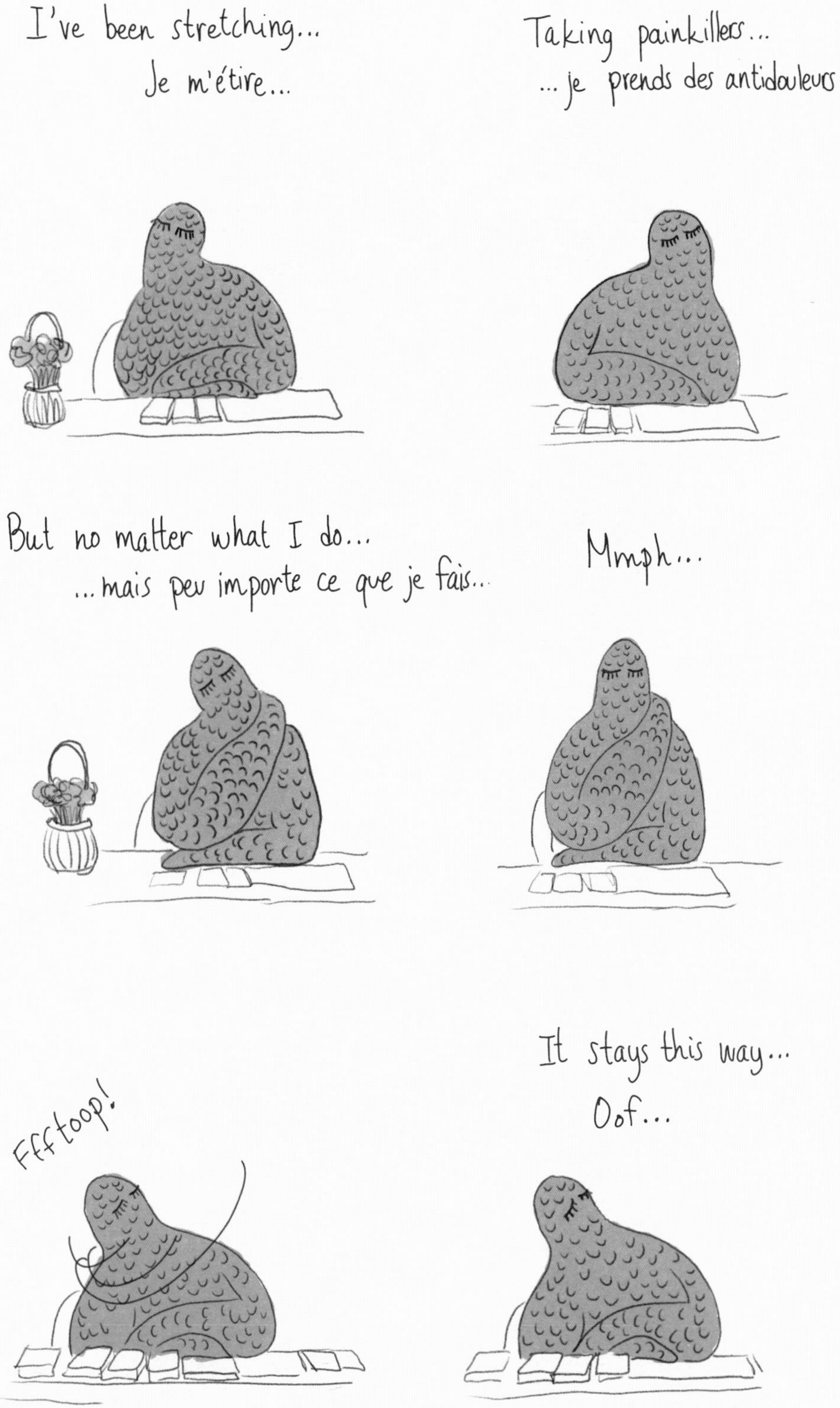

I've been stretching...
Je m'étire...
Taking painkillers...
...je prends des antidouleurs
But no matter what I do...
...mais peu importe ce que je fais...
Mmph...
Fffftoop!
It stays this way...
Oof...

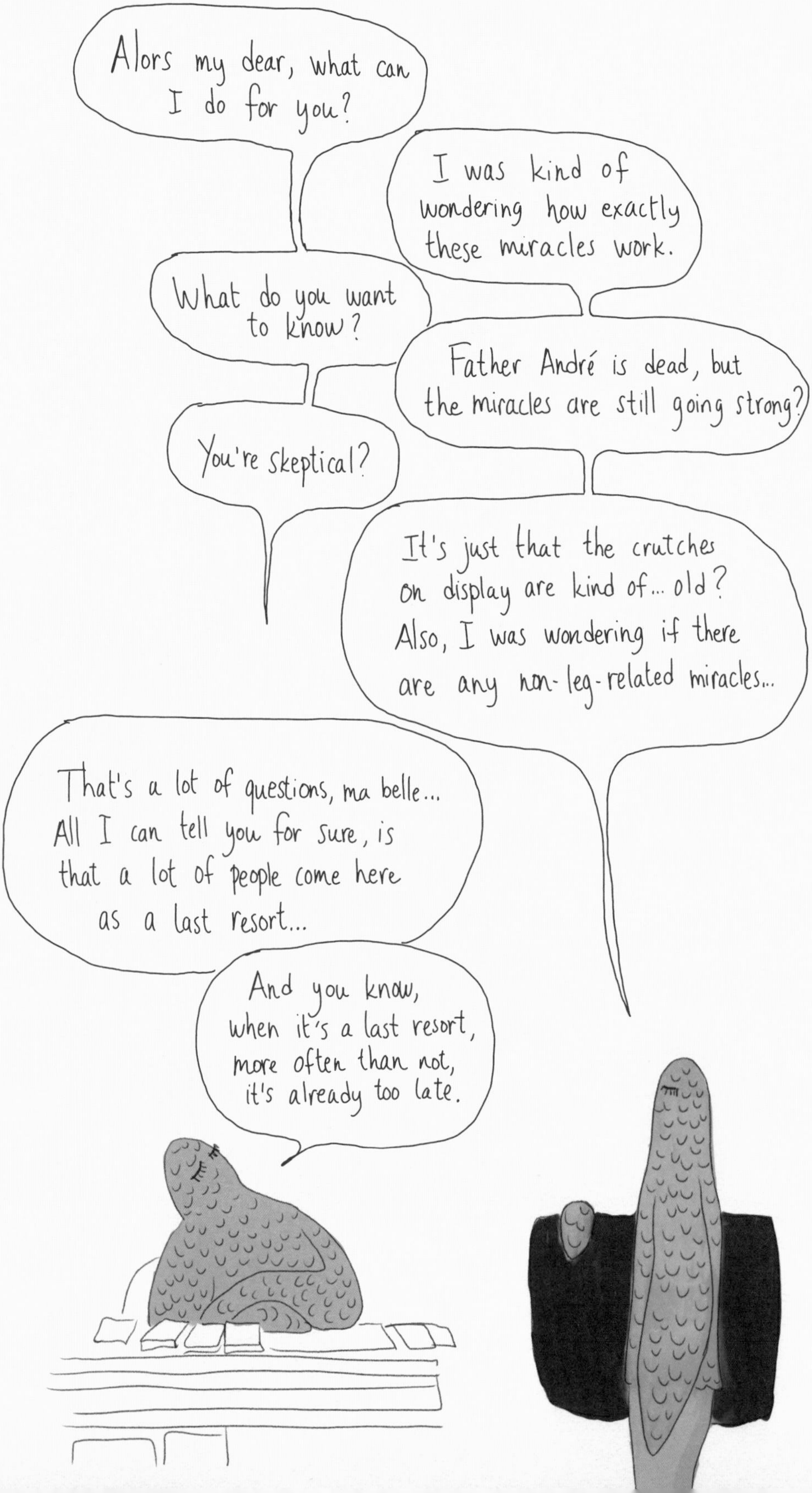
Alors my dear, what can I do for you?
I was kind of wondering how exactly these miracles work.
What do you want to know?
Father André is dead, but the miracles are still going strong?
You're skeptical?
It's just that the crutches on display are kind of... old? Also, I was wondering if there are any non-leg-related miracles...
That's a lot of questions, ma belle... All I can tell you for sure, is that a lot of people come here as a last resort...
And you know, when it's a last resort, more often than not, it's already too late.

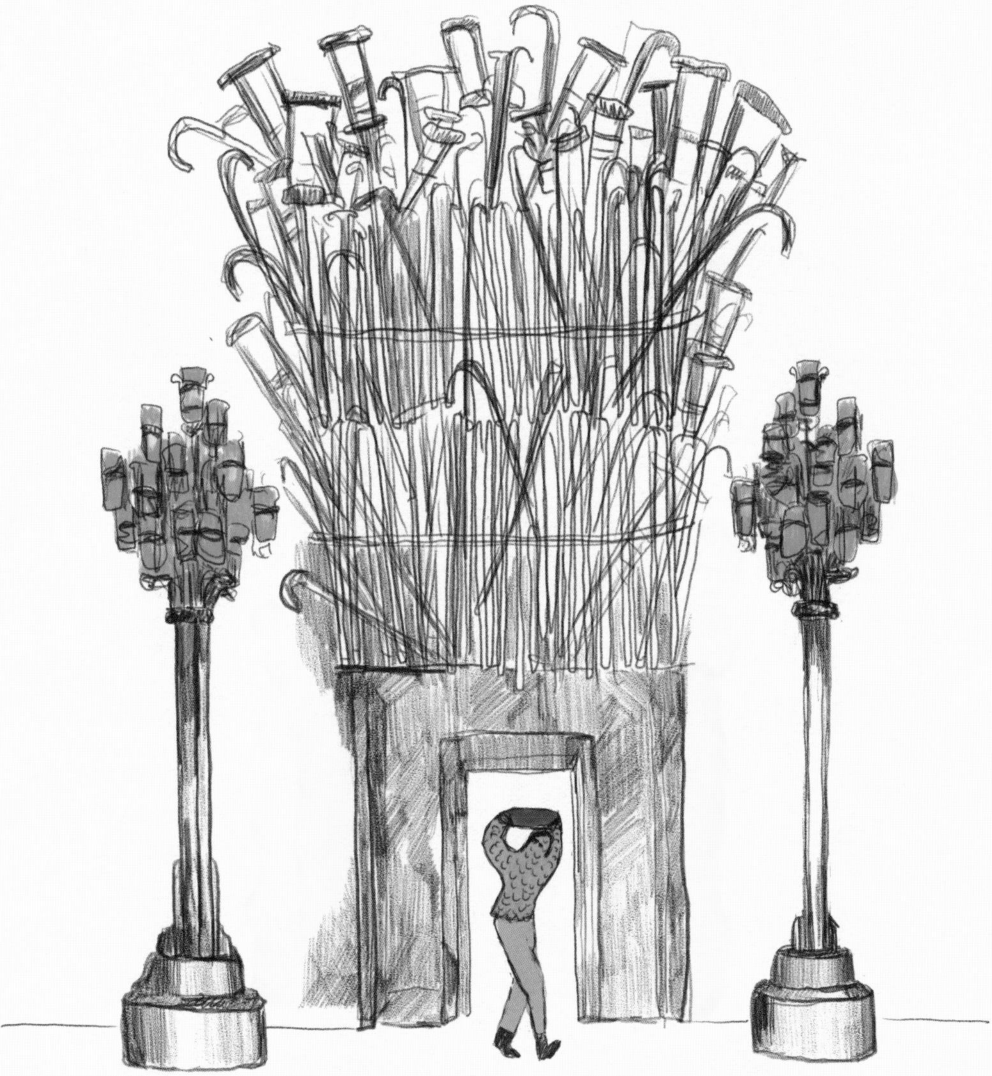

You will find all
these items for sale
at the main gift shop

Micheline

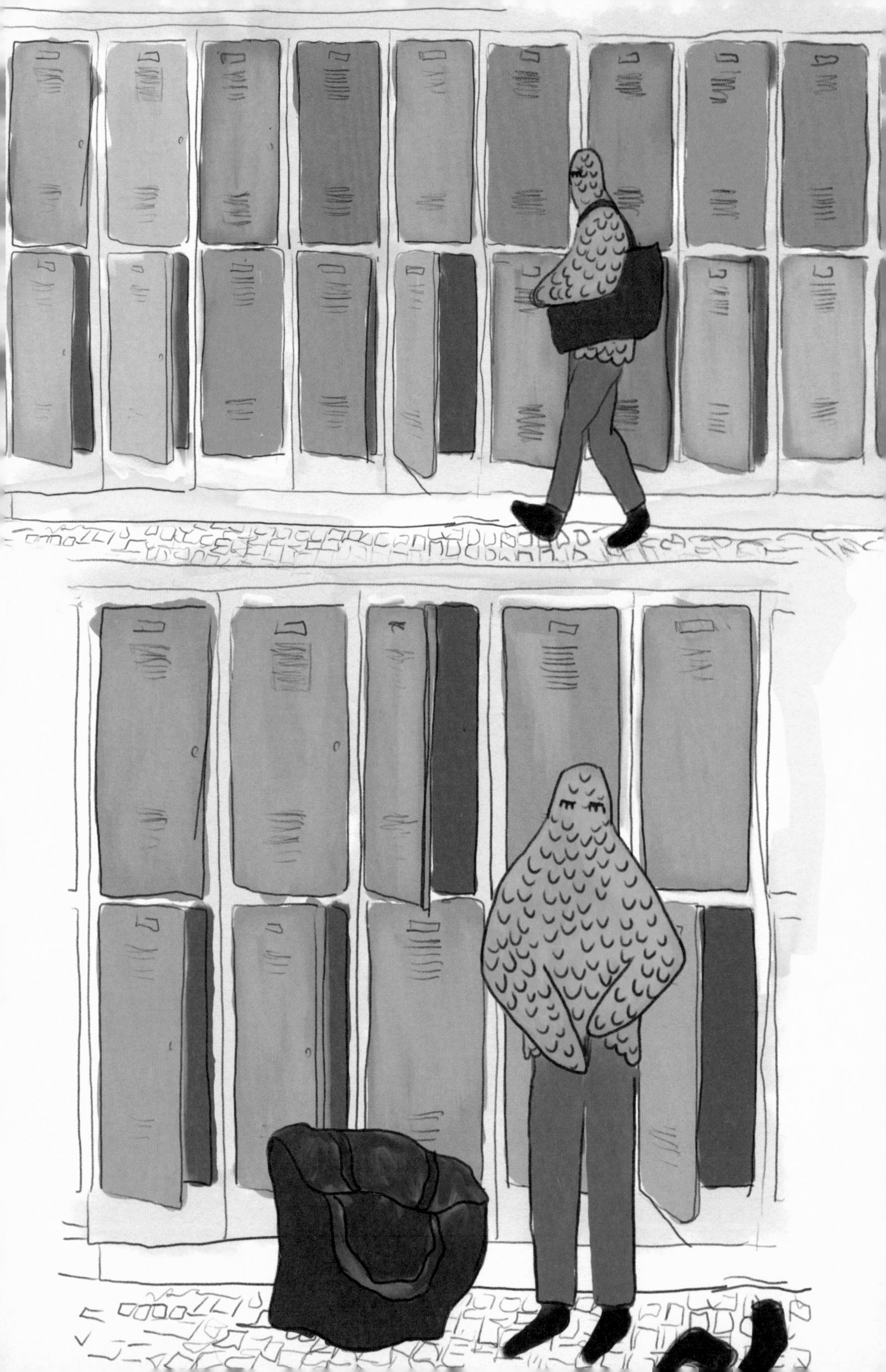

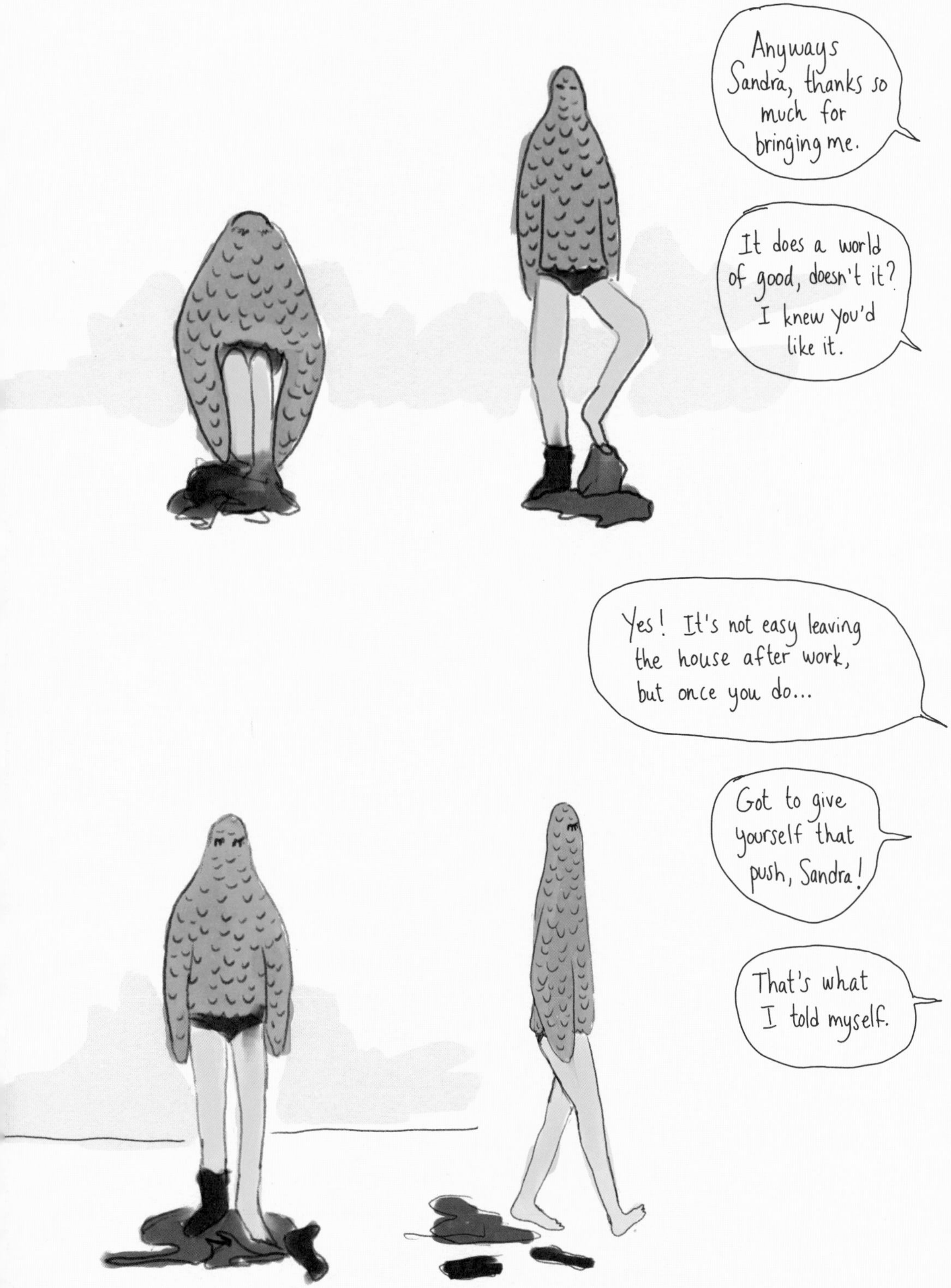
Anyways Sandra, thanks so much for bringing me.
It does a world of good, doesn't it? I knew you'd like it.
Yes! It's not easy leaving the house after work, but once you do...
Got to give yourself that push, Sandra!
That's what I told myself.

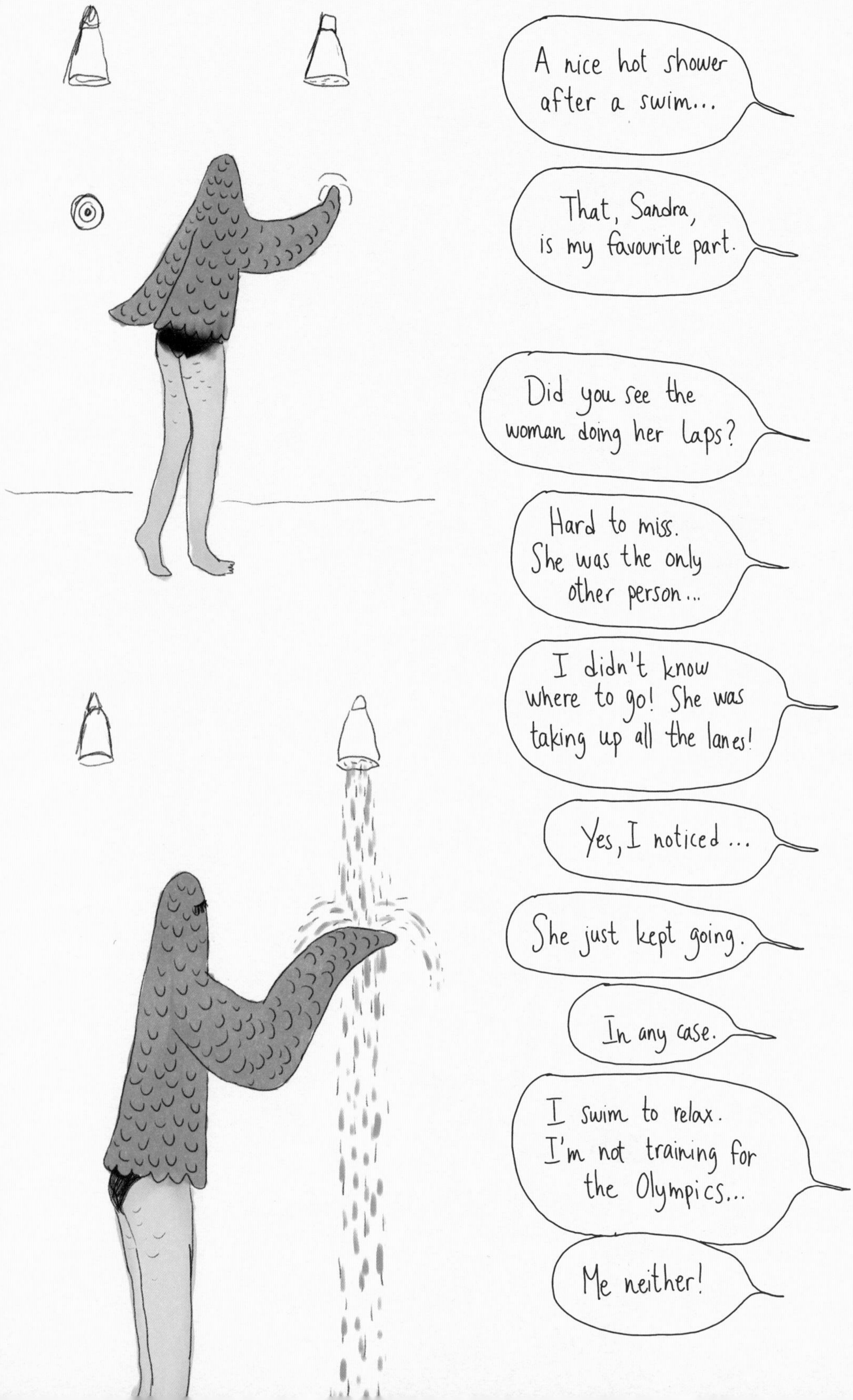
A nice hot shower after a swim...
That, Sandra, is my favourite part.
Did you see the woman doing her laps?
Hard to miss. She was the only other person...
I didn't know where to go! She was taking up all the lanes!
Yes, I noticed...
She just kept going.
In any case.
I swim to relax. I'm not training for the Olympics...
Me neither!

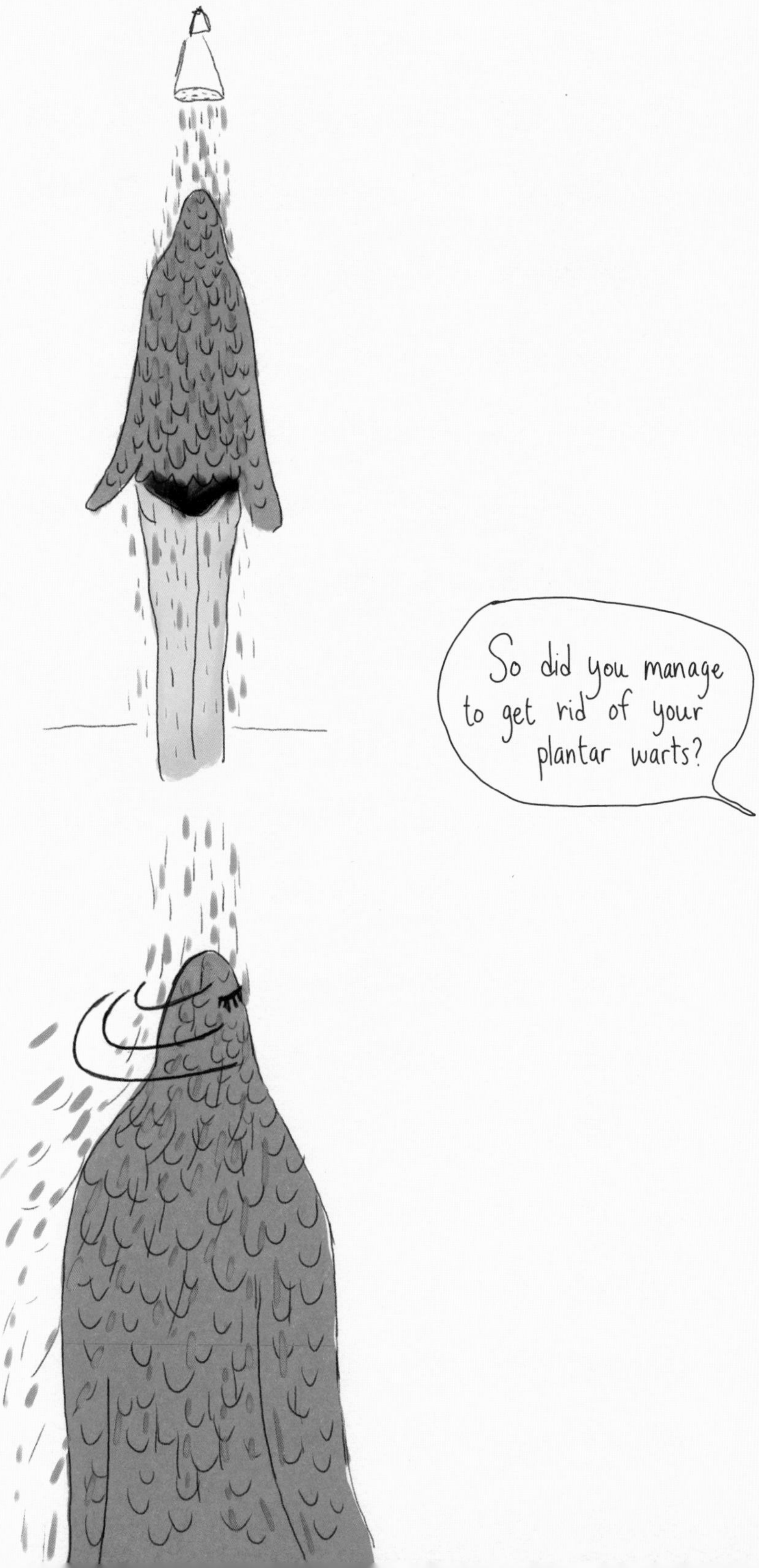
So did you manage to get rid of your plantar warts?

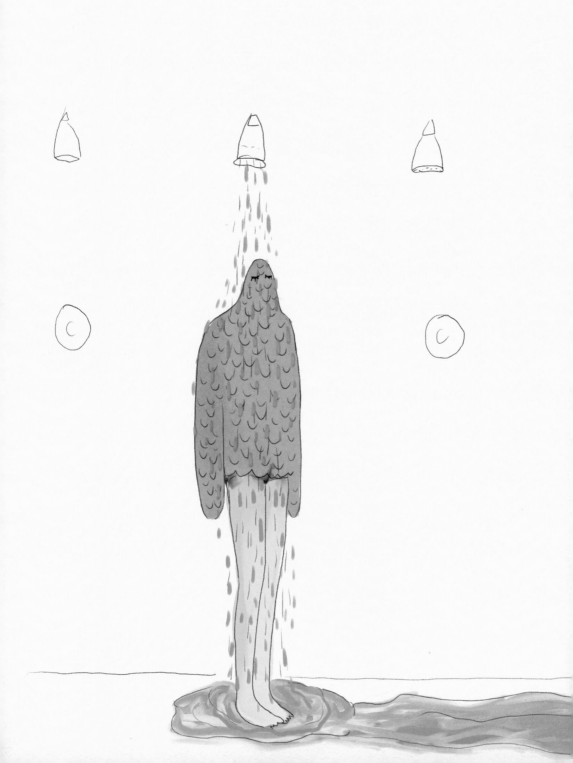

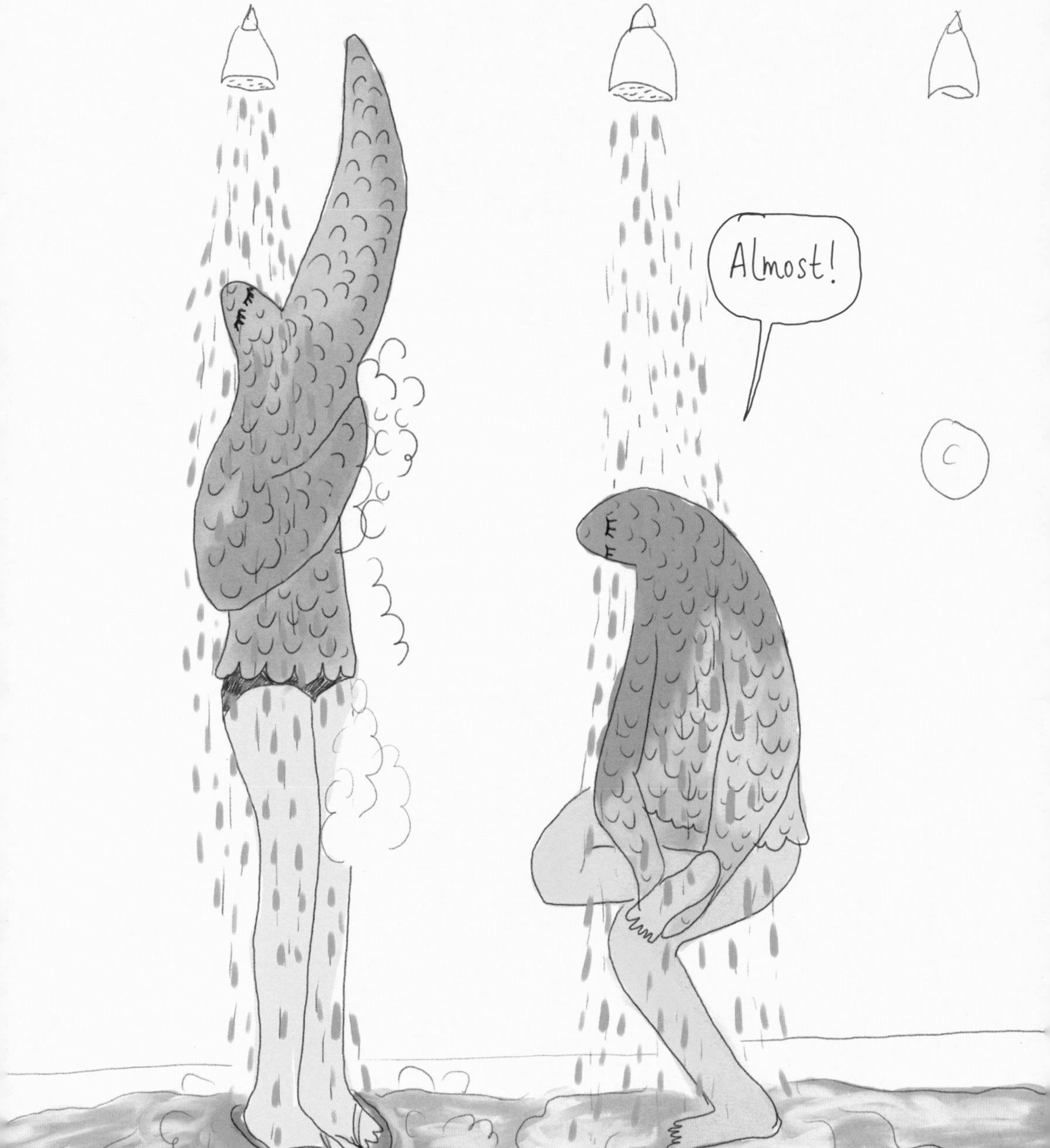
Almost!

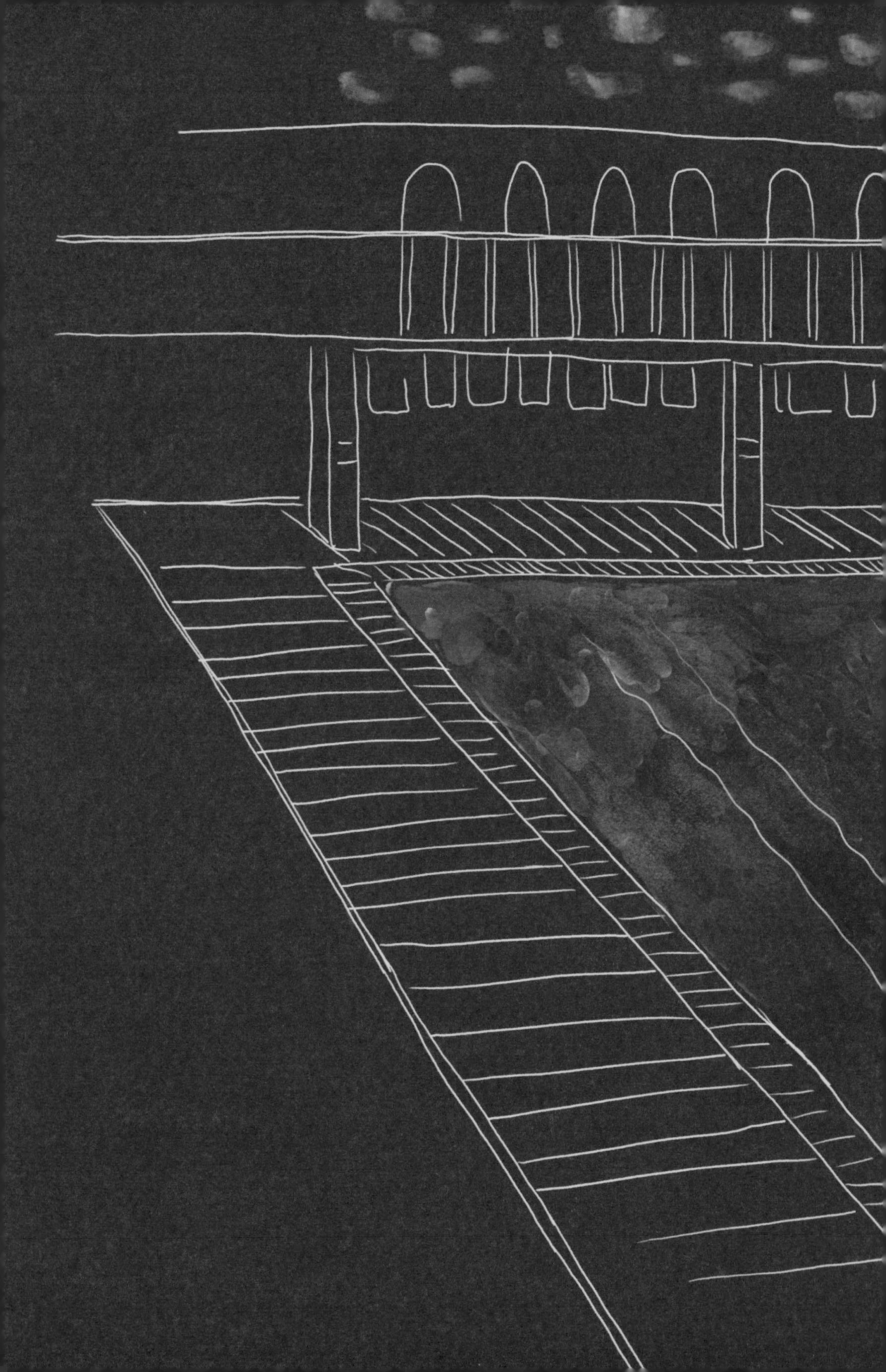

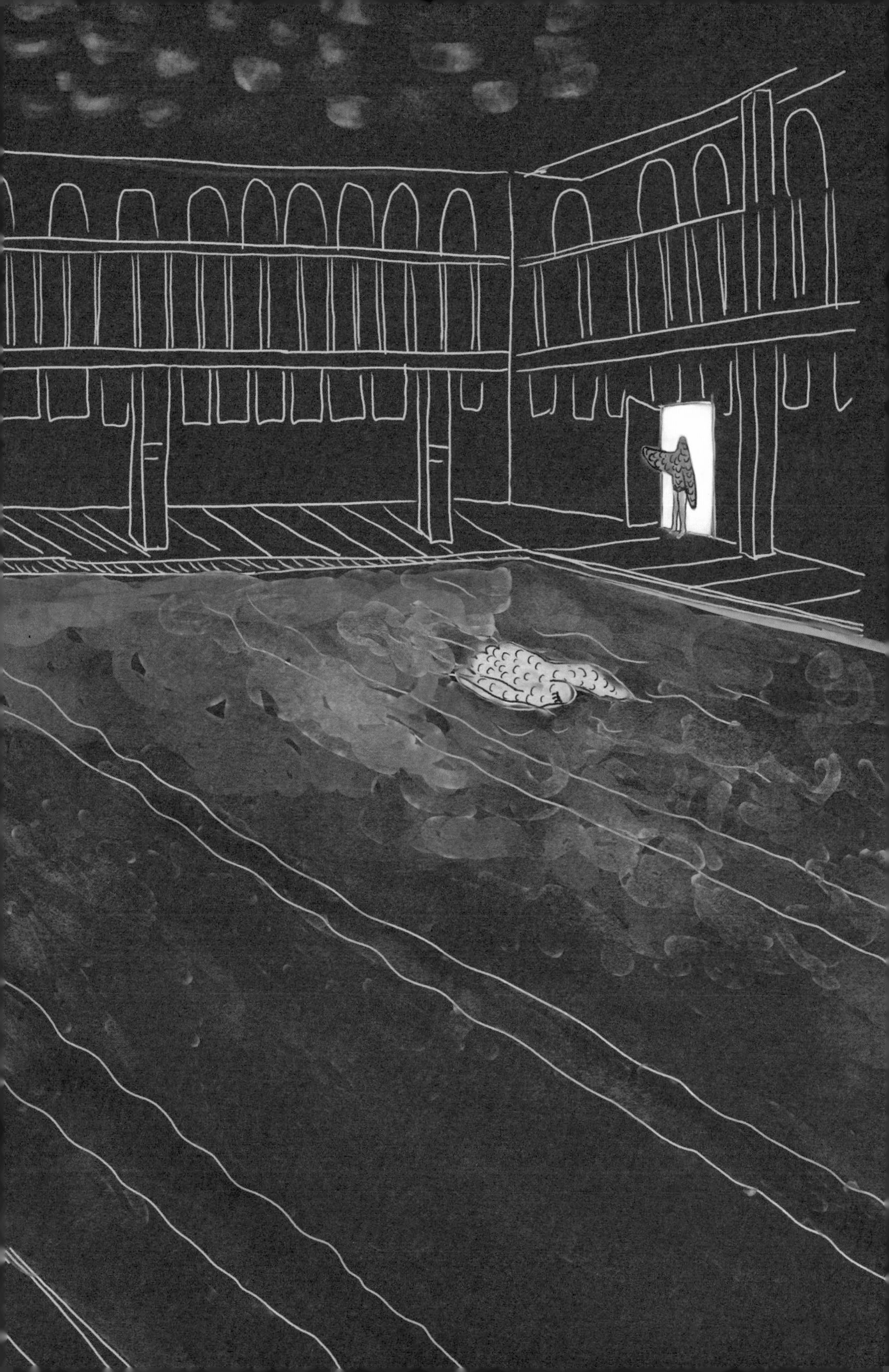

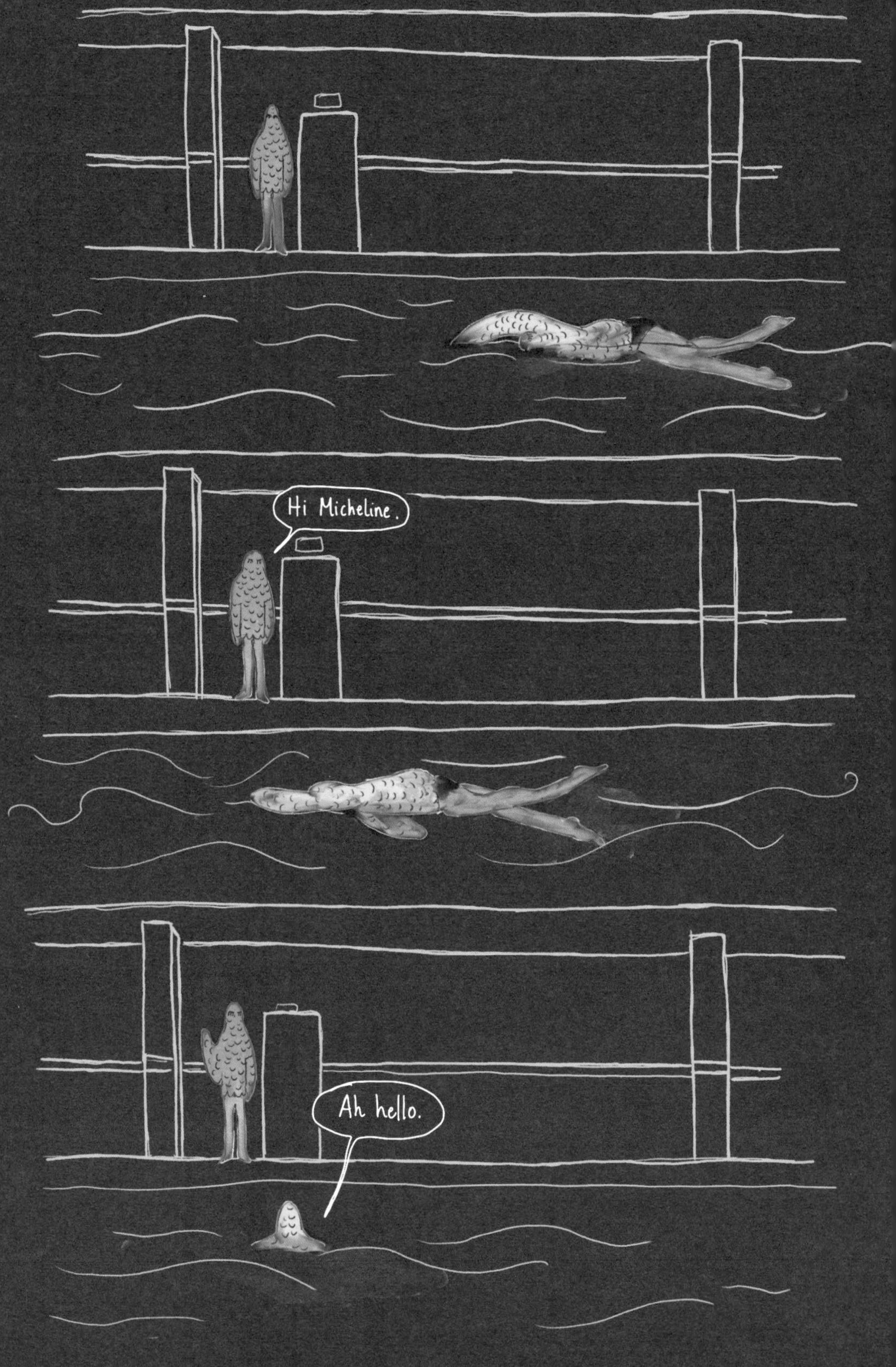
Hi Micheline.
Ah hello.

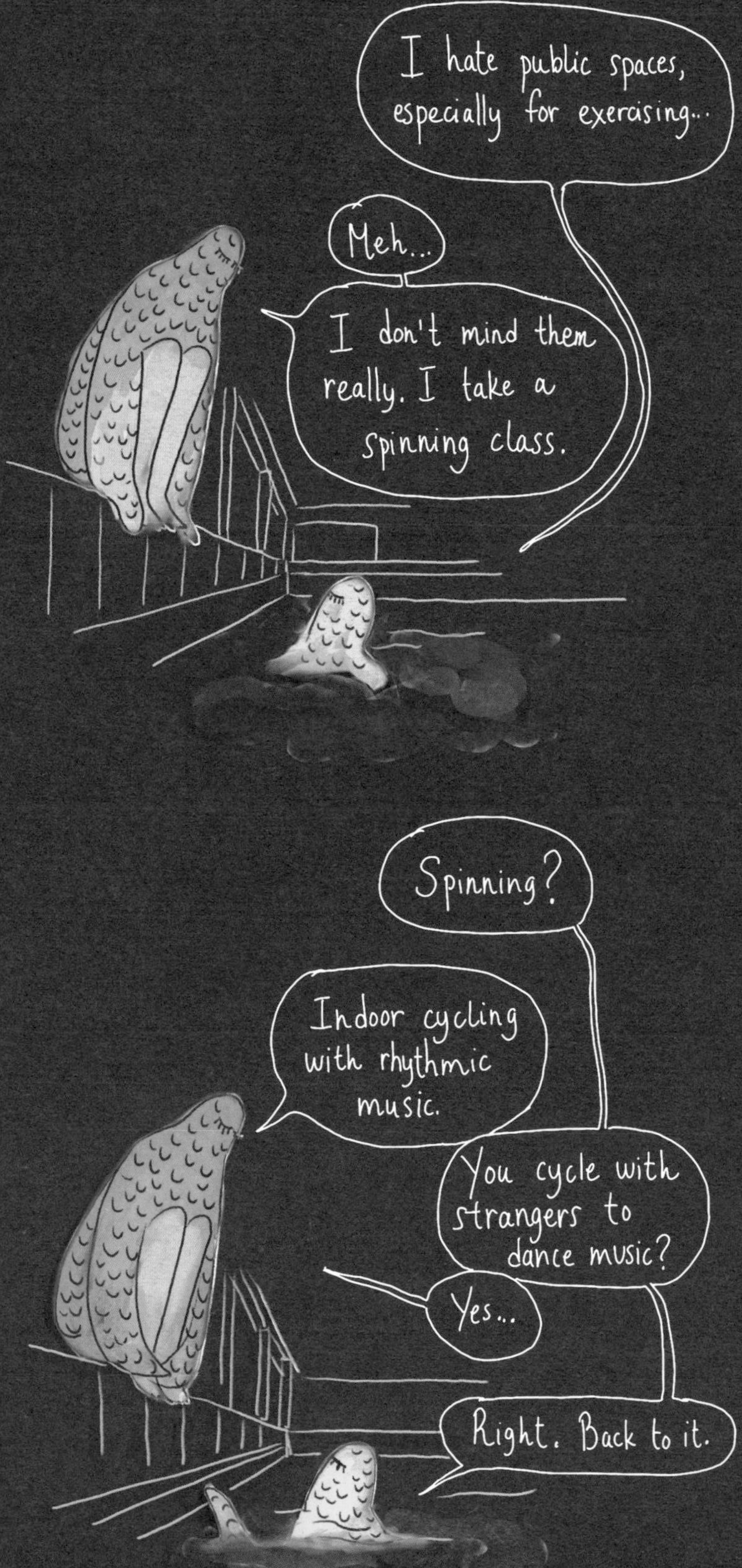
I hate public spaces, especially for exercising..
Meh...
I don't mind them really. I take a spinning class.
Spinning?
Indoor cycling with rhythmic music.
You cycle with strangers to dance music?
Yes...
Right. Back to it.

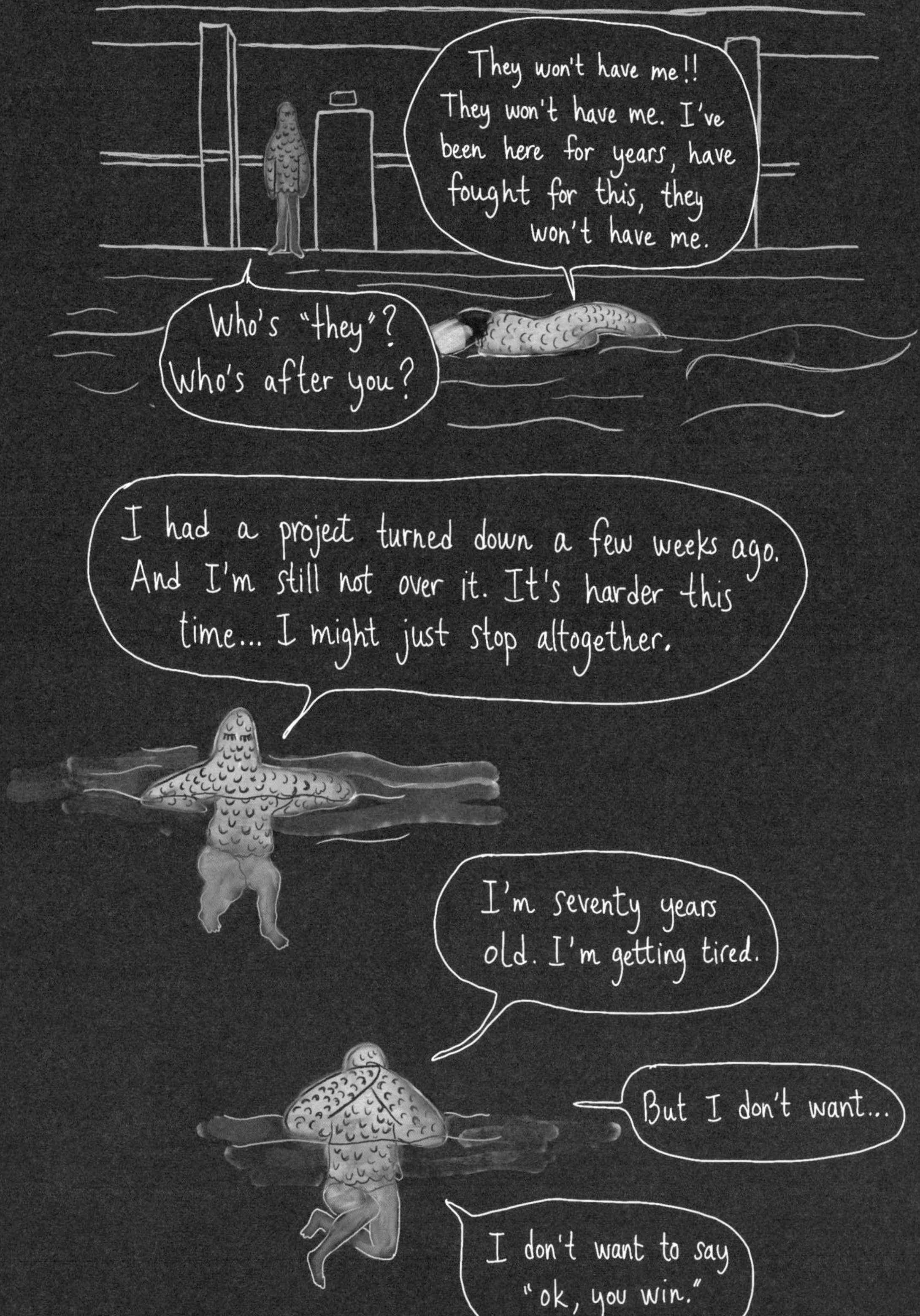
They won't have me!! They won't have me. I've been here for years, have fought for this, they won't have me.
Who's "they"? Who's after you?
I had a project turned down a few weeks ago. And I'm still not over it. It's harder this time... I might just stop altogether.
I'm seventy years old. I'm getting tired.
But I don't want...
I don't want to say "ok, you win."

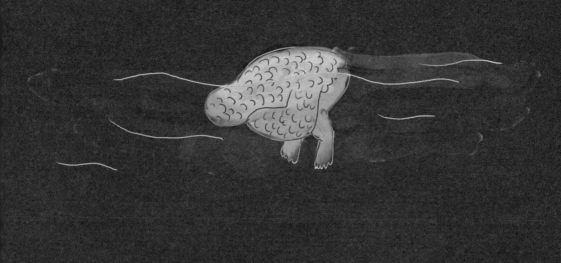

I won't let them win.

That's always been my motto:
"I won't let those bastards win."
When they turned down a movie pitch,
I came back with another one, a
cheaper one. I'm a pit bull. I grab
onto a leg and I don't let go till
I've got the money.

But now...

Now I'm tired.

And I'm fed up.

It's hard to take. Extremely hard.

I've been lucky. My acting work won me a lot of public admiration, which has balanced out how hard it's been to be a filmmaker.

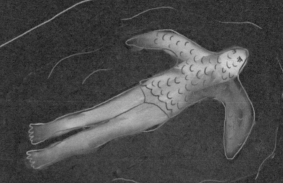

My movies have won prizes in other countries...

...I don't want to dwell on a failure...

My self-respect will save me...

Maybe...

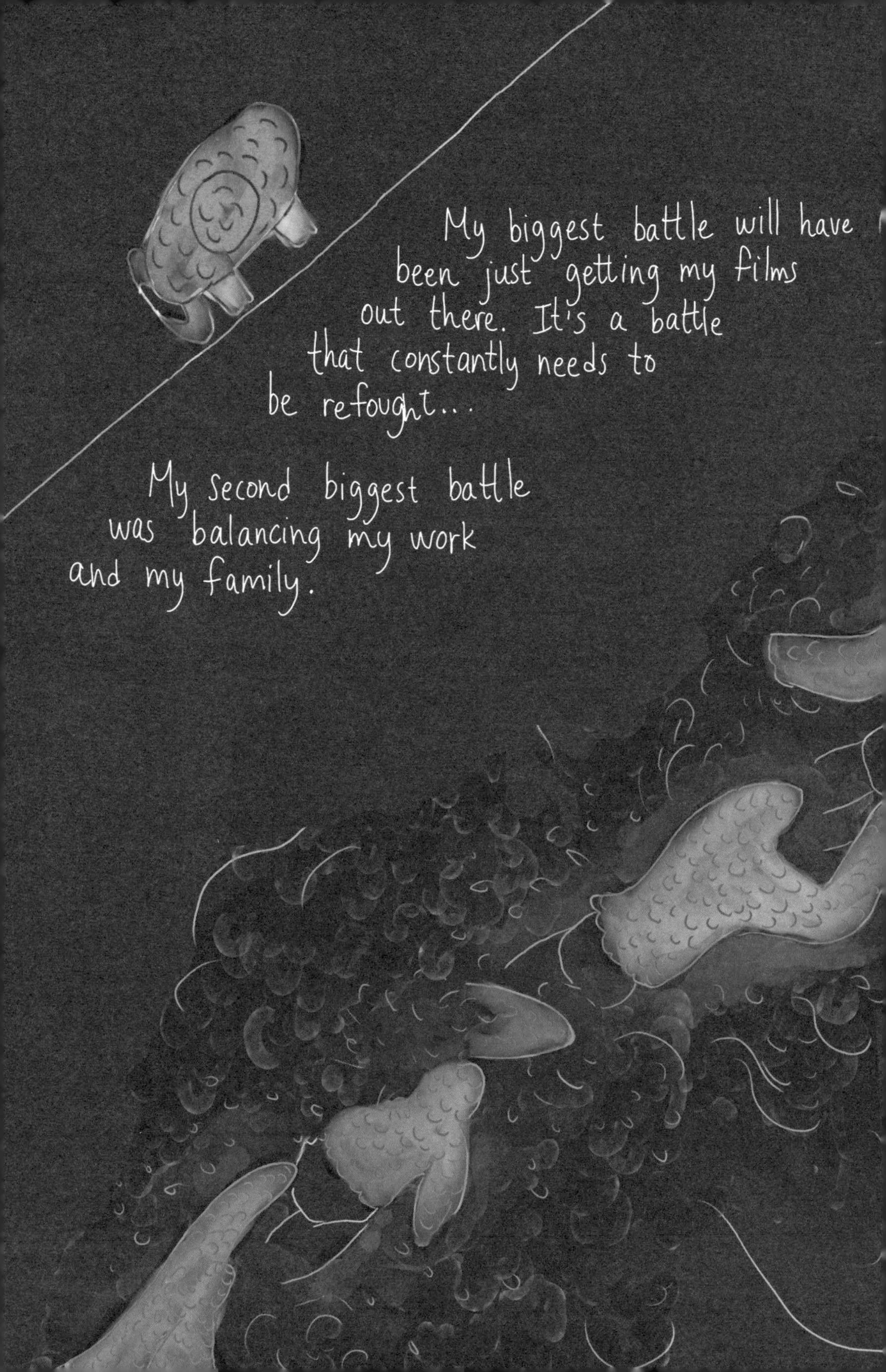
My biggest battle will have been just getting my films out there. It's a battle that constantly needs to be refought...
My second biggest battle was balancing my work and my family.

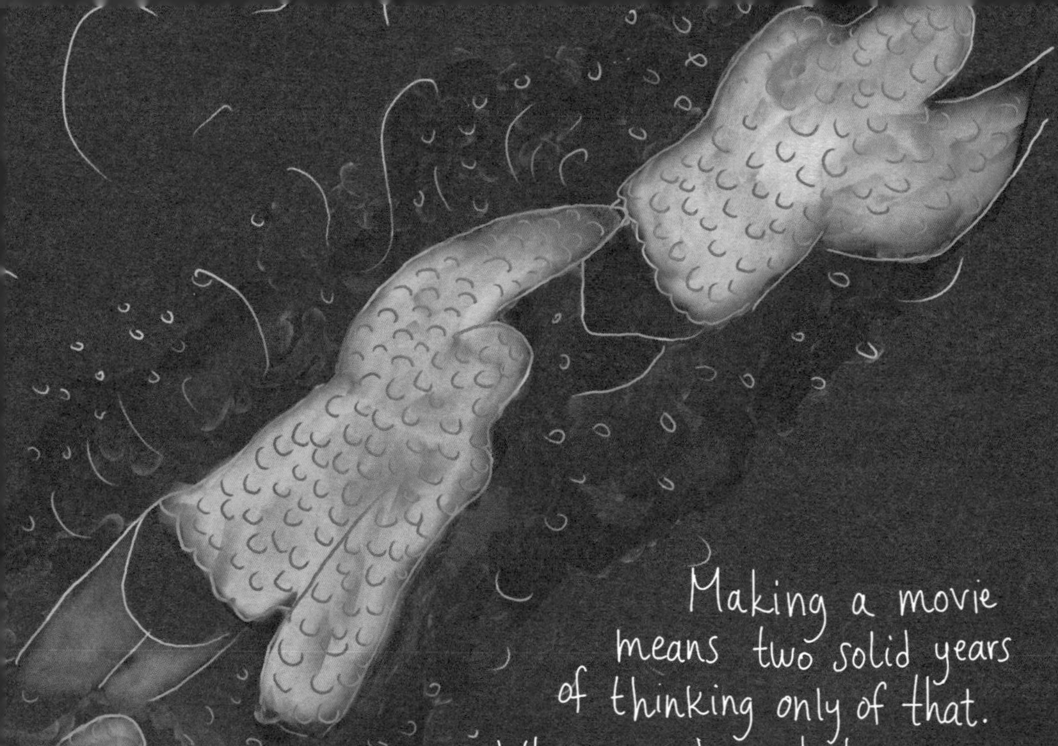

Making a movie means two solid years of thinking only of that. When you have kids, you can't let yourself follow an idea without being constantly pulled back to real life, to the concrete, to managing the family. All of that makes it hard to stay inspired and keep creating fresh new work.

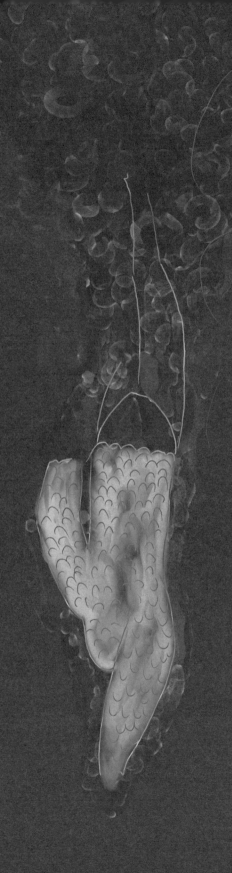

Artists are all
battling something
or other.

Whether we're
waging political
wars...

...or struggling
with ourselves...

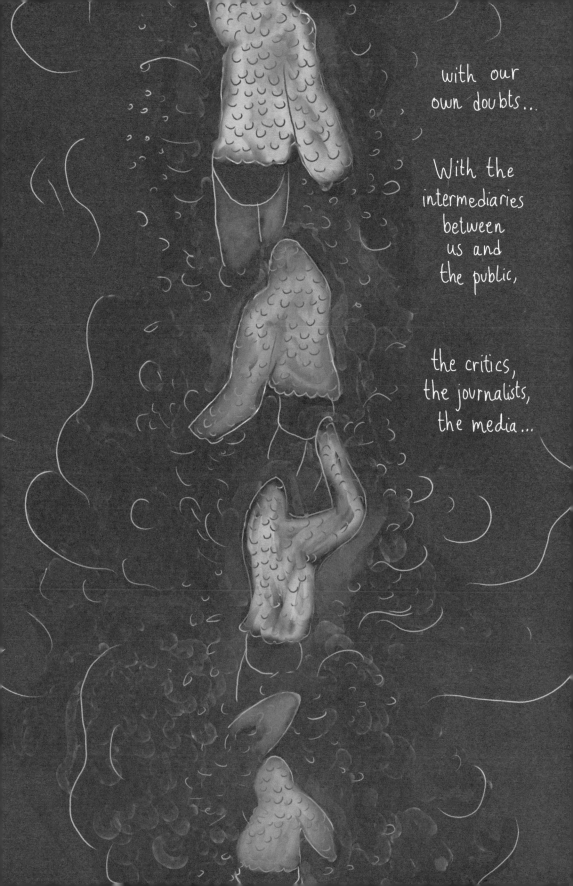

with our
own doubts...

With the
intermediaries
between
us and
the public,

the critics,
the journalists,
the media...

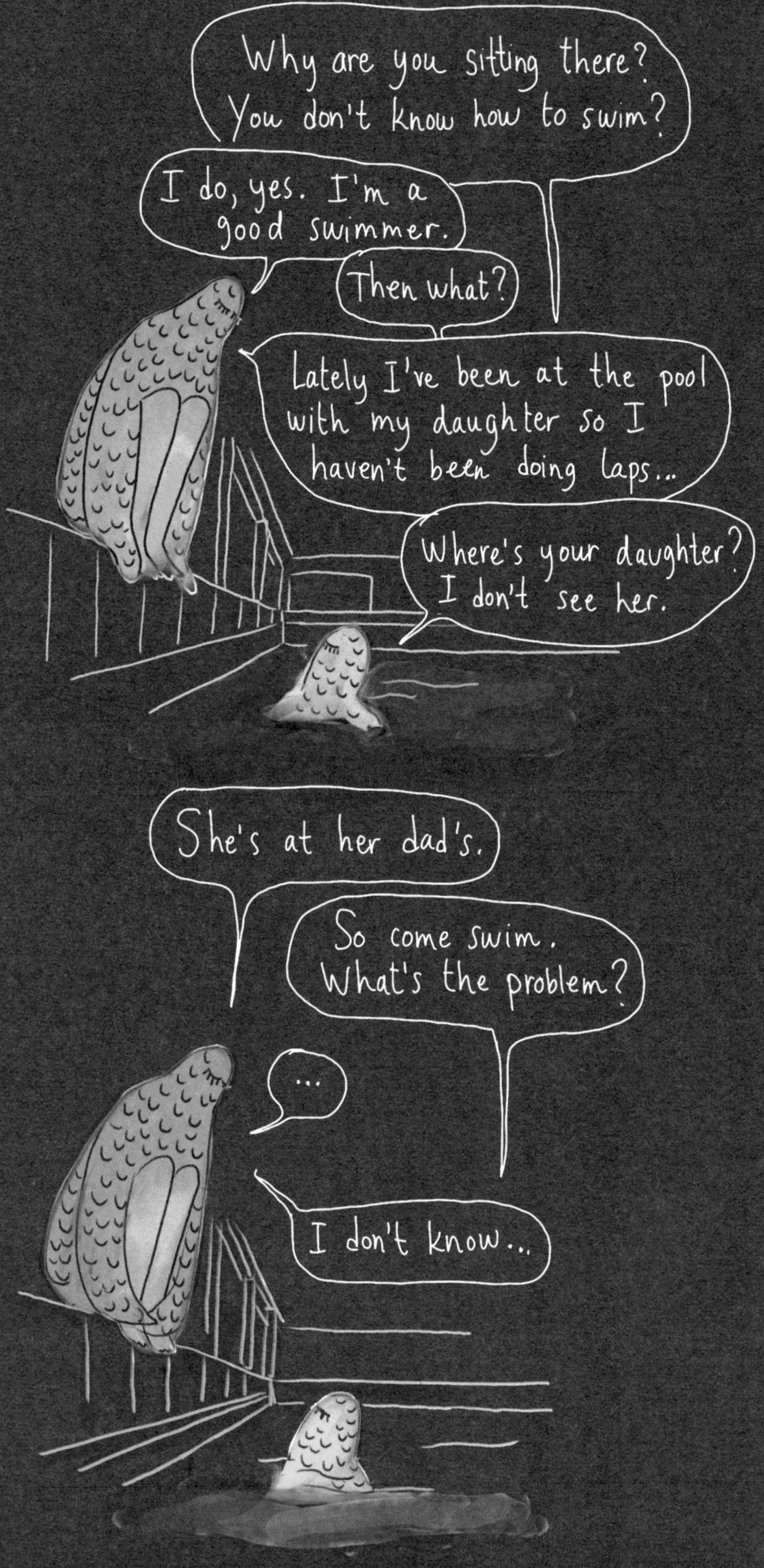
Why are you sitting there? You don't know how to swim?
I do, yes. I'm a good swimmer.
Then what?
Lately I've been at the pool with my daughter so I haven't been doing laps...
Where's your daughter? I don't see her.
She's at her dad's.
So come swim. What's the problem?
...
I don't know...

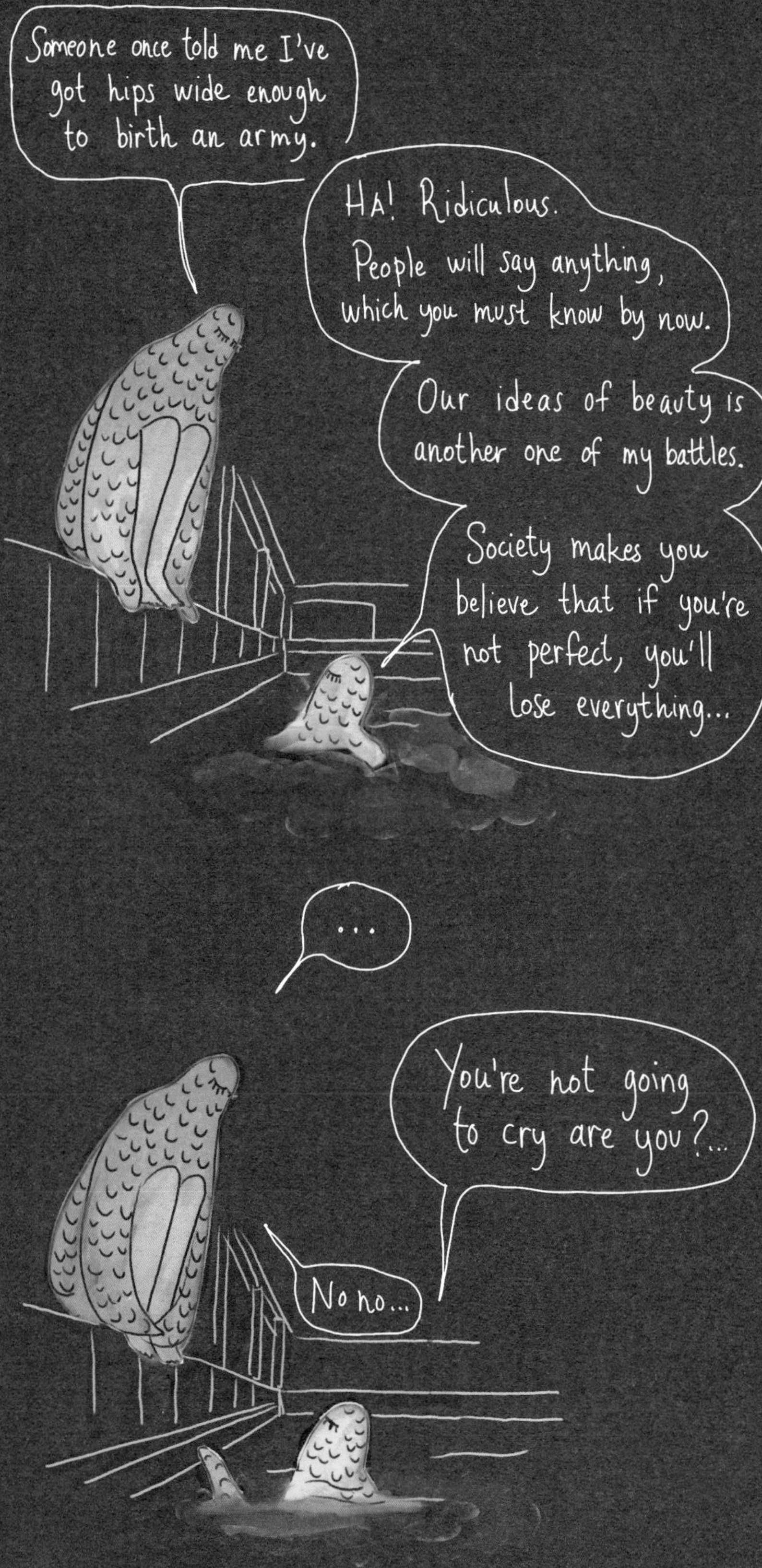
Someone once told me I've got hips wide enough to birth an army.
HA! Ridiculous. People will say anything, which you must know by now.
Our ideas of beauty is another one of my battles.
Society makes you believe that if you're not perfect, you'll lose everything...
...
You're not going to cry are you?...
No no...

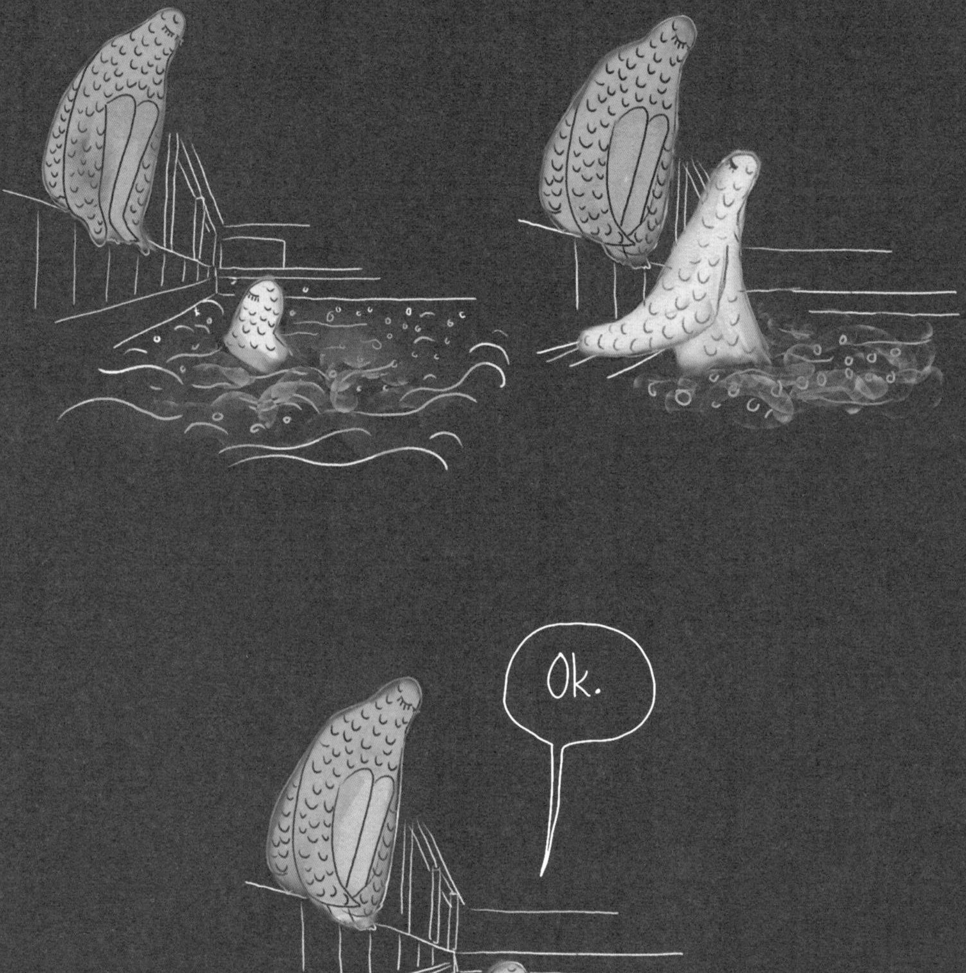
Ok.

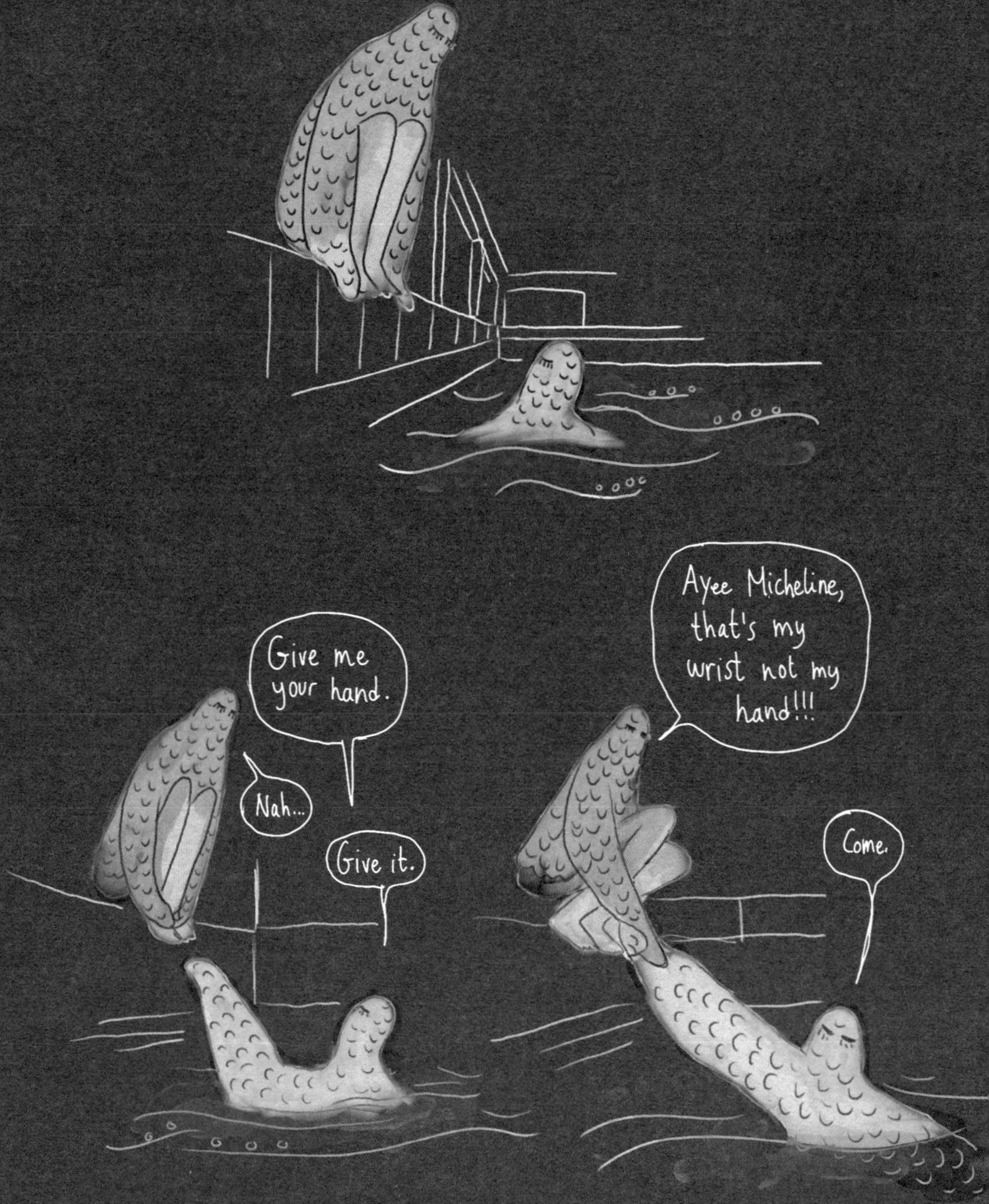
Give me your hand.
Nah...
Give it.
Ayee Micheline, that's my wrist not my hand!!!
Come.

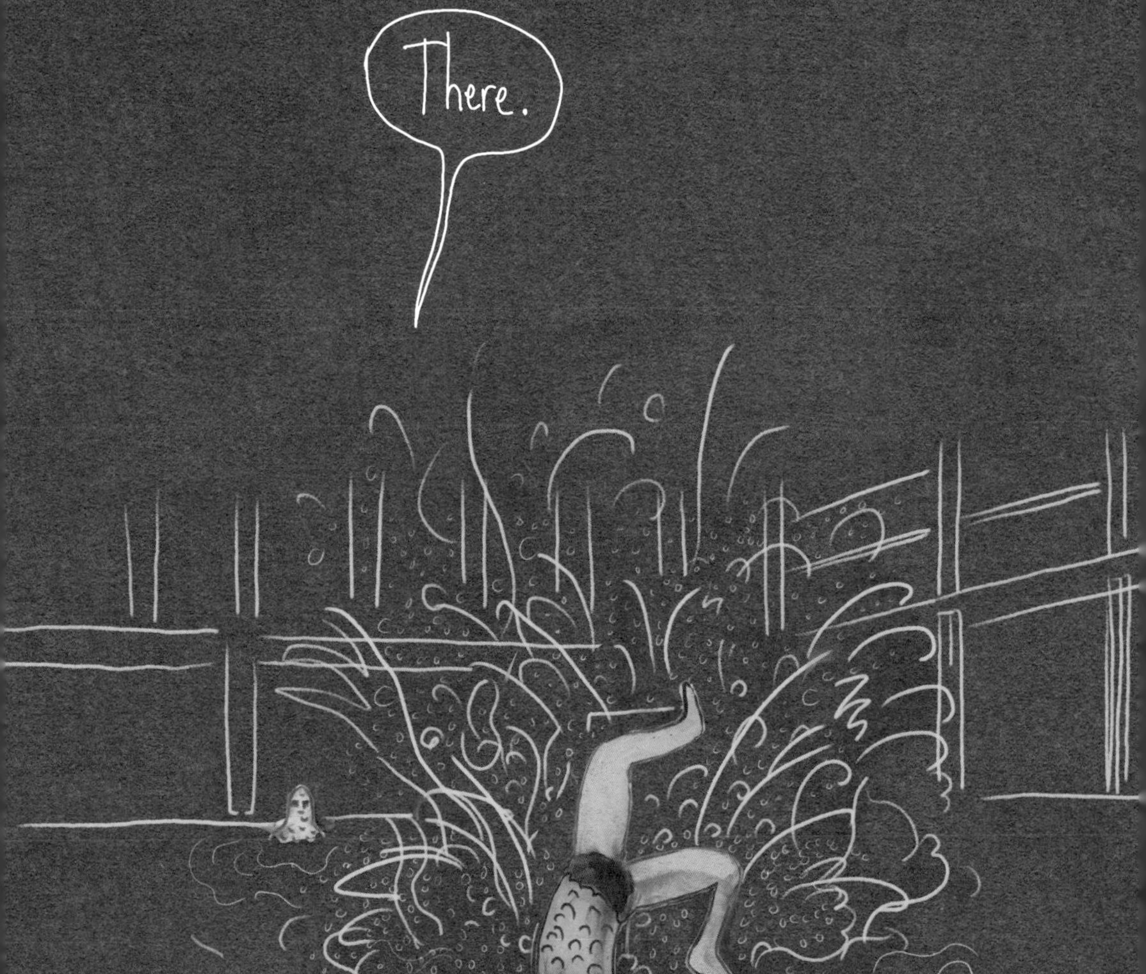
There.

Catherine

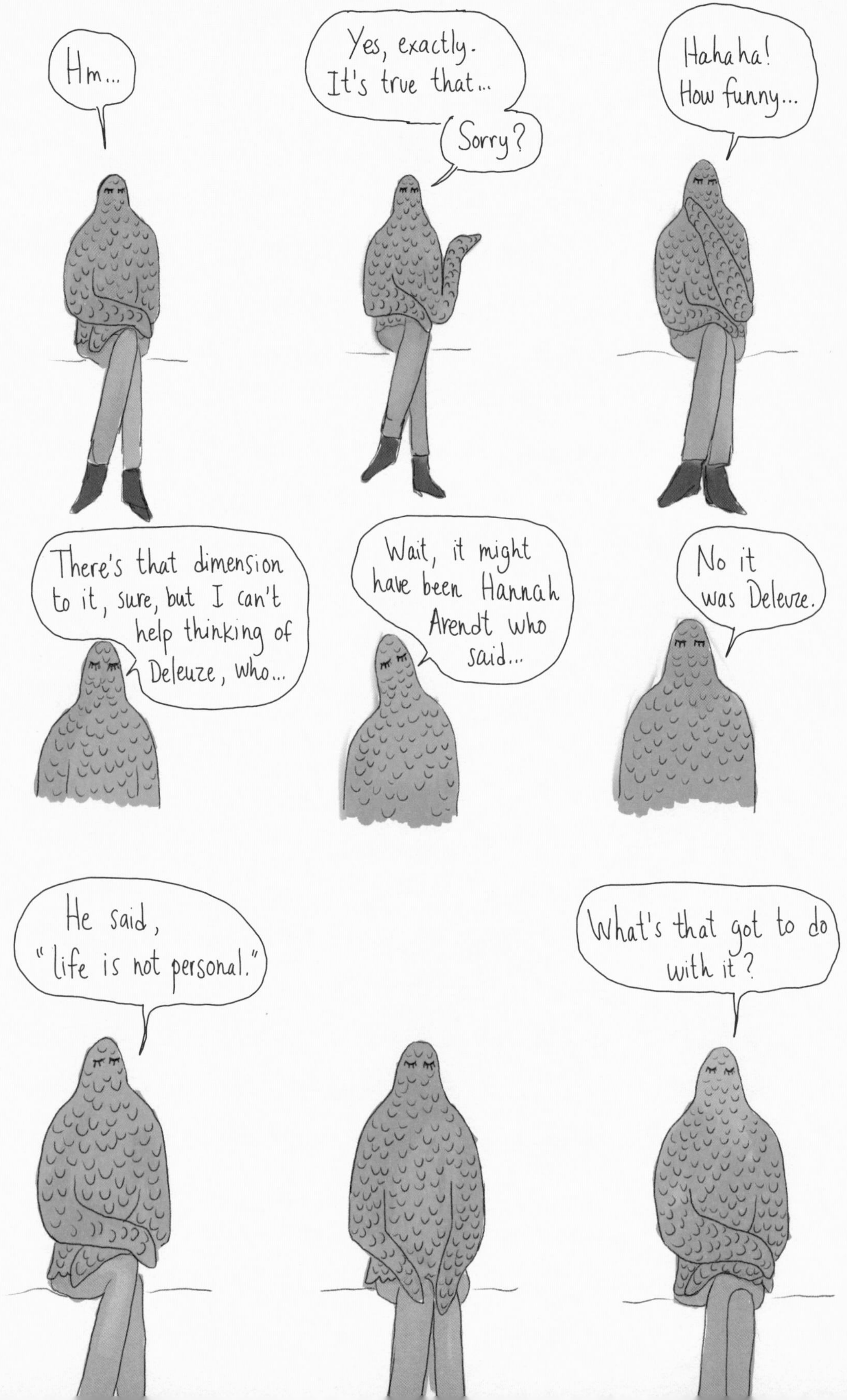
Hm...
Yes, exactly. It's true that...
Sorry?
Hahaha! How funny...
There's that dimension to it, sure, but I can't help thinking of Deleuze, who...
Wait, it might have been Hannah Arendt who said...
No it was Deleuze.
He said, "life is not personal."
What's that got to do with it?

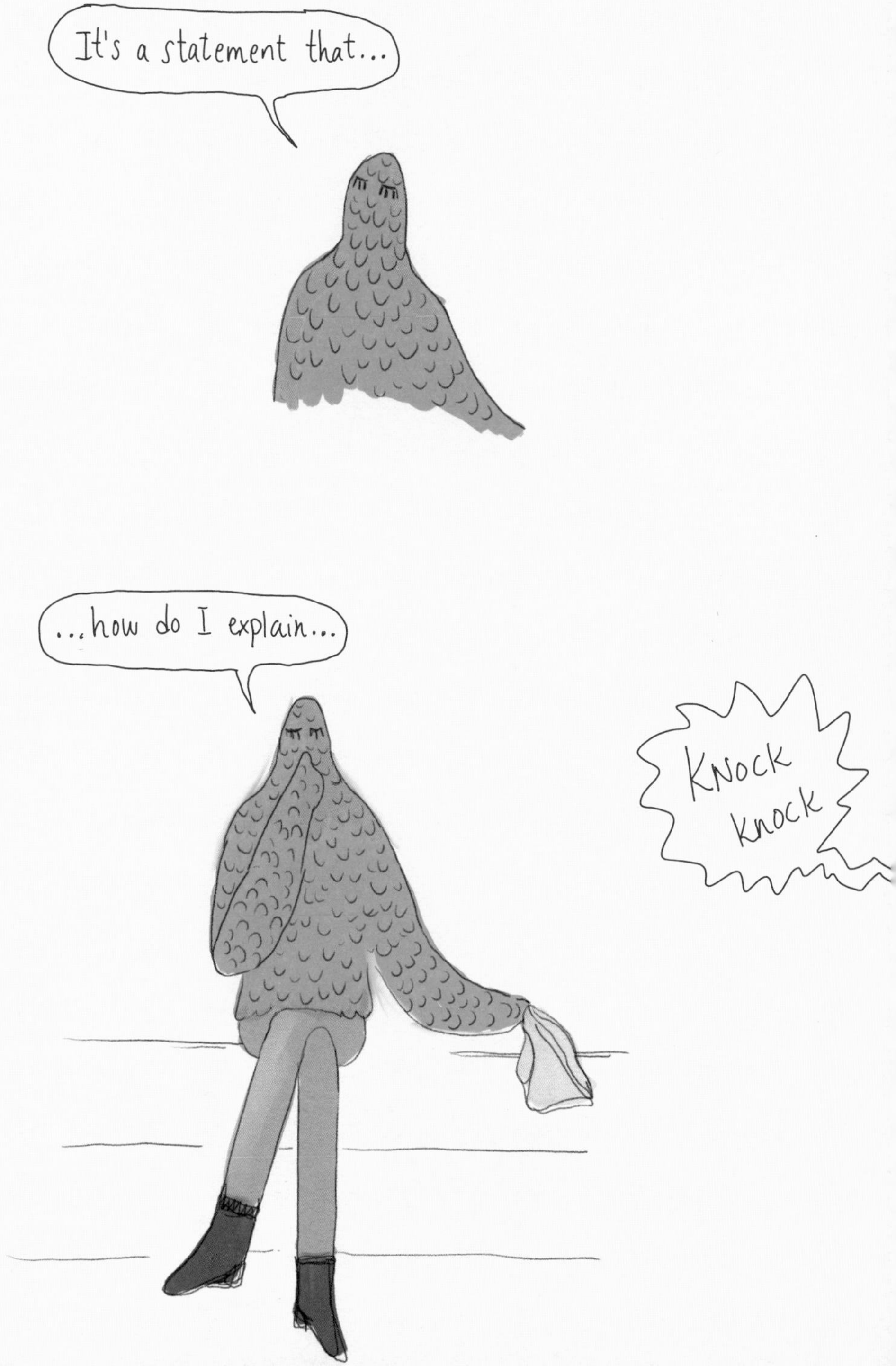
It's a statement that...
...how do I explain...
KNOCK knock

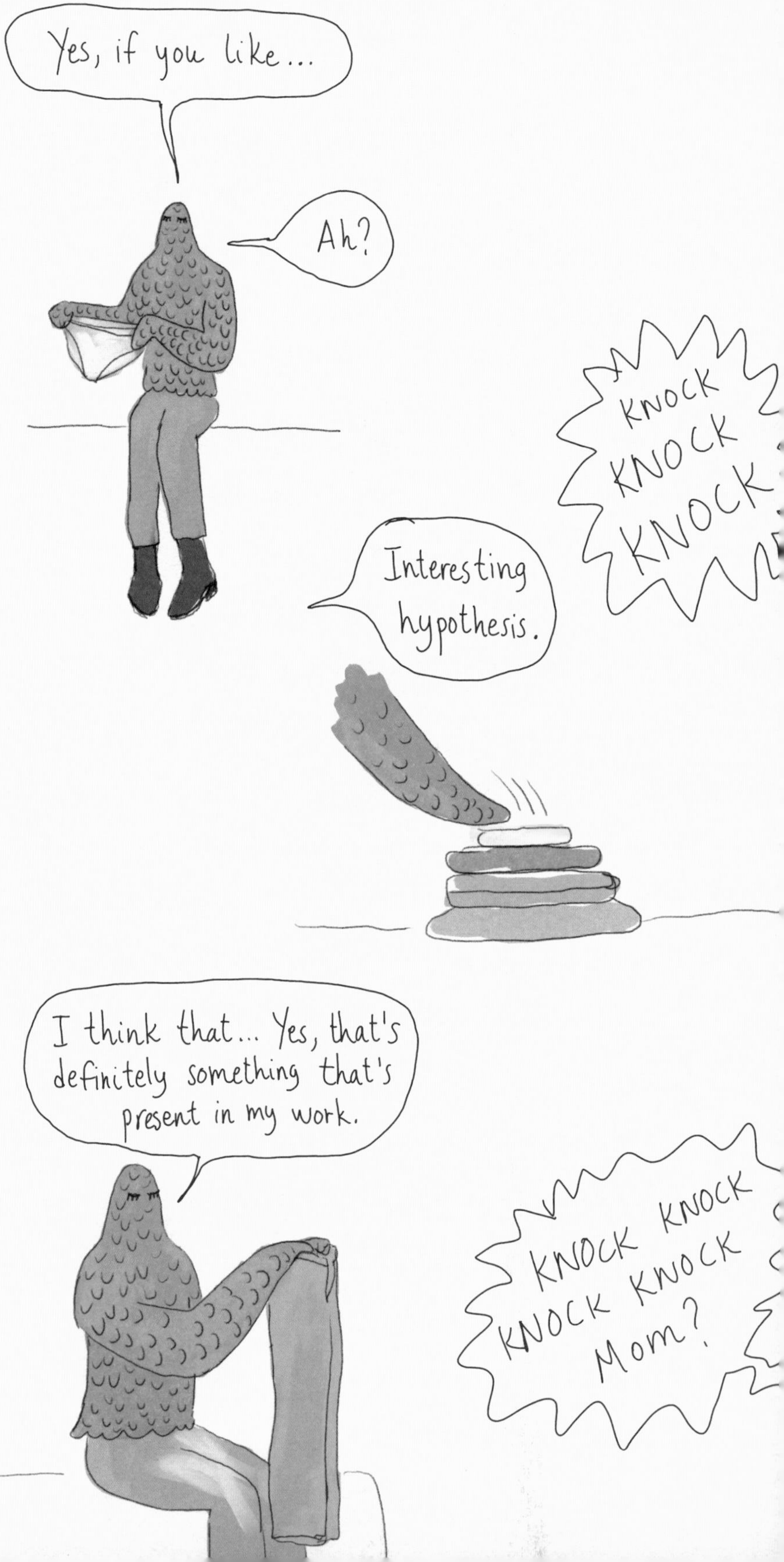

Yes, if you like...
Ah?
KNOCK KNOCK KNOCK
Interesting hypothesis.
I think that... Yes, that's definitely something that's present in my work.
KNOCK KNOCK KNOCK KNOCK Mom?

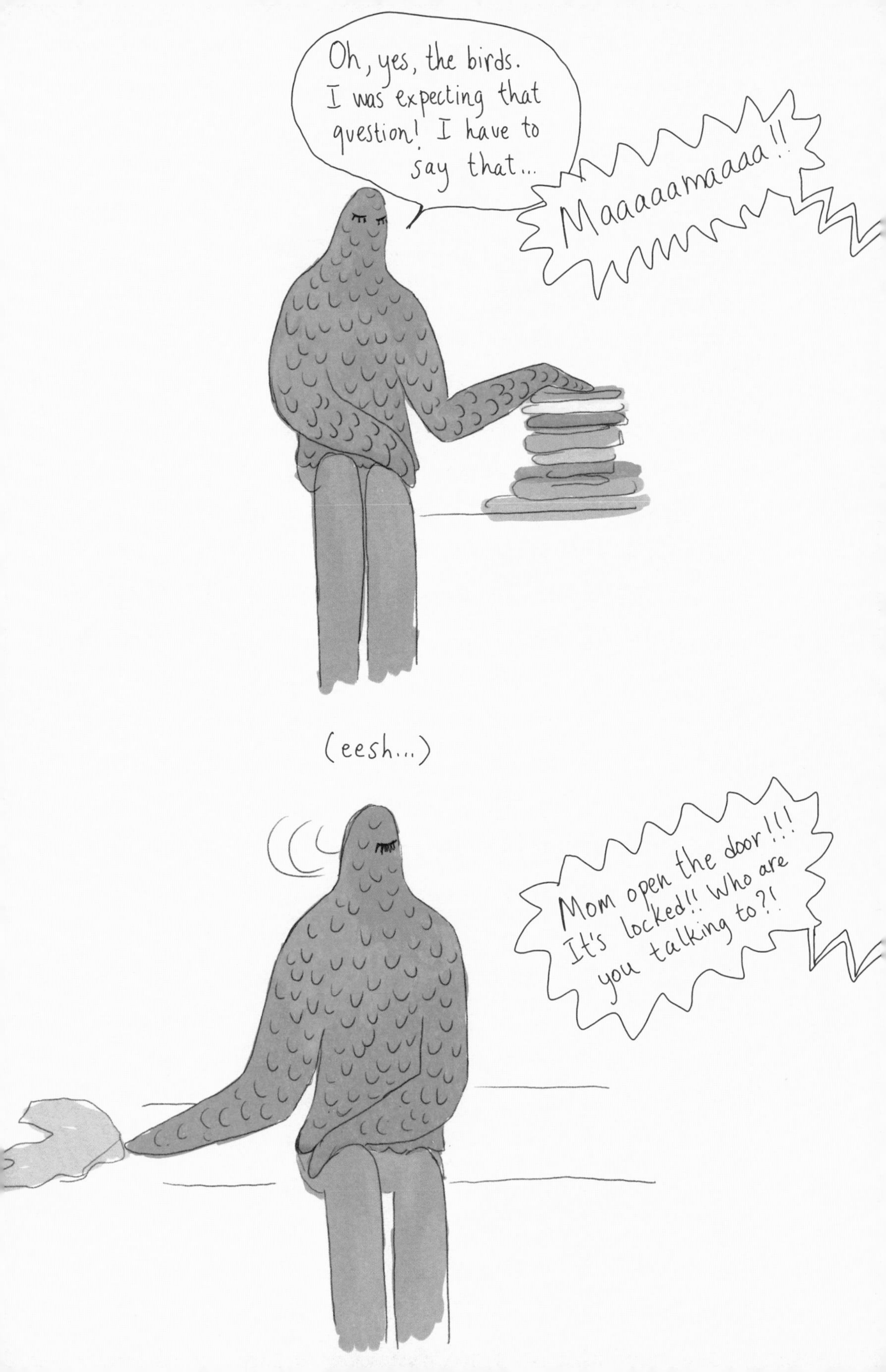
Oh, yes, the birds. I was expecting that question! I have to say that...
Maaaaamaaaa!!
(eesh...)
Mom open the door!!! It's locked!! Who are you talking to?!

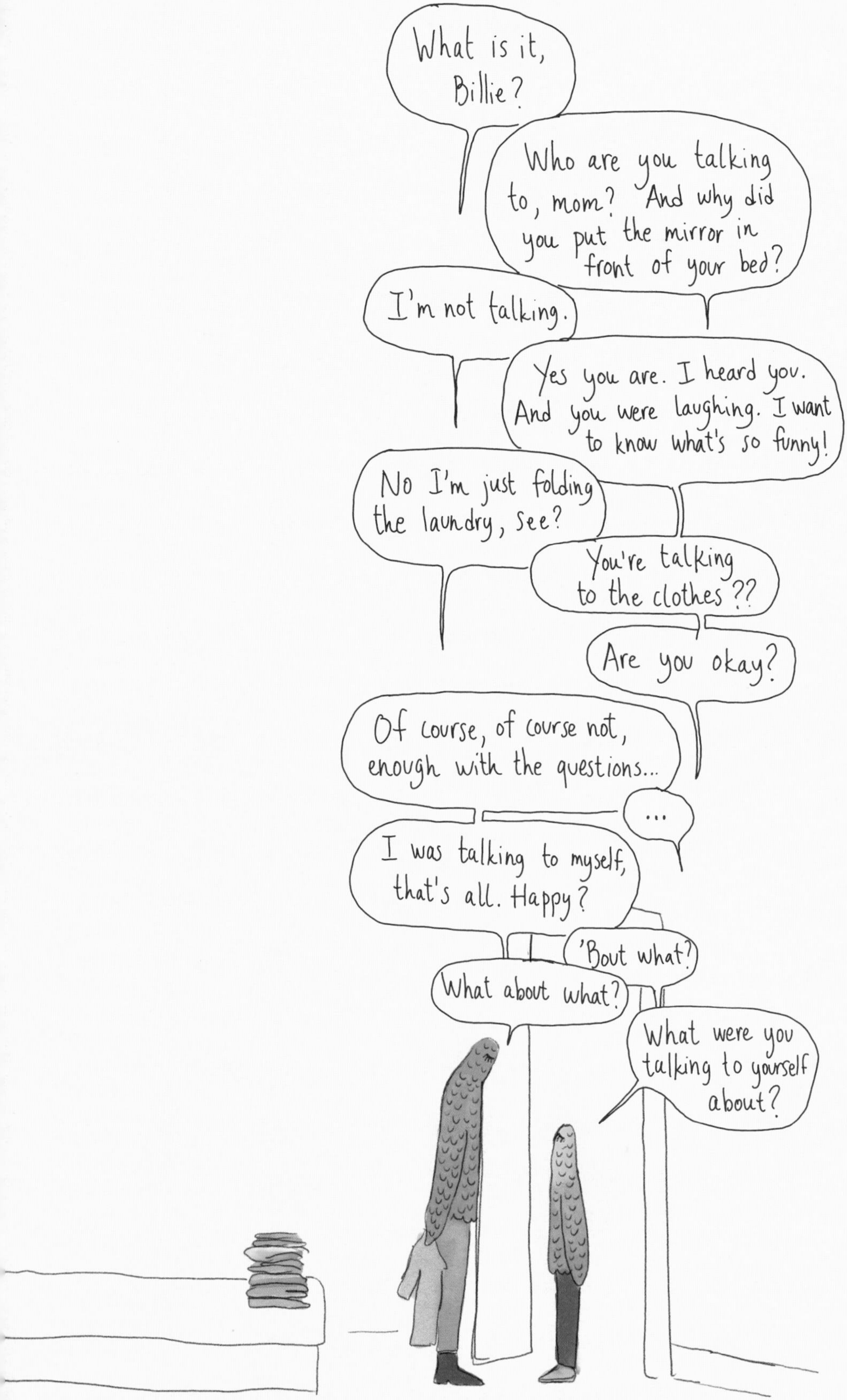
What is it, Billie?
Who are you talking to, mom? And why did you put the mirror in front of your bed?
I'm not talking.
Yes you are. I heard you. And you were laughing. I want to know what's so funny!
No I'm just folding the laundry, see?
You're talking to the clothes??
Are you okay?
Of course, of course not, enough with the questions...
...
I was talking to myself, that's all. Happy?
'Bout what?
What about what?
What were you talking to yourself about?

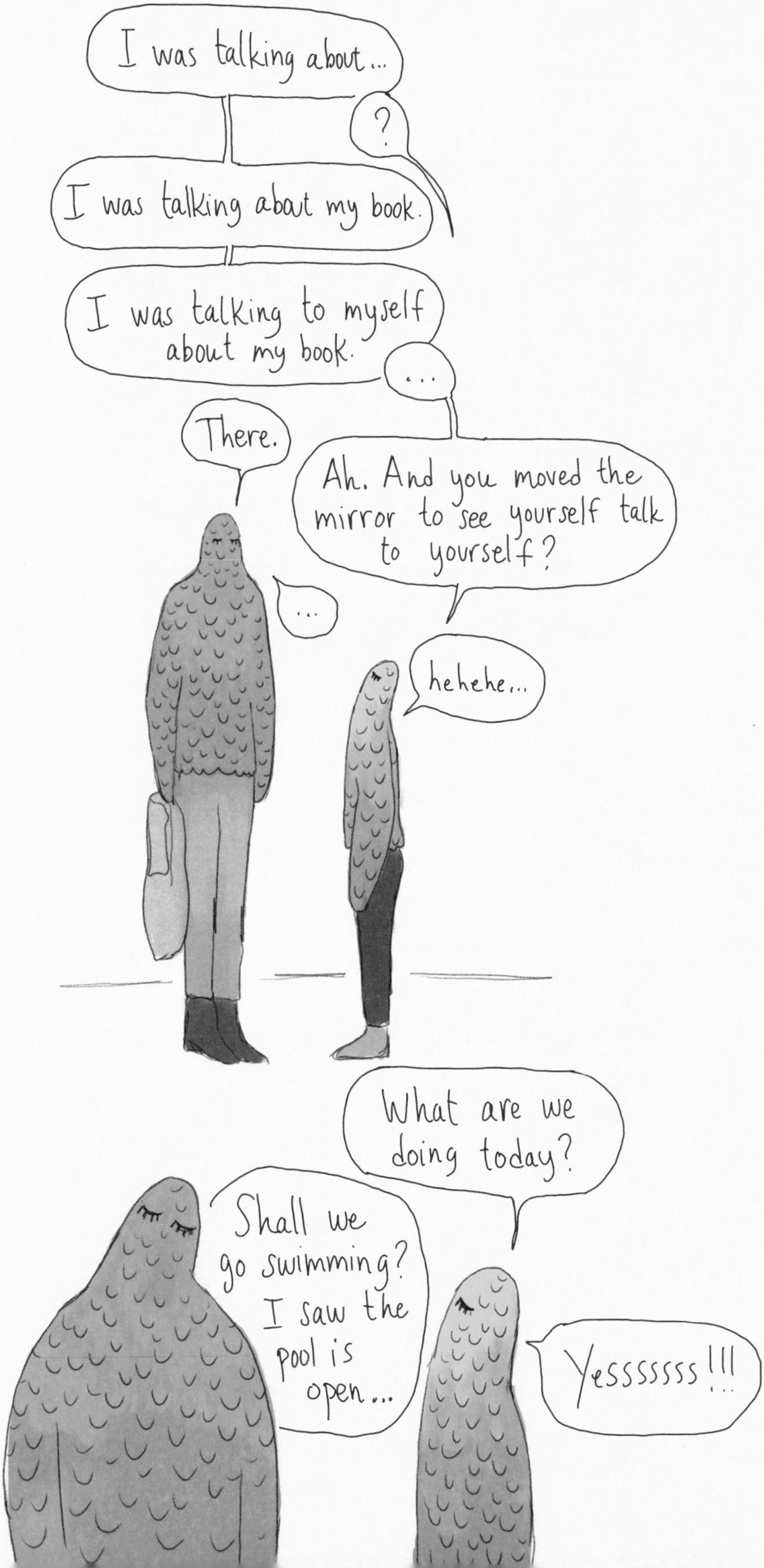
I was talking about...
?
I was talking about my book.
I was talking to myself about my book.
...
There.
Ah. And you moved the mirror to see yourself talk to yourself?
...
hehehe...
What are we doing today?
Shall we go swimming? I saw the pool is open...
Yessssss!!!

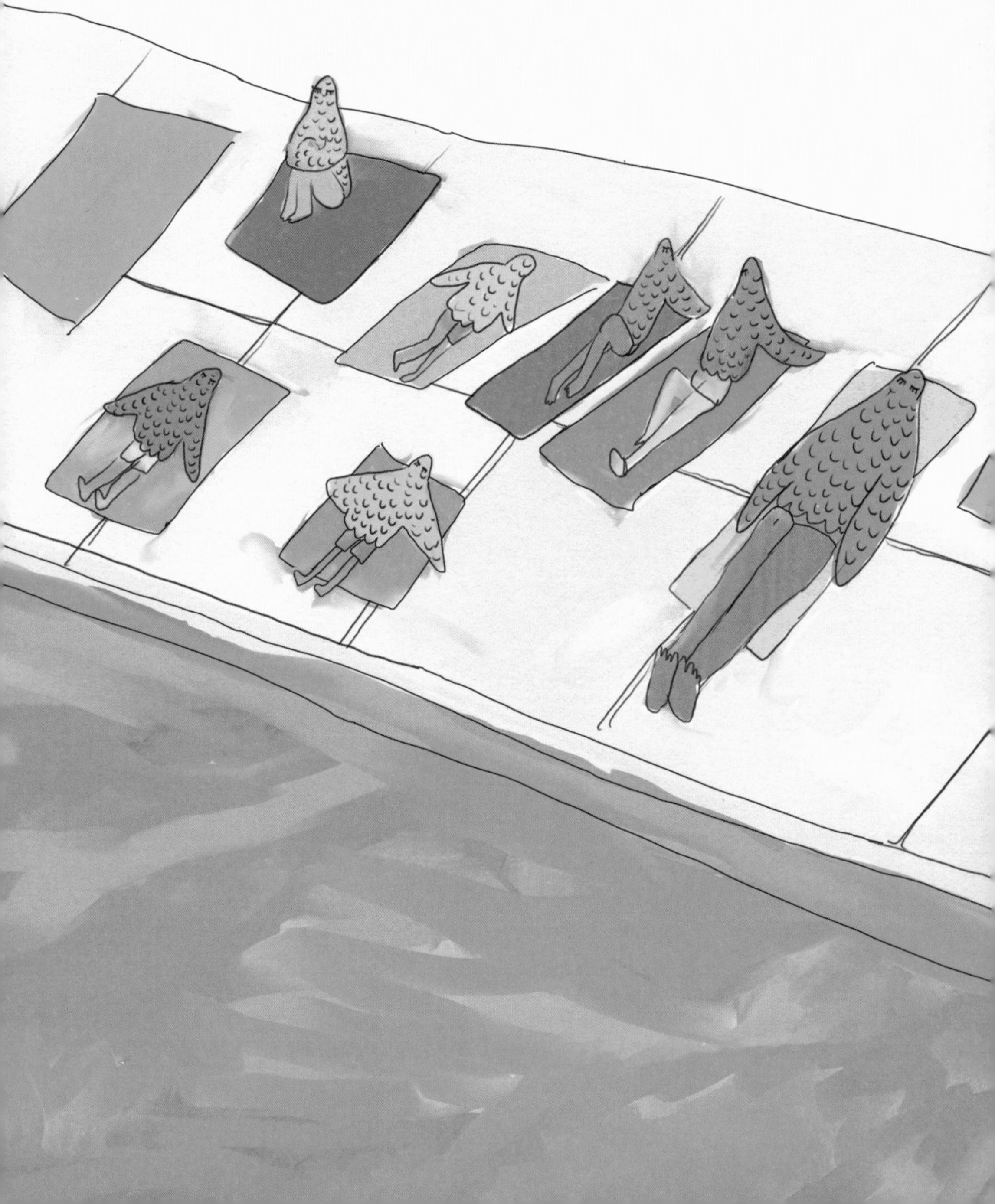

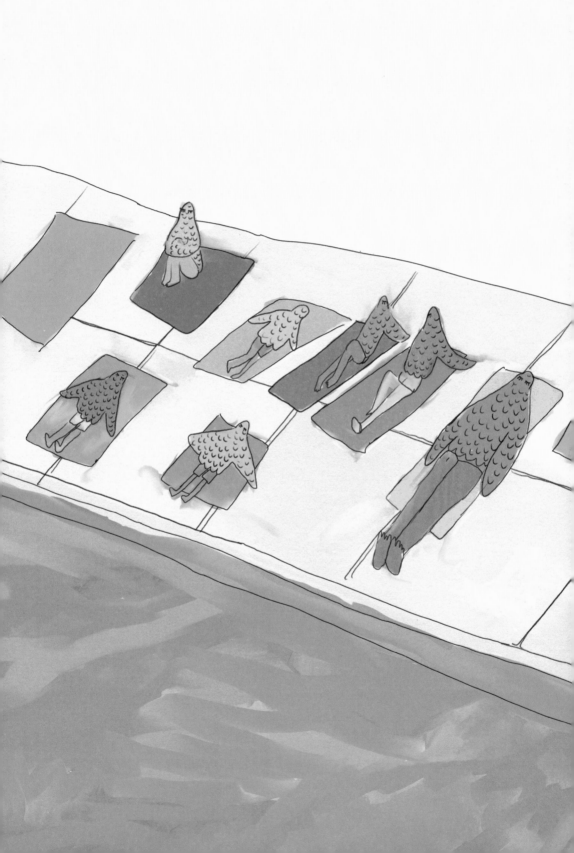

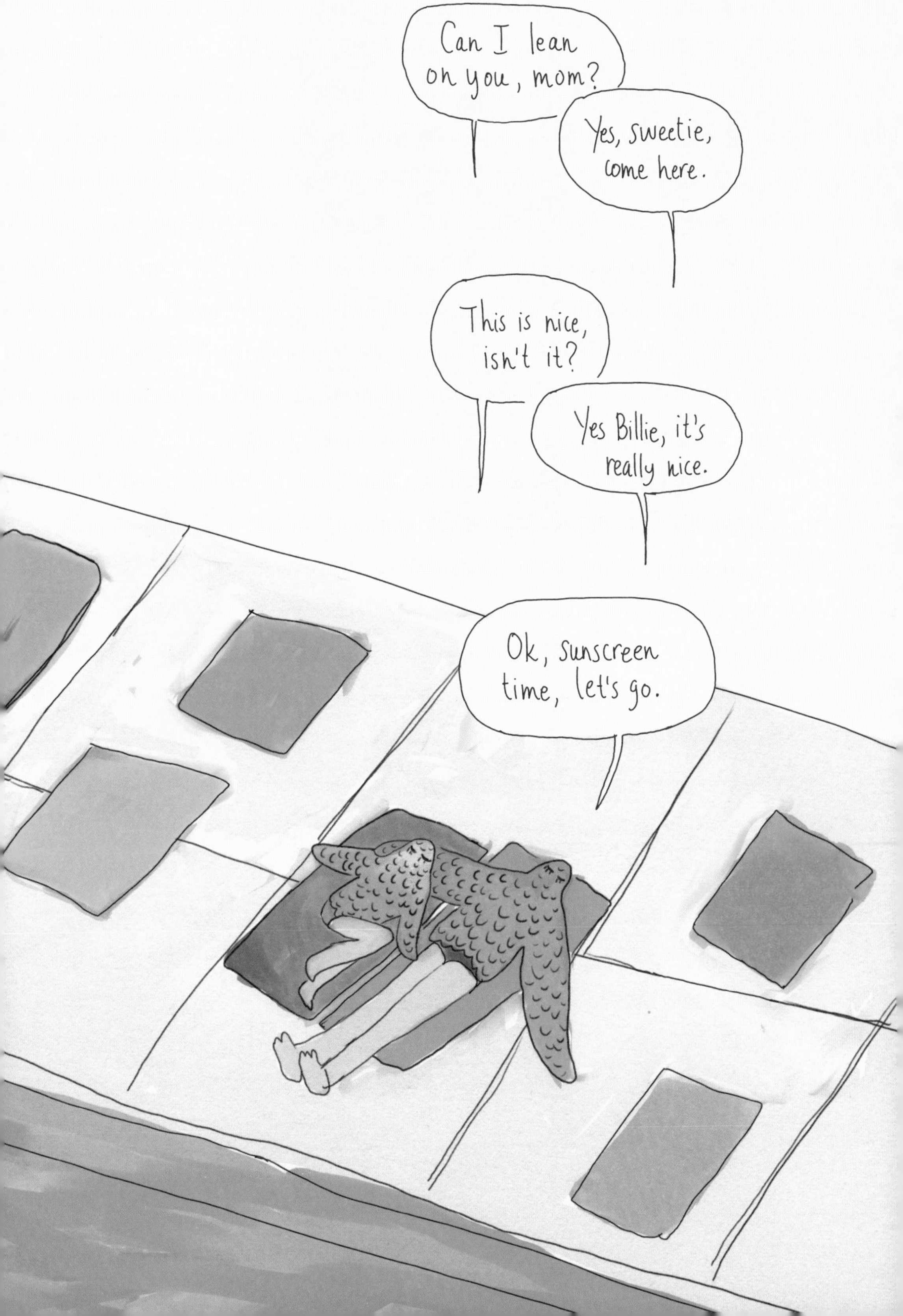
Can I lean on you, mom?
Yes, sweetie, come here.
This is nice, isn't it?
Yes Billie, it's really nice.
Ok, sunscreen time, let's go.

A very special thanks to Rose.

♥

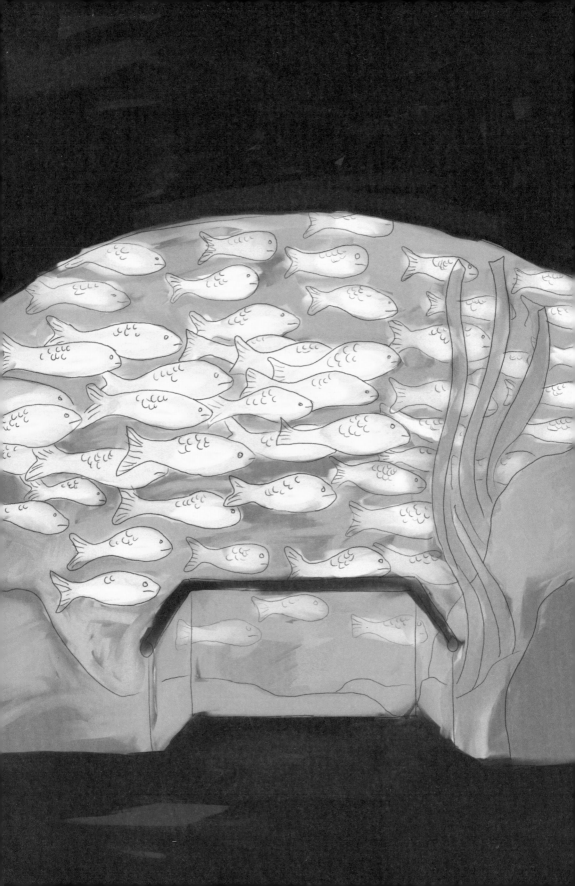